CLASSIC MOTORCYCLE ENGINES

VIC WILLOUGHBY

CLASSIC MOTORCYCLE ENGINES

A NEW PERSPECTIVE ON
20 OUTSTANDING DESIGNS

MRP

MOTOR RACING PUBLICATIONS LTD
Unit 6, The Pilton Estate, 46 Pitlake, Croydon CR0 3RY, England

ISBN 0 947981 10 1
First published 1986

Photoset and printed in Great Britain by
Netherwood Dalton & Company Ltd
Bradley Mills, Huddersfield, West Yorkshire

Contents

Introduction

For more than 40 years, one of the most fascinating series of articles to appear in the motorcycle press were the analyses of outstanding engines published in *The Motor Cycle, Motor Cycle* and *Motor Cycle Weekly* (same journal, modified title). Written by my predecessors and me following interviews with the designers and development engineers, and illustrated by the drawings of our staff artists, these features were popular not only with ordinary enthusiasts, who gained an insight into the innermost details of world-famous power plants, but also with the engineers themselves, who were able to compare notes; indeed some engineers from other automotive fields relished them.

The series ran well into three figures, starting with an anonymous exposition of the Sunbeam high-camshaft singles on January 5, 1939 and ending with my story on the exciting 500cc desmodromic Ducati Pantah 90-degree twin on May 23, 1981.

In bringing together a selection of 20 of the more stimulating of these analyses in this book, it would have been easier to reproduce them as originally published, but that would merely have duplicated many an enthusiast's scrapbook. Instead, I have rewritten and expanded the articles in the light of hindsight, subsequent engineering developments, and, in many cases, further interviews with the original designers and development engineers.

In this way, I hope my stories will appeal not only to the older, but also to the younger reader, who will gain an understanding of why the engines were conceived and the less obvious reasons for some of their design features. Such readers may also acquire a better perspective on some modern designs, especially the Japanese.

It should be clear that this book does not purport to be a historical review of overall design trends. Nevertheless, the text plainly identifies several influences on design — in some cases the constraints of a price-sensitive market, in others the desire for the prestige of, say, a world championship. Arbitrary regulations — as in grand-prix and speedway racing — also affect design, either directly or through some inadvertent bias; so too does the exploration of new technologies — and so does fashion. Whatever the overriding constraints, however, the motorcycle industry has never lacked sound design and development talent.

A word of warning should perhaps be given about bhp figures. Neither the press nor anyone else has had the opportunity to test various makes of engine on an independent dynamometer. Consequently, quoted power figures are usually those claimed by the makers. Any seeming discrepancies may reflect exaggeration or even modesty on the makers' part — or the fact that peak power does not relate infallibly to road or lap speed, where power *characteristics* are often more significant.

1986   Vic Willoughby

Acknowledgements

The author and publishers are grateful to East Midlands Allied Press for permission to re-produce most of the drawings and photographs in this book and to Brian Woolley for his diligent searches in the archives. For other pictorial help thanks are due to photographers Don Morley and Trevor Meeks and to Peter Glover (Harglo).

For settling one or two historical queries we are indebted to Dr Joe Bayley and Jeff Clew. Also appreciated is the willing help of John Greenwood, Brian O'Reilly (Honda), Rex White and Martin Ogbourne (Suzuki) and the late Dave Collins (Ricardo).

Finally, this book could not have been written without the co-operation of all the engineers mentioned, both in the original analyses of their creations and, where feasible, in reviewing their work in the searching light of hindsight.

V W

An explanation

The word Classic in the title of this book does not signify any specific period such as, say, the late 1950s to late 1960s; that is a misuse of the word that has gained currency this past decade or so. In relation to the designs discussed here the word is used in its literal sense to imply engines of outstanding merit — whether in concept, achievement or potential — regardless of their time. The 20 engines selected for this volume span half a century and five nation-alities.

CHAPTER 1

The last Rudge Ulster

Sired by a grand-prix winner, the sporting big single with the most ingenious four-valve configuration

In the TT races and European championships of the early 1930s, George Hack's spectacular achievements as development engineer and race chief for Rudge Whitworth were based on two distinct types of four-valve cylinder head. These were the pent-roof head, with parallel pairs of inlet and exhaust valves, 'reinvented' by Honda some 30 years later for their highly successful grand-prix programme; and the part-spherical head, with radial valves, also reinvented by Honda (initially for a 350cc roadster) more than 50 years after Rudge Whitworth pioneered it. To catch up with Rudge and Hack, Honda now have only to reinvent the semi-radial head (parallel inlets, radial exhausts) that was a patented feature of the Ulster engine analyzed by *Torrens* of *The Motor Cycle* in the issue dated May 25, 1939.

Launched some 10 years earlier as a 499cc (85 × 88mm) supersports single, the Rudge Ulster was so named to commemorate Graham Walker's popular victory in the previous year's (1928) Ulster 500cc Grand Prix, the first classic road race to be won at more than 80mph. Although its exhausts were always widely splayed, the Ulster engine initially inherited the parallel valves of the racer, with an angle of approximately 60 degrees between the planes of the inlet and exhaust stems — an early example of the trend towards narrower included angles for compact combustion chambers.

Naturally enough, *Torrens'* opening question when interviewing George Hack was: 'Why do you use four valves, for in this respect your engines are just about unique?' Hack conceded that Rudge were indeed unique in the motorcycle world (where the few other four-valvers had fallen by the wayside) but pointed out that four-valve heads were almost universal in high-performance aircraft engines.

So far as Rudge were concerned, he summed up the various advantages by saying that duplicating the valves made it much easier to obtain reliability in a high-output engine. More specifically, reliability was

enhanced because two small exhaust valves ran cooler than one large one; small valves were mechanically stronger than large ones; and their much lighter reciprocating weight banished valve float, even with return springs giving a pressure (in the Ulster engine) of only 83lb at half lift. As for performance, the larger total opening area meant deeper breathing, despite relatively short timings and slowish opening and closing rates, while the sparking plug could be placed in the middle of the head, to give the shortest possible flame path, hence more efficient combustion.

Mainspring of Rudge's adoption of paired valves was the company's boss, John Pugh — a sound engineer in his own right who recognized and encouraged the young Hack's talent from the start. By the time I had the good fortune to meet him (through a mutual acquaintance, John Greenwood) George Hack was 18 years into a well-earned retirement. Yet his recollection of Rudge affairs was almost crystal clear, although he'd had no connection with the motorcycle industry since 1939.

'Since a central plug position was an important factor in your design change,' I began, 'why did your early four-valvers have the plug low down on one side of the cylinder head?'

'In their Ricardo model,' Hack recalled, 'Triumph had gone to four valves a few years before us; and rumours had reached us of many cracked cylinder heads there. So, for safety's sake, we changed only the valve gear at first. Of course, the side plug had its own attraction — accessibility.'

Soon, however, Hack moved the plug to the middle, whereupon Rudge too suffered from head cracking, both between the plug hole and the exhaust seats and between the two exhaust seats themselves.

When, for the 1927 TT, all four ports of the racing engine were enlarged as part of a development programme that boosted peak power to 28bhp at 5,200rpm, the opportun-

ity was taken to splay the hitherto-parallel exhaust ports outward and thus provide space between them for more finning and a freer airflow.

To the extent that Rudge then began to make their mark in the European 500cc championship (culminating in a one-two by Tyrell Smith and Graham Walker at Francorchamps in 1930) and in the Senior TT, where Wal Handley scored a most emphatic victory in pouring rain the same year — to that extent those splayed exhaust ports seemed to have banished the pent-roof four-valver's problems. In fact, however, the move was only partially successful as a cure for head cracking; and Hack's decisive remedy, on the works 500cc racers in 1931, was twofold. First, he disposed the exhaust valves radially, which allowed more metal between the seats and a further increase in finning; second, he persuaded the sparking plug manufacturers to reduce thread diameter from 18 to 14mm, which gave an extra 2mm of metal between the plug hole and the valve seats.

That semi-radial arrangement — in which the parallel inlet valves were opened by a conventional rocker with two fingers while the exhausts were actuated by an ingenious system of three separate rockers — was adopted on the Ulster engine for 1933 and retained until the end of production. Only briefly, in 1932, were all four Ulster valves radially disposed, with actuation by six rockers.

Nevertheless, Rudge's first departure from the pent-roof configuration was, in fact, a full-radial arrangement — for the 1930 Junior (350cc) TT in which they scored a resounding hat-trick, straight from the drawing board, through Tyrell Smith, Ernie Nott and Graham Walker. 'The chief object of the layout,' to quote George Hack, 'was to secure the most compact combustion chamber, with a central plug to obtain complete combustion with relatively small optimum ignition advance. Incidentally, there was less

George Hack (Rudge Whitworth).

heat loss to the chamber walls and better cooling for the exhaust valves.'

A pedant might point out that this thermodynamic advantage was obtained at the cost of a slight increase in the reciprocating weight of the valve gear, compared with the pent-roof engine. In effect, however, any increase was negligible and all three of Rudge's four-valve layouts were superior to comparable two-valvers in terms of ease of valve control.

As further proof of the soundness of Rudge thinking on combustion, their devastating Junior TT performance was reinforced by Nott's victory in the European 350cc championship at Francorchamps. Then, for the following year's racing (1931), they scaled down the radial engine to 250cc and came within an ace of scoring another TT hat-trick when a slack tappet locknut on the final lap dropped Nott from first place to fourth, leaving Walker to win from Tyrell Smith.

Walker also won the European 250cc championship, at Montlhéry, where Nott retained his 350cc title. And so competitive were those radial two-fifties that — more than a year after the factory quit racing for financial reasons — they gave the marque another TT hat-trick (in the 1934 Lightweight) through a private syndicate comprising Jimmy Simpson, Nott and Walker.

Why, then, did the 500cc racer not benefit similarly from the full-radial layout? And why did the Ulster engine revert to parallel inlet valves after only a year in six-rocker guise? Simply because the combination of a single carburettor and radial inlet valves impaired the volumetric efficiency of the big cylinder — which breathed more deeply through parallel inlets and their straighter ports.

Hack preferred a single carburettor for simplicity, so the inlet tract was divided, by a knife-edge wall, into two branches to feed the separate valves. With the valves radially disposed, the branches needed much more curvature to bring them in line with the valve heads than was the case with parallel valves — and the larger the cylinder bore, the more the curvature. There was no problem with the 62.5mm bore of the two-fifty, or even the 70mm bore of the three-fifty; but with the five-hundred's 85mm bore the porting was too curly.

'I tried two carburettors on a fully radial five-hundred,' George Hack told me, 'but never got anywhere.' It should be noted, however, that in this and other areas of development, Hack's scope was increasingly constrained, long before the outbreak of war, by the company's looming liquidation.

Another question in my mind, not raised by *Torrens,* concerned the nature of the contacts between the first, second and third rockers — and was equally relevant to the radial and semi-radial valve gear. As the exploded drawing of the Ulster engine shows, both contact surfaces on the second (middle) rocker were ground flat, while the mating contacts on the first and third rockers were ground cylindrical.

On the face of it, one might expect the first contact to have been the more troublesome, since the rockers operated in planes at 90 degrees to one another; and the second contact to have presented no problem, with both rockers operating in the same plane. In fact, it was the other way round.

Graham Walker (Rudge Whitworth) leads Charlie Dodson (Sunbeam) in the 1928 Ulster 500cc Grand Prix. Walker's eventual victory gave the name Ulster to the four-valve sports machine Rudge introduced the following year.

The first Rudge Ulster with semi-radial valve gear — the 1933 model.

By the ingenious method of grinding the cylindrical form on the first rocker *so that its axis bisected the angle between the first and second rocker planes,* a substantially rolling contact was obtained. But to the rolling contact between the flat surface on the other end of the second rocker and the cylindrical radius on the third rocker was added an inevitable sliding contact, since the rocker axes were fixed.

So long as the valve gear was exposed to the elements and unlubricated, as on the racing machines, it was the second contact that suffered from rapid wear — and, as a palliative, an H-section slipper was inserted to halve the rubbing speed. But the true solution, adopted on the Ulster engine, was to enclose the valve gear and flood it with oil — in which case the slipper was discarded.

At school, Hack's favourite subject was chemistry, and his consequent flair for metallurgy was invaluable to Rudge in the selection of materials and heat treatment. At the time of *Torrens'* visit to the factory, the Ulster cylinder head had just undergone its second change of material — from aluminium bronze to RR50, a high-duty aluminium

alloy of considerable strength and relatively low thermal expansion.

Besides saving some 10lb in weight, the new head conducted surplus heat away much faster than did its predecessor, thus greatly extending the advantages the bronze head had itself brought when it superseded the original cast-iron head several years earlier. But whereas aluminium-bronze was tough enough to form seats for the valves, the light-alloy head needed inserts, for which austenitic iron was chosen for its resistance to hammering and a thermal expansion rate approaching that of the head itself.

For retention, a 0.005in interference fit was used — *ie,* measured separately at atmospheric temperature, the seat rings were 0.005in larger in diameter than their recesses in the head. For ease of fitting, the head was heated to some 100 degrees C by immersion in a trichlorethylene degreaser while the rings were cooled to about minus 20 degrees C in solid carbon dioxide; these measures reduced the interference below 0.001in, so that the rings·could be driven home without much pressure.

With the engine running, the interference was only a shade less than at atmospheric

temperature, due to the slightly greater expansion of the head. But, in the case of the exhaust seats, extra security was ensured by chamfering their outer edges and rolling the head material over the chamfers with a rotary tool piloted in the valve guides.

A similar method of shrink-fitting was used for the five screwed bronze bushes (chosen for thread strength and high expansion) that accepted the long holding-down studs. In that case, however, the inserts were screwed in very quickly, by means of a drill, to prevent premature locking as they expanded under heat. To obviate any possibility of their turning in the head, two flats were formed at the bottom of each bush and the head material was punched against the flats by a Brinell hardness tester. The fifth clamping point was situated midway between the exhaust ports, to obviate an earlier tendency for the head joint to blow there.

When it came to the valve guides, the carbon dioxide/trichlorethylene technique was unsuitable because it would have made it impossible for the home mechanic to renew them when worn. Instead, they were an ordinary hot-water fit. The material was a

Enclosure of the valve gear, from 1937, enhanced the engine's neat appearance.

nickel-chrome cast iron — a high-grade material that takes a good finish and wears well. All four guides had a knife-edge chamfer at the top to prevent too much oil from getting down the stems, particularly the inlets.

Valve material followed racing practice, with KE965 (an austenitic steel) chosen for the exhausts for its retention of strength at high temperatures, while the inlets were made of 3 per cent nickel steel, hardened and tempered, enabling the stem diameter to be reduced to $\frac{1}{4}$in. This, together with a reduced radius under the head, arrived at by air-flowing tests, gave increased volumetric efficiency.

The shapes of the valve heads more-or-less matched the combustion-chamber profile insofar as the inlets were flat while the exhausts were semi-tulip; the important point there was that the tulip shape gave slight flexibility, hence freedom from breakage.

Stem clearance (in the guides) was a mere couple of thou for the inlets, so minimizing the chance of oil being sucked into the combustion chamber; the exhaust stems, however, needed a larger clearance because they ran hotter and their material had a higher thermal expansion rate. Stem diameters were only $\frac{1}{4}$in (inlet) and $\frac{5}{16}$in (exhaust), so contributing to low reciprocating weight. Both the valve stems and the top collars were tapered, so the spring load was taken by the tapers and not by the small shoulder at the top of the stem.

Inlet-port diameter at the valve seat was $1\frac{1}{8}$in, so providing a pretty hefty total opening area. During manufacture, port diameter was checked by rolling steel balls of various sizes right through them. No bush was used for the sparking plug thread, the head material proving amply strong considering the length of the thread, $\frac{3}{4}$in. To avoid pockets of stagnant air, the massive cluster of vertical fins between the exhaust ports was separated from the valve tray by a $\frac{1}{8}$in gap, which was formed by coring, not machining. There was a direct passage between the exhaust ports to get a draught of air to the plug.

Before leaving the cylinder head and proceeding downward, *Torrens* asked George Hack what the valve rockers were made of. 'Three per cent nickel case-hardening steel,' he was told, 'because it is easier to machine than nickel-chrome steel and has proved very satisfactory.'

All three exhaust rockers pivoted on bronze bushes clamped in forked bosses formed integrally with the head. 'You will notice,' Hack added, 'that a separate banjo union feeds oil to each pivot pin and so, through drillways, lubricates its bush. The floor of the valve tray slopes down towards the $1\frac{1}{4}$in-diameter pushrod tube, thus draining the oil down over the timing gear on its way to the sump for return to the tank.'

Like the valve guides, the cylinder was made of nickel-chrome cast iron and the bore was ground only, not honed. Why so? First, because honing was at that time insufficiently reliable and any hone material left in the bore would cause excessive wear if not removed in its entirety; second, the final fine-grinding gave the bore a matt finish, with a useful oil-retaining property. The joint at the head was made with a plain copper washer, clamped between the inner faces so as to preclude any possibility of an annular gas trap.

A thickness of nearly $\frac{3}{4}$in ensured ample strength in the base flange — and the effect was enhanced by placing the six retaining studs in the crankcase mouth as close as possible to the cylinder wall. This entailed not only providing six small scallops in the cylinder for clearance, but also making the studs small in diameter. For that reason they were made of an alloy steel that ensured they would neither strip nor break.

The $7\frac{1}{4}$in-diameter, 1in-wide flywheels were drop-forgings in 0.35 per cent carbon steel, chosen because it was tough enough to resist stretch in the holes for the crankpin and mainshafts; thus they could be renewed during a major overhaul without risk of a slack fit.

For the drop-forged connecting rod 5 per cent nickel case-hardening steel was chosen, heat-treated to a tensile strength of 75 to 80 tons/sq in. 'Considering its potential strength,' Hack told *Torrens,* 'this material is particularly easy to machine while in the annealed condition. The subsequent heat-treatment, too, is simple — case-hardening (in the bores only) to a depth of 0.05

to 0.06in.' The hardening was necessary because both the gudgeon pin and the big-end rollers ran directly in the con-rod eyes — the absence of bushes saving both weight and bulk.

Unusually, the rod had a smooth dumbell section rather than a pronounced H-section. 'We have always raced with this section,' Hack revealed, 'and it has proved very effective.'

For a tough core that would take a hard bearing surface, the crankpin was made of 2 per cent nickel case-hardening steel. Bearing diameter for the three rows of rollers was $1\frac{5}{16}$in, while the axles were of only $\frac{7}{8}$in diameter. Separating the different diameters were two large flanges that pulled up against the inner faces of the flywheels to give the necessary rigidity. 'Given a really rigid junction between the crankpin and flywheels,' Hack explained, 'the axles do not need to be any larger since they are mainly in shear.' The crankpin nuts (like those securing the taper-fit mainshafts) were locked by hexagon-hole washers and set-screws.

For strength and lightness, the big-end roller cage was in duralumin. And, since the softer metal invariably wears the harder one, the cage was located on the crankpin flanges, leaving the bearing tracks untouched. Fed in

the usual way through the timing-side mainshaft, the crankpin oil hole faced forward at top dead centre.

There were three main bearings. Close up to the flywheel assembly on each side was a single-row caged bearing with 0.4in-long rollers, its outer race a press fit in the diecast crankcase; outboard of the drive side-roller bearing, and separated from it by a spacer, was a ball bearing retained in the case by a threaded lock ring. To simplify cleaning, the race-pattern crankcase ribs that characterized earlier Rudge Ulsters had been discarded in favour of a smooth exterior. No loss of stiffness was entailed, for wall thickness tapered outward from a maximum of approximately half an inch around the bearings.

To minimize the reduction in mainshaft diameter, the drive to the transmission shock absorber was taken through shallow serrations, with a 55-degree flank angle, rather than the more conventional splines; it was a feature Rudge had used with considerable success on their detachable car wheel.

Housed at the base of the timing chest, the worm-driven rotary plunger of the oil pump had a considerably larger diameter at the rear than at the front. As a result, the capacity of the scavenge side was $2\frac{1}{2}$ times

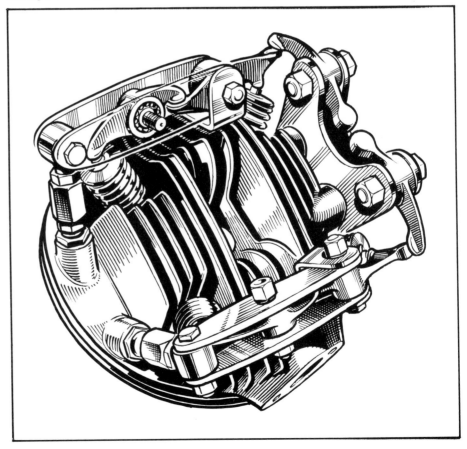

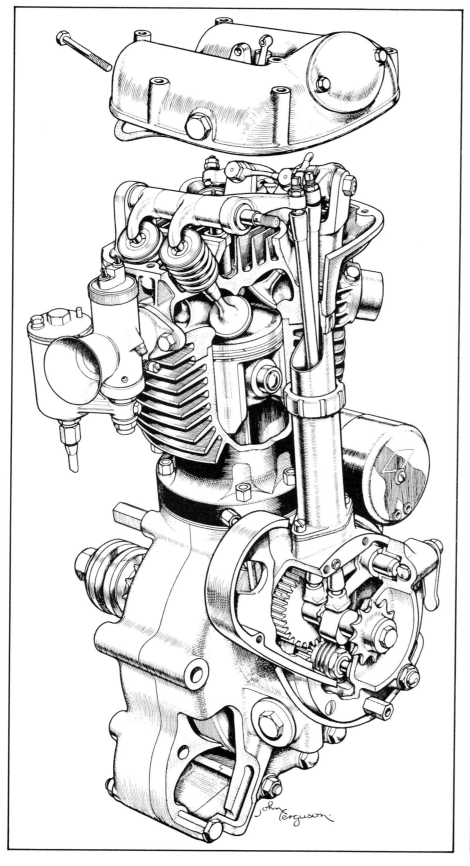

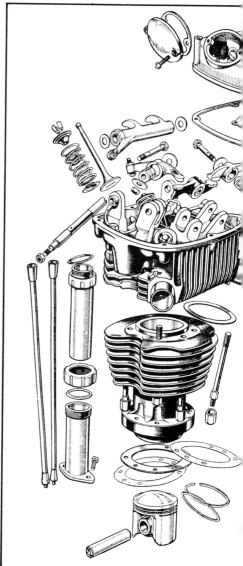

Sectioned drawing of the 1937 engine, showing the inlet-port bifurcation and full-length pushrods.

that of the delivery side, so preventing an accumulation of oil in the sump. Plunger material was KE805 oil-hardening steel, which suffered minimum distortion in hardening and gave very strong teeth.

'At the time we enclosed the valve gear,' Hack informed *Torrens*, 'we doubled the pump capacity. It now delivers almost half a pint a minute at an engine speed of 5,000rpm. The feed goes three ways — to the big-end bearing, the rear of the cylinder wall and the valve gear — and, once the oil is hot, the big end gets 13 pints an hour, the valve gear 12 pints and the cylinder 2½.'

'From a cold start, however, the cylinder gets appreciably more at the expense of the valve gear, because the long external pipe to the cylinder head restricts the flow of cold oil.'

I asked George Hack why it had been necessary to feed oil to the cylinder anyway, since that flung out of the big-end bearing is usually found to be ample. 'The need arose in the TT,' was the answer. 'In those days we were not allowed to warm-up the engine just prior to the race; without a cylinder feed, a full-throttle start with cold oil could scuff the thrust face of the piston straight away.'

In view of the direct cylinder feed, albeit greatly reduced once the engine was hot, I was surprised to learn that the piston had only the usual two compression rings and no oil scraper. 'We just didn't find a scraper necessary,' Hack told me. 'Anyway, the plain rings gave a pretty high specific pressure, being thick radially, only 1½mm wide and hardened. We found that hard rings were kinder to the cylinder bore than were soft ones, which tended to fritter away and provide a lapping powder.'

The piston itself was a shallow-domed, slipper-type diecasting in Y-alloy — a nickel aluminium alloy combining high structural strength with low thermal expansion and a good finish. For roundness at running temperatures, it was ground elliptically, with the fore-and-aft diameter some 0.006 to 0.007in greater than that across the skirt edges; and to control skirt expansion there were circumferential slots just below the lower ring groove.

Standard compression ratio was 6.8:1, though this was raised as high as 7.5:1 for competition purposes, in conjunction with racing cams and a larger-bore carburettor.

Of ¾in diameter, the lapped gudgeon pin was made of 3 per cent nickel steel and well supported in piston bosses only an inch apart. Mistrusting circlips for long-term use, Hack located the pin by end pads pressed out

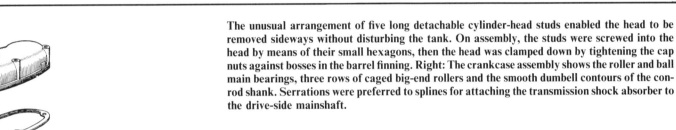

The unusual arrangement of five long detachable cylinder-head studs enabled the head to be removed sideways without disturbing the tank. On assembly, the studs were screwed into the head by means of their small hexagons, then the head was clamped down by tightening the cap nuts against bosses in the barrel finning. Right: The crankcase assembly shows the roller and ball main bearings, three rows of caged big-end rollers and the smooth dumbell contours of the conrod shank. Serrations were preferred to splines for attaching the transmission shock absorber to the drive-side mainshaft.

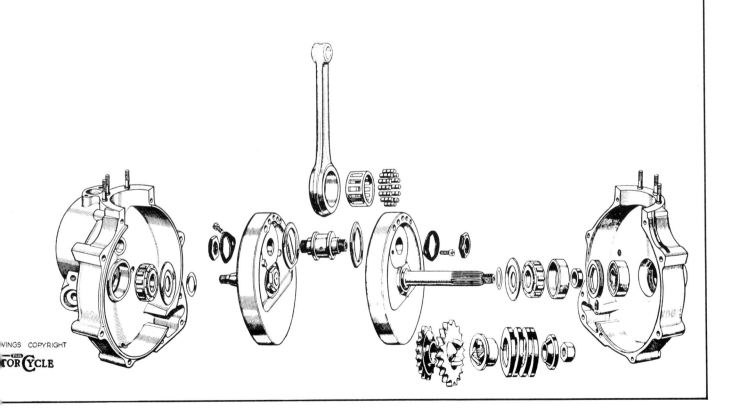

15

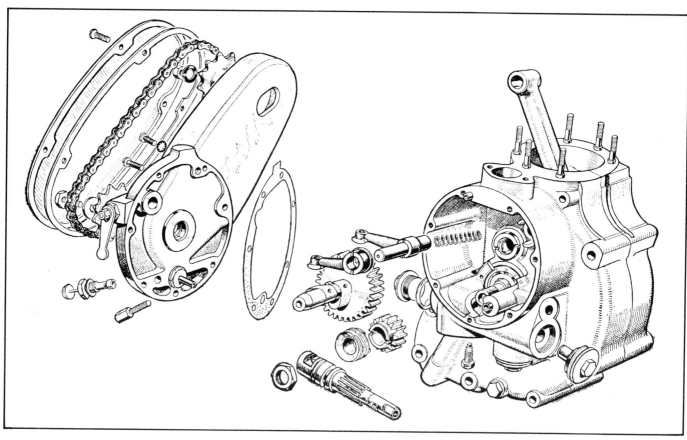

The magneto was chain-driven from the cam-shaft, and the oil pump worm-driven from the mainshaft. Between the two cam lobes was a small decompressor cam.

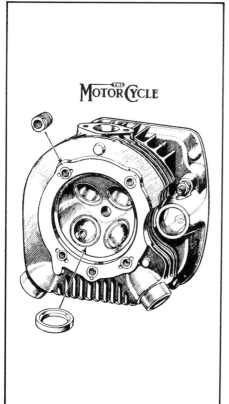

Underhead contour was flat for the inlet valves, part-spherical for the exhausts. The four austenitic-iron valve seats and five screwed bronze bushes were shrunk in position.

of sheet bronze and pushed up to internal shoulders in the pin.

Ground after hardening, the timing gears were paired selectively to achieve minimum backlash. Made of manganese case-hardening steel in order to obtain a hard enough surface, the cams were formed integrally with their shaft, which was pressed into its wheel (and had a taper on its outer end to accept the chain sprocket for the drive to the rear-mounted magneto).

Pivoted cam followers actuated the push-rods direct. As a contribution to low reciprocating weight with adequate stiffness, the rods were made from $\frac{3}{8}$in-diameter RR56 aluminium-alloy tubing, with the oil-hardened steel ends pressed on. A happy consequence of the use of light alloy for both cylinder head and pushrods was that valve clearances differed hardly at all, hot or cold.

The four-valver's inherent ability to extract sporting performance from modest valve timings enabled Rudge to endow the Ulster with commendable mechanical quietness and longevity. Measured with a clearance of 0.020in, the inlet valves opened 10mm before top dead centre and closed 13mm after bottom dead centre, while the exhausts opened 16mm before bdc and closed 10mm after tdc. Converted into the more usual terms of crankshaft rotation,

Tyrell Smith rounds Quarter Bridge on the way to a great victory in the 1930 Junior TT on Rudge's first machine with a radial-valve engine.

those figures give (approximately) an inlet period from 35 degrees early to 50 degrees late and an exhaust period from 55 degrees early to 35 degrees late — a valve overlap of about 70 degrees. (For racing, the overlap was just about doubled, while the inlet-closing and exhaust-opening points were extended by about 15 degrees.) Ulster ignition advance, dependent on compression ratio, ranged from 12 to 14mm (*ie,* a little more or less than 40 degrees).

Transforming an out-and-out racer into such a civilized sportster was a great credit to George Hack, especially in view of the increasing constraints imposed by the company's deteriorating financial position.

For racing purposes, there was and still is a limit to how far any designer can exploit the mechanical and thermodynamic advantages of the four-valve head in a big single — because taming the valve gear merely transfers the engine's Achilles heel to the big-end bearing as the power peak is pushed farther up the rpm scale.

When I asked George Hack whether Rudge had considered extending the limit by cutting cylinder size (which not only reduces mechanical loadings but also increases relative port sizes) he told me of the radial-valve 250cc V-twin he designed for racing in the early 1930s. Since supercharging was then permitted (and catching-on fast), the cylinders were fed by an eccentric-vane compressor. Alas, the project had to be dropped as liquidation loomed. Another promising racing development that suffered the same fate was a 500cc engine with the stroke shortened to about 61mm to make an oversquare three-fifty.

The circumstances in which Honda adopted the pent-roof four-valve cylinder head as the cornerstone of their grand-prix challenge in the early 1960s differed profoundly from those in which Rudge Whitworth operated several decades earlier; indeed, it was almost inevitable that Honda would have to exploit the potential of the layout to a greater degree than Rudge had been able to.

For a start, since supercharging had been outlawed for classic racing, the only reliable road to increased specific power lay through a combination of higher engine speeds and adequate breathing — hence shorter strokes leading to smaller cylinders and more of them, twin overhead camshafts for even lighter reciprocating masses in the valve gear and squish segments front and rear for even more compact combustion chambers.

Then, the unparalleled challenge of the disc-valve two-stroke (together with rapid advances in tyre grip) propelled Honda ever faster along that road; diminishing returns notwithstanding, individual cylinder size shrank from 62.5 to 25cc, cylinder groups multiplied from two to four, five and six and peak revs climbed from 13,000rpm to nearly 20,000.

Unlike Rudge, Honda had almost unlimited resources to back their engineering efforts. But in the annals of the four-valve engine no name is prouder than that of Rudge — and not least the Ulster.

CHAPTER 2

DKW three-cylinder racer

Highly competitive 350cc two-stroke whose off-beat cylinder layout was
an evolutionary accident

In its mid-fifties heyday, the strange-looking three-cylinder DKW two-stroke was one of the most praiseworthy grand-prix machines never to achieve the supreme accolade of a world championship. Technically, it was a brilliantly pragmatic conversion from a disappointing rotary-valve 250cc parallel twin to a piston-ported 350cc flier that pushed the all-conquering Moto Guzzi flat singles to the limit.

Nearly 30 years later, following the NR500 fiasco, Honda salvaged their sporting pride with an equally peculiar three-cylinder two-stroke — the NS500 on which Freddie Spencer won the 1983 world 500cc championship. The sad irony of the situation was that the journalists of the day made an entirely false comparison. Seemingly unaware of the real (and well documented) reasons for the Deek's off-beat cylinder layout — the middle one prone, the others rampant — they interpreted the middle cylinder position instead as a cunning ploy to lower the machine's centre of gravity. (At best that would have been a drop in the ocean, considering the 36-litre fuel load above the engine.) By inference, Honda had resurrected the idea — indeed, improved on it by widening the cylinder spacing from 75 to 112 degrees.

Clearly Honda appreciated the benefits of a low centre of gravity because — in the NSR500 V4 that succeeded Spencer's three in 1984 — they put the fuel load below the engine and the much lighter exhaust boxes above it. Doubtless, too, they staggered the three's middle cylinder to bring the other two closer together and so make the engine narrower than a three-abreast without cramping the size of the transfer passages or twisting the cylinders appreciably on their axes to overlap adjacent passages (as on the Suzuki GT750). In contrast, however, DKW never even set out to design a three-cylinder engine. Both the middle cylinder and its position were simply quirks of the engine's rapid evolution — albeit the arrangement naturally allowed ample transfer space.

The highest praise for the Deek came from Fergus Anderson, Moto Guzzi's shrewd team manager, in 1955. The German three, he said, had sufficient speed and acceleration to have won the world championship; it was simply outgunned by the Italian team's riding talent, particularly that of the year's 350cc king-pin, Bill Lomas. That assessment may have been a trifle generous, since the Deek's high and heavy fuel load tended to make it a handful in fast bumpy bends, whereas the low, light Italian singles handled impeccably.

In part, too, Anderson's respect for the three-cylinder engine may have been a reaction to his scathing opinion of DKW's race strategy before the war, when he accused them of 'brute force and ignorance' for exploiting high-pressure supercharging (mostly of piston type) to blow the opposition extremely noisily into the weeds in the European 250 and 350cc championships.

For a few years after the war those ingenious and thirsty racers — with two out-of-phase pistons per combustion chamber (to close the exhaust ports before the transfers) — still lorded it over the opposition in German national races. But when the FIM readmitted Germany to international competition in 1951, supercharging had already been banned in road racing for five years. Consequently, the DKW engineers (in their postwar Ingolstadt home) had no option but to abandon their 26-year-old tradition and design an unblown racing engine. It was for them the end of the line for the pumping type of two-stroke and the beginning of reliance on gas resonances to charge and scavenge the cylinder.

Their first effort was a 125cc single. The earlier double-piston layout, with its articulated connecting rods, was abandoned — partly because much higher revs would be required in the absence of supercharging and partly because separation of the exhaust and transfer ports low down in adjacent cylinder bores was hardly conducive to the best use of

exhaust resonances for cylinder filling. For charging the crankcase, however, they rejected piston control of the inlet port, with its necessarily short (symmetrical) opening period, in favour of a gear-driven cylindrical rotary valve across the back of the crankcase, giving longer (asymmetrical) timing without blowback through the carburettor. (Such a valve had been used to feed the compressor of the blown split-single two-fifty on which Ewald Kluge dominated the 1938 Lightweight TT and the European 250cc championship in that and the following year.)

Soon the little postwar single was doubled-up into a 250cc parallel twin with the rotary valve lengthened to feed both crank chambers alternately from a common carburettor at one end. To the engineers' dismay, however, the considerable difference in the lengths of the two induction tracts resulted in an uncompetitive performance, and so the rotor was turned through 90 degrees to lie fore-and-aft between the two crank chambers. In that way the tract lengths were equalized and shortened. The carburettor fed the rear of the rotor while the other end drove the magneto, which protruded horizontally from the front of the crankcase. It needs little imagination to see in that revised parallel-twin layout the first glimmerings of the three-cylinder engine.

Be that as it may, the changed rotor position boosted engine performance sufficiently for Siegfried Wünsche — one of the team's prewar stars, who was familiar with the TT course — to finish third in the 1953 Lightweight 250cc race, albeit more than 4 minutes behind winner Fergus Anderson (Moto Guzzi) and newcomer Werner Haas (NSU).

However, engineers Erich Woolf and August Jacob had already recognized that the cylindrical inlet valve — so successful in a comparatively low-revving supercharged engine with late-closing transfer ports — was far from ideal in a design which, under the new rules, could achieve competitive power

Helmut Görg (DKW).

only through high rpm and gas resonances. Compared with the crankshaft-mounted disc valve then being developed by MZ's Walter Kaaden in Zschopau (DKW's prewar home), the cylindrical valve not only required a power-absorbing gear drive; it also provided both a long, tortuous gas tract with a lower resonant frequency and — because of its smaller effective diameter — slower port opening, hence a weaker pressure pulse.

So, in 1952, Woolf and Jacob abandoned their rotary valve in favour of piston-controlled porting, put a horizontal cylinder (with longitudinal finning) in place of the magneto and reduced the bore and stroke to 53 × 52.8mm to give a total capacity of 349cc. In short, the third cylinder and its crank assembly were simply put in the space vacated by the magneto, and discarded inlet valve. End of 'mystery'.

Each cylinder had its own carburettor, of course, and sparks were initially provided by a six-cylinder magneto driven at half engine speed from the right-hand end of the crankshaft.

It was DKW's first racing engine with symmetrical timing of all ports. For nearly 30 years they had used mechanical means to circumvent the restrictions inherent in that feature — through supercharging, reed valves and rotary valves on the inlet side, and through out-of-phase pistons on the exhaust/transfer side. Now, at last, the regulations had outdated those methods and the way ahead lay in controlling gas movements by harnessing the natural resonances in the exhaust and inlet tracts.

To suit the magneto, if for no other reason, the firing intervals had to be equal — ie, 120 degrees. Whereas, with three cylinders in line, that merely involves spacing the crankpins equally around the crankshaft, the 75-degree offset of the middle cylinder necessitated an equally peculiar layout for the crankpins. Those for the end cylinders were, of course, disposed at 120 degrees to one another, but the middle pin trailed the right-hand one by only 45 degrees. (In the Honda three-cylinder engine, this figure is reduced to a mere 8 degrees.)

Initially the new three gave a modest 31.5bhp and lacked reliability (Wünsche rode it in the 1953 Junior TT but retired). Its rapid rise to world class soon afterwards is a classic example of what can be achieved by first-class development engineering — in this case by the eager and talented Helmut Görg, who took over in March 1954.

Within little more than a year he had raised peak power to 42bhp at 9,700rpm, reliability was a byword, fuel consumption by no means disgraceful at about 30mpg — and August Hobl finished second to Lomas in both the German and Belgian Grands Prix. (It was the day after the latter race that I rode south-east to Ingolstadt to study the engine.) Before the month (July) was out Hobl had consolidated the German 350cc championship; by the season's end he was third in the world rankings to Lomas and his Moto Guzzi team-mate, Dickie Dale. A further three bhp were rumoured to be in the kitty in 1956, when Hobl improved his world-championship performance by splitting the Moto Guzzi pair. At the end of the season, alas, DKW pulled out of grand-prix racing, a year ahead of Moto Guzzi.

If there was one feature, besides his enthusiasm, that impressed me about Görg's work it was his painstaking attention to detail. Externally, the chief change to the engine seemed to be the absence of the bulky magneto. In its place was a contact-breaker assembly for a 6-volt battery-and-coil system, chosen for its better sparks, reduced rotating mass and slight power saving. Inside the engine, however, vital improvements had been made to the bearing layout, shaft rigidity, port timing, piston and cylinder-head design and lubrication.

In stiffening the crankshaft and its main bearings, Görg had arrived at dimensions of 22.5mm (just over $\frac{7}{8}$in) for the shaft itself and 55mm for the outside diameter of the four

DKW's solitary entry in the 1956 Junior TT, Cecil Sandford finished fourth in wet and windy conditions.

The caged-roller main bearings incorporated gas seals and were located by rings trapped in crankcase grooves.

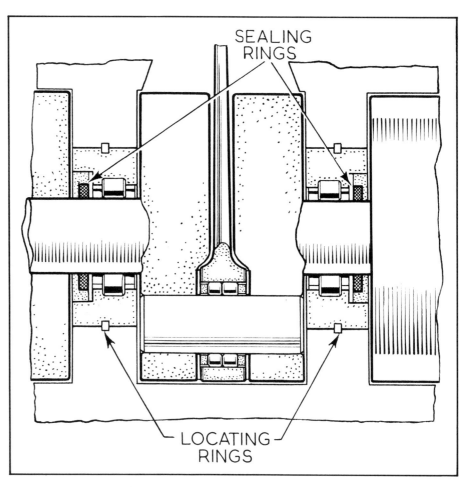

SEALING RINGS

LOCATING RINGS

roller bearings supporting it in the Elektron (magnesium alloy) crankcase. These sizes, I noted, were appreciably larger than those for the famous 350cc Mark 8 KTT Velocette *single,* with three times the individual cylinder capacity. And whereas aligning the KTT mainshafts to within 'half a thou' (*ie,* 0.0005in) was a matter for self-congratulation — and perfectly satisfactory with only two closely spaced main bearings — shaft alignment on the DKW was checked with a gauge reading to a thousandth of a millimetre; that is 0.00003937in or, in Imperial engineering slang, appreciably less than 'half a tenth'!

Naturally alignment was more critical in an 11in-long pressed-up shaft with four evenly spaced bearings; but when Görg checked an assembly for me that had completed the German GP, the indicator needle remained virtually motionless.

The main-bearing outer races were located laterally by split rings fitted in matching grooves in the races and crankcase walls; differential expansion of the shaft and case was accommodated within the bearings. Each bearing also incorporated a metal gas seal, developed to obviate excessive shaft wear caused by rubber seals. Lateral location of the complete shaft assembly was by a ball thrust bearing on the left-hand end, in the primary drive cover.

To minimize crankcase volume (in the interest of a high primary compression ratio) the highly polished, 3½in-diameter flywheel discs had a bare working clearance in their crank chambers. Moreover, there was only 6mm (less than ¼in) between each pair for the slender oval-section connecting rod; and the two 24mm-diameter balance holes in the outer face of each disc were plugged by thin light-alloy blanks.

In the big-end bearings, two rows of caged 4 × 5mm rollers ran directly on the 17.5mm-diameter crankpins, while the con-rod eyes were slotted and scalloped for lubrication. Plain small-end bushes, even when allowed to float in the con-rods, wore rapidly at high rpm and were replaced by steel-caged needle rollers.

Forged in aluminium alloy, the pistons had the usual shallow domes and the skirts cut away at the sides to avoid masking the transfer passages at bottom dead centre. For

flywheel clearance at the same point the bottom skirt edges were ground; and since skirt length on the inlet side was critical for port timing too, a special grinding jig was made for the purpose. Görg had not got around to trying only one ring per piston but was progressively reducing the thickness of the two plain alloy-steel rings, which was 1.25mm (about 0.050in) at the time.

With 6in-square finning on the end ones and radial finning to a diameter of 6in on the middle one, the cylinders comprised cast-iron liners shrunk in aluminium-alloy jackets. To ensure accuracy of port profiles and consistency as between all cylinders, Görg had abandoned hand grinding in favour of the use of internal and external cylinder jigs during manufacture. Inlet and exhaust ports, both oval, were then carefully blended into the bolted-on adaptors for carburettor and exhaust pipe, respectively. A change in the induction-tract contour, to aim the ingoing charge more directly at the main bearings, was claimed to have permitted a reduction in the proportion of SAE50 vegetable oil in the petrol from 6 to 4 per cent.

After port shaping was finished, each cylinder was bolted to a dummy crankcase

and its port timing checked by means of a protractor on the end of the crankshaft.

At the time, the benefits of the third transfer port (and its variations) — both in power and small-end life — had yet to emerge from Zschopau. Accordingly, the DKW cylinders had the customary rectangular transfer port at each side, directing the charge tangentially backward and upward against the cylinder wall. A crescent-shape squish band with a bare working clearance from the front of the piston crown confined the combustion space to the rear of the head — and there the rising gas column was given the loop flow pattern required, first for scavenging, then for turbulence. Calculated from bottom dead centre, secondary compression ratio was 12:1 — probably around 7:1 in Japanese terms (measured from exhaust-port closure). To obviate distortion, the sleeve nuts retaining the cylinders and heads were tightened with a torque-indicating wrench.

Driven by a tongued plastic coupling, the contact-breaker unit was housed in a light-alloy casting on the right-hand end of the crankcase. All three sets of points were independently adjustable for gap and timing,

The compact power unit weighed only 75lb, including the five-speed all-indirect gearbox. Plastic sleeves insulated the carburettors from heat and intake gauzes were claimed to stabilize airflow. A ball bearing in the primary drive cover located the crankshaft laterally. The small generator outboard of the cover powered the 15,000rpm tachometer.

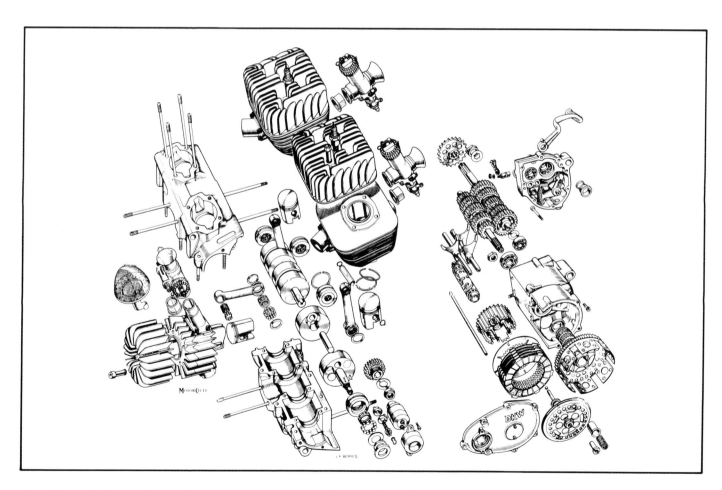

The differential finning of the cylinders and heads was designed to suit the airflow. Note the shallow-dome piston-crowns, the pressed-up construction of the crankshaft and the grooves in the crankcase webs for main-bearing location. Primary drive was by spur gears on the left to a five-speed all-direct gearbox bolted to the back of the crankcase.

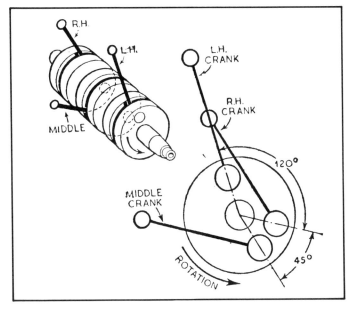

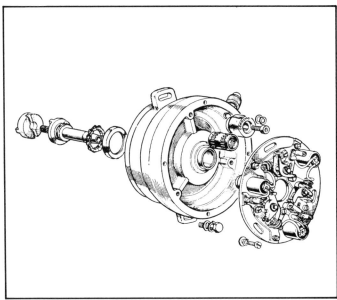

Firing intervals were 120 degrees, but because the middle cylinder lay 75 degrees forward of the parallel cylinders the crankpins were not equally spaced. The outer pins were disposed at 120 degrees to one another but the middle pin was only 45 degrees out of phase with the right-hand one.

Driven by a plastic coupling, the triple contact breaker had individual and overall adjustments. A long, double-row needle bearing stabilized the cam; the lobe was drilled to reduce unbalanced mass.

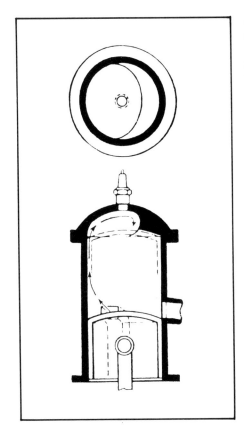

This sketch from a DKW patent specification shows the effect of the half-moon squish band on gas flow during the transfer phase.

while slotted mounting lugs provided for overall adjustment.

Grand-prix two-strokes are notoriously sensitive to ignition timing and it was no surprise to learn that each cylinder was timed (within a range of 3 to 4mm advance) with a lamp and battery and a dial indicator on the piston crown reading to a hundredth of a millimetre (0.0003937in), again less than our old friend 'half a thou'.

An earlier tendency for the timing to advance at high rpm was traced to fling of the cam lobe. The solution was to reduce the out-of-balance mass of the cam by drilling several holes through the lobe and then to stiffen the support of the camshaft by adding a long double-row needle bearing to the original ball bearing in the housing and discarding the plain outrigger bush in the Elektron cover. Incidentally, an ignition cut-out button was provided for full-throttle, clutchless upward gear changes — primarily to prevent interruption of the oil supply to the engine, though faster changes resulted anyway.

Two measures were taken to keep charge temperature down, hence density up. First, the 28mm Dellorto carburettors were insulated from their adaptors by plastic sleeves; second, warm air from the cylinders was deflected away from the rear mixing chambers by light-alloy shields. Each carburettor intake was covered by a large, domed gauze strainer; these were obviously

effective in keeping grit out of the engine, but Görg made the surprising claim that they also stabilized the airflow.

Considering the lengths DKW had gone to in their supercharged engines to close the exhaust port before the transfers, they were obviously keenly aware of the potential charge loss inherent in the opposite sequence, which follows from symmetrical

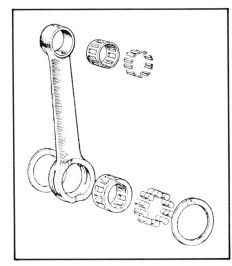

One of the slim connecting rods with two needles side-by-side in each slot of the steel small-end cage and two rollers end-on in each slot of the light-alloy big-end cage.

23

timing of those ports. It was to be expected, therefore, that Görg was one of the first race engineers to experiment extensively with the double-taper sort of exhaust box calculated to harness both negative and positive pressure pulses to pull as much burnt gas as possible out of the cylinder without losing too much of the next charge in the process.

The pursuit of consistency as between individual cylinders was not confined to manufacture. In the test house, too, each cylinder was brake-tested on its own, then matched to others of identical output in a complete engine. The normal operating range extended from 7,500 to 10,000-10,500rpm, where the power curve was relatively flat. Maximum engine speed for indefinite use was 11,000rpm; but so eagerly and sweetly would the revs sing up beyond 15,000 that Görg had to specify a dead hand in the electric revmeter. Since this was pushed round by the live hand and could be brought back only with a magnet, it showed the highest revs reached and so enabled Görg to decide whether any subsequent failure warranted serious investigation or was simply due to inadvertent overrevving. A valuable adjunct to development, though less popular with some riders!

Complete with carburettors and ignition apparatus, the engine was commendably light at 75lb. Unusually for a non-British engine, the five-speed, all-indirect gearbox was not integral with the crankcase, but bolted to the back of it by four long studs. Nevertheless, primary drive was by gears.

When DKW quit the grands prix, there was no sign that Görg had exhausted his ideas. Indeed, he was hoping for a 15-percent improvement in all-round efficiency from a change to fuel injection. Given the further opportunity, the 350cc Deek, like the 125cc MZ, might well have been the first two-stroke to win a world road-racing championship, rather than Ernst Degner's 50cc Suzuki in 1962.

In the 1956 Ulster 350cc Grand Prix Cecil Sandford, on the three-cylinder DKW, leads Moto Guzzi stars Dickie Dale and Bill Lomas into Tornagrough.

CHAPTER 3

Mark 8 KTT Velocette

Last and greatest of an illustrious line of production replicas of the
works single-knocker racers

It would be unrealistic to expect any manufacturer to market racing machines of identical specification and performance to those provided for their contracted riders. Quite apart from wanting to ensure that the team riders are never embarrassed by the best privateers, the makers would be unable to keep the retail cost of such ultra-specialized machines down to a level that the market would stand.

But some manufacturers were always more altruistic than others and the credit for consistently keeping the performance margin between their works and catalogue racers smallest probably belongs to Velocette, whose 350cc overhead-camshaft KTT model — from the birth of the Mark 1 in 1929 to the death of the Mark 8 in the early 1950s — was the nearest thing to a pukka works racer that the amateur could hope to ride.

Indeed, the £80 Mark 1 KTT was the first out-and-out racing model ever marketed and was based on the works machines (with the revolutionary feature of positive-stop foot gear change) on which Alec Bennett and Harold Willis (the factory's development engineer) had filled the first two places in the previous year's Junior TT (1928). Likewise the £120 Mark 8 KTT — star exhibit in the 1938 Earls Court Show — was a much closer copy than seemed possible of the handsomely impressive black-and-gold steeds on which Stanley Woods and Ted Mellors had finished first and second respectively in the Junior TT a few months earlier.

Those Junior TT successes were by no means isolated instances of Velocette prowess on the world's most demanding race circuit. Bennett had already won the race in 1926 (by nearly 10½ minutes) and Willis had first been runner-up in 1927. In 1929 Freddie Hicks brought the company its third Junior victory in four years, with Bennett third. And Woods repeated his 1938 win the following year, when most of the private finishers rode the exciting new Mark 8 KTT. This 350cc dominance continued for a few years after the war, when the Junior TT was

won by Bob Foster in 1947, then by Freddie Frith in 1948 and '49. They also won the first two world 350cc championships — Frith in 1949, Foster in '50.

Externally, the Mark 8 KTT looked positively futuristic compared with the Mark 1. The original model had a comparatively skinny iron cylinder and head, a separate cambox, exposed coil springs for the valves, an 18mm plug, a plain exhaust pipe and no rear springing. In contrast, the last of the noble line had an enormous aluminium cylinder muff topped by 9in-square finning on the head and integral cambox, enclosed hairpin springs, a 14mm plug, megaphone exhaust, magnesium cone hubs and oleo-pneumatic rear springing. Internally, too, there was an equally marked contrast, for the original compression ratio of little more than 7:1 had rocketed to almost 11:1.

Yet many basic features survived the whole KTT series to underline the soundness of Percy Goodman's original ohc design (which first appeared as the Model K roadster in 1925). For rigidity, the crankcase was extraordinarily slim, so enabling the lipped roller main bearings (only one each side) to be closely spaced, directly in line with the walls of the case and cylinder. Similarly, the flywheel assembly itself was equally slim and rigid. And, in view of the use of single main bearings, flexure of the drive-side mainshaft under transmission loads was minimized by placing the primary drive inboard of the secondary, so as to keep the shaft as short as possible and the chain sprocket close up to the bearing.

Although this transmission layout necessitated a rather complex clutch withdrawal mechanism, which was particularly sensitive to correct adjustment, it greatly simplified gearbox-sprocket changes to alter overall gearing — a boon for the racing man. Other unchanged features included the use of bevel gears and vertical shaft to drive the cams, chain drive to the rear-mounted magneto, and cylinder dimensions of 74mm bore and 81mm stroke.

The first batch of Mark 8s had yet to reach the dealers when *Ubique* (the pen-name of Henry Teage, *The Motor Cycle*'s first technical editor) visited the Hall Green, Birmingham, factory to have the whys and wherefores of the engine explained to him by Percy Goodman and Harold Willis. Almost overwhelmed by the gleaming array of parts laid out for his inspection, Teage was eventually persuaded to start at the top and work downward. Nevertheless, the size of the cylinder barrel so impressed him that he started there and asked what the materials were and how they were mated.

To his surprise, he was told that the silicon-aluminium-alloy jacket, with its deep radiating ribs, was cast on the pre-heated nickel-cast-iron liner, the outer surface of which was corrugated to prevent any vertical creeping in service. Willis did not think there was much to choose between that method and the alternative of pressing-in a plain liner (or shrinking-on the jacket) — a method used on the works cylinders with their even larger-diameter fins. (It should be remembered that the superior Wellworthy Al-Fin technique of bonding the two components together, so providing a much freer heat path, was a wartime development, hence not available for the Mark 8.)

The cylinder head, a truly beautiful casting, was made of heat-treated Y-alloy — chosen, *Ubique* was told, for its light weight, strength and high thermal conductivity. The importance of a lightweight material was clear enough from the comprehensive nature of the casting, which included the camshaft-and-rocker housing and two large boxes for the valves and their double hairpin springs. But it was when *Ubique* suggested that it must be well-nigh impossible for a worth-while flow of air to reach the roots of the fins that he learned why high conductivity was so important. For Harold Willis replied that careful tests had shown it was much more effective to get a large cooling surface right out into the draught than to rely on such air as might possibly pass the wheel, mudguard,

25

Harold Willis (Velocette).

The legendary Stanley Woods chalking up his second successive Junior TT victory for Velocette in 1939. The Mark 8 KTT was a production version of Woods' works machine.

fork and frame eventually reaching the fin roots.

(That impressive pattern of head finning was first used on the 1937 works racers and went into production the following spring on the Mark 7 KTT, which was virtually a lower-compression (8.75:1), unsprung precursor of the Mark 8. Full valve enclosure and integration of the cambox with the light-alloy head, however, appeared earlier on the Mark 6 KTT, which inherited the layout from the KSS roadster in 1936. Prior to that, all KTTs had exposed valve gear, while the heads were of aluminium-bronze on the Mark 5 and later Mark 4s, cast iron up to and including the early Mark 4s.)

Noticing the pale-gold hue of the exhaust-valve seat ring, *Ubique* asked why different materials were used for that and the inlet seat. The answer was that the exhaust seat was made of a hard aluminium-bronze alloy because the high thermal conductivity of that metal helped keep the valve cool, while the high coefficient of expansion ensured that the ring maintained firm contact with the head at high temperatures. For the inlet valve, though, where the seat was vulnerable

to grit, a nickel cast iron was preferred for its hardness.

As for fitting the rings, the head was first heated in an electric furnace to 200 degrees C, after which the seatings — previously mounted on special jigs — were pushed home very quickly. Speed was essential, for as soon as the rings made contact with the hot head they expanded and locked in position.

Aluminium-bronze was used for the valve guides too — not only for its high conductivity and expansion, but also for its excellent bearing properties. These characteristics, along with the very high finish on the valve stems and guides, plus ample lubrication from the cambox, kept wear to a negligible level over long periods. Stem clearance, incidentally, was unusually small — 0.0015in inlet, 0.003in exhaust.

Valve materials were a high-tensile cobalt-chrome steel, with a hard-wearing surface for the inlet; and KE965 steel for the exhaust, because it had to retain great strength at very high working temperatures. (Unfortunately, in extreme circumstances, the standard solid

26

Original KTT engine — the Mark 1 of 1929. Though comparatively primitive in its appearance, it is clearly recognizable as the sire of the illustrious line of overhead-camshaft Velocette racing singles.

valve could still get hot enough to lose strength disastrously, as I discovered to my cost. My first few meetings on a Mark 8 were at Brooklands, where full throttle in top gear was often sustained for up to 30 miles at a stretch — and not on cool-running alcohol, but on 50/50 petrol-benzol. Nowhere in road racing did an exhaust valve suffer such unrelenting thermal stress. Early signs of stretching — *ie,* reduced running clearance — were misinterpreted as 'bedding down' until, at top speed on the long Donington straight, the head broke off the stem and dropped into the cylinder. To prevent such a disaster, the works exhaust valves were hollow and partially filled with sodium; splashing up and down in use, the molten sodium transferred heat from head to stem, where it was dissipated through the guide.)

I suspect *Ubique* knew the answer he would get when he asked why the inlet valve was larger than the exhaust. It was, of course, because it was much more difficult to fill the cylinder, by atmospheric pressure, than it was to empty it, with a residual pressure approaching 100psi at exhaust-valve opening, then a rising piston and finally a megaphone-induced depression in the port around top dead centre.

Throat diameter of the inlet valve (a more significant measurement than outside diameter) was $1\frac{9}{16}$in (although a $\frac{1}{8}$in-larger valve was fitted later in conjunction with a bigger inlet port and an increase in carburettor choke size from $1\frac{3}{32}$ to $1\frac{5}{32}$in). To minimize port obstruction, stem diameter was as small as safety would allow – $\frac{5}{16}$in. (With the same object, the guide was cut off flush with the port roof.) Exhaust-port diameter was $1\frac{7}{16}$in while the valve stem was thicker at $\frac{3}{8}$in. Lift of both valves was $\frac{3}{8}$in. (Later on, the original K17/8 cam was superseded by the K17/11, giving an inlet lift of just over 0.4in and a 5-degree earlier inlet closure.)

To resist hammer, the tip of the inlet stem was hardened — a technique that was not applicable to the exhaust stem, which was fitted with a hardened cap instead. Checked cold, running clearances were 0.015in inlet, 0.025in exhaust.

For setting the valve timing during assembly, however, both clearances were changed to 0.020in — in which case the inlet valve opened 55 degrees before tdc and closed 65 degrees after bdc, while the exhaust valve

opened 75 degrees before bdc and closed 45 degrees after tdc. Thus valve overlap around tdc was 100 degrees.

Ubique noticed the slightly elaborate way in which the ends of the hairpin springs were attached to the valve stems. Instead of the plate bridging the spring loops itself having a small taper bore to accept the split cotter on the valve stem, it was a loose fit round a separate collar that had the necessary taper bore. Thus the valve and collar together could rotate in the plate. The reason for this arrangement, he learned, was that the makers set great store by the valves being free to rotate, in order to prevent distortion, even though it meant a slight increase in

reciprocating weight. Spring pressure, with the valve seated, was 110lb; each rocker, however, had its own hairpin return spring exerting a pressure of 25lb on the cam base circle.

Velocette were among the pioneers of total valve enclosure for racing and *Ubique* wondered if it had caused overheating. On the contrary, the valve boxes had a large external area exposed to the draught while the interior was cooled by a liberal circulation of oil.

When asked why the makers had reverted to a single-ohc layout following a brief double-knocker experiment on a Mark 5 engine in 1936, Percy Goodman said that,

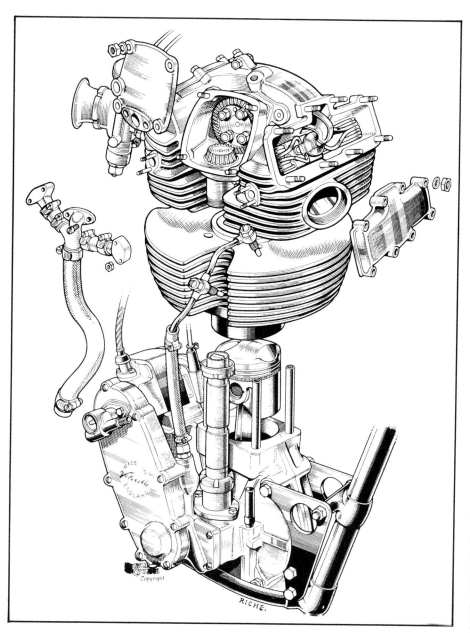

Immediate predecessor of the Mark 8 KTT engine was this Mark 7, catalogued for 1938 and chiefly distinguishable by its low-crown piston giving a compression ratio of 8.75:1.

their shaft were made separately and pressed and keyed together. The cams were of straight carbon steel, deeply case-hardened with 1 per cent carbon in the case. But 3 per cent nickel steel was used for the shaft, which was case-hardened to form a track for the caged rollers just behind the large bevel gear. The end-thrust from the bevels was taken by a ball bearing supporting the left-hand end of the shaft.

Except that the lower pair of bevels was strengthened to cope with high revs and heavy valve springs, the cam drive was standard. Why strengthen only the lower bevels and not the upper ones? Because the shape of the small-diameter bevels, of approximately equal size, was less favourable to tooth strength. At the top, the four stud holes through which the large bevel was bolted to the camshaft flange were elongated to provide a fine timing adjustment.

To distribute the loading evenly around the vertical bevels, each had 23 teeth, as distinct from 22 on the crankshaft bevel (hence 44 on the camshaft bevel), a technique known as the hunting tooth. The bronze bushes supporting the vertical bevels (in which they were located by pressed-on steel rings) were flanged to take the end-thrust. Joining the two bevel shafts was a solid vertical shaft with a double-tongued Oldham coupling, in oil-hardened nickel-chrome steel, at each end. The vertical shaft ran in plain bronze bushes pressed into a tube that was secured to the vertical-bevel housings by an asbestos-packed gland nut at each end — an arrangement that ensured a necessary trace of flexibility without oil leaks.

Internally, the crankcase halves were flat and smooth — and such was the inherent rigidity of the case that only the shallowest of external radial ribs were provided. Only $1\frac{13}{16}$in thick, the flywheels too were exceptionally smooth, and made of heat-treated carbon steel as a precaution against stretch in the mainshaft and crankpin holes.

Of 3 per cent nickel steel, the $\frac{7}{8}$in-diameter mainshafts were pressed into the wheels and located by a pin, which took the form of a screw, half in the shaft and half in the wheel. A slight taper on each shaft ensured that the inner race of its caged roller bearing was firmly locked when driven home. Shrunk into the case, the lipped outer races had a

despite its theoretical attractions, the twin-camshaft arrangement had presented difficulties in providing readily accessible tappet adjustment and full valve enclosure. Worse still, cam-drive failure had been encountered for the first time.

Harold Willis took up the story, which was one of quick-fire problem solving rather than long-term scientific investigation. For example, while hindsight suggests that the cam-drive failure may well have been caused by high-frequency cyclic vibrations in the greatly extended gear train, a series of experiments showed that the best all-round results came from a single-camshaft layout — provided the rockers could be kept in constant contact with the cams. That was

why the rocker return springs were introduced.

At first, however — despite the jet of oil directed on to the cam/rocker rubbing faces — the springs caused scoring and rapid wear of the rocker heels and cams — a problem that was solved by giving the rocker heels a Stellite surface.

Made from stampings of air-hardening nickel-chrome steel, with a tensile strength of 100 tons, the rockers were supported on eccentric pivot pins (for clearance adjustment), with a fully floating bronze bush between each rocker and its pin to more than double the effective bush area.

Because the metallurgical requirements of the two parts were different, the cams and

28

The crankcase assembly was a model of rigidity, with a massive crankpin stiffening the flywheels, while the main bearings were little more than 2in apart and directly in line with the crankcase and cylinder walls.

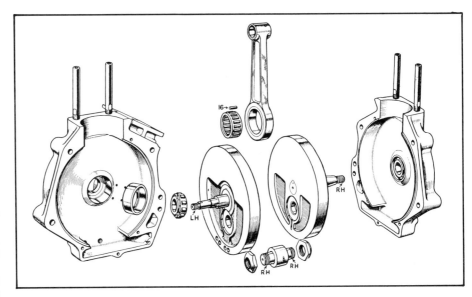

brass shim adjustment so that end-float could be kept to a minimum consistent with free running at working temperatures.

Contributing greatly to the rigidity of the flywheel assembly was a massive nickel-chrome steel crankpin with a journal diameter of $1\frac{3}{8}$in; slightly tapered at the ends, it was pulled into the wheels against its wide shoulders by heat-treated nickel-steel nuts. To form an inner track for the $16\ \frac{9}{16} \times \frac{3}{16}$in rollers of the big-end bearing, the pin was case-hardened.

Locating the rollers was a slotted duralumin cage, with the inner surface of the bars relieved so that only the end rings of the cage bore on the crankpin. In that way, damage to the roller track was prevented; one has only to examine the underside of a used KTT crankpin to see that, under centrifugal loading, the soft cage wears the hard pin much more than the rollers do. The outer race of the bearing was pressed into the connecting rod, as was a bronze bush at the small end.

Revealing that the robust connecting rod was forged from an oil-hardening nickel-chrome steel, heat-treated to some 80 tons tensile, Harold Willis explained that they could easily have specified an even higher tensile strength, except that great toughness was also required. The rod was machined all over and polished on the outside, not only to remove surface scale and weight, but also to reveal potentially dangerous surface cracks or flaws.

No less than $\frac{13}{16}$in in diameter, the case-hardened, nickel-chrome-steel gudgeon pin was not only hollow, but taper-bored at the ends to save weight. The ends were also chamfered externally so that any sideways movement would tend to jam the plain wire retaining circlips in their grooves in the piston bosses rather than displace them.

Sandcast in heat-treated Y-alloy, the slipper-type piston had the lofty crown inevitable in the achievement of a high compression ratio with a deep, part-spherical cylinder head and widish valve angle (70 degrees). So lofty, indeed, that much of the crown surface was machined away to provide clearance for the valve heads.

Although the consequent 'orange-peel' shape of the clearance volume, and its high surface/volume ratio, would bring a frown to the brow of a modern thermodynamicist, the structural design of the piston was first class. Vertical ribs braced each gudgeon-pin boss to the crown, while the shape of the front and rear slippers was maintained by a circular rib at the mid-height of the bosses. Compression was sealed by two narrow Wellworthy Thermocrom rings (heat-formed, not hammered) while oil control was effected by a slotted scraper. On assembly, each engine had its combustion-chamber volume adjusted to 35cc by means of shims under the cylinder, so giving a compression ratio of 10.94:1 for the 50/50 petrol-benzol mixture stipulated for road racing.

Lubrication was by the jet system introduced on the Mark 5 KTT in 1935. On the Mark 8 there were three carefully calibrated metering jets — the largest (of 0.052in diameter) feeding the big-end bearing; the next (0.046in) directed to the cam/rocker contacts, as mentioned earlier; and the smallest (0.033in) aimed at the point of mesh of the upper bevels. Circulation, by a double gear-type pump, was at a rate of 10 gallons an hour.

On the standard engine, all the oil drained to the sump for scavenging. On the works engines, however, the drain from the lower bevel box to the sump was blanked off and an additional pump incorporated to scavenge the bevel box separately — a modification I and other privateers also carried out as a precaution against plug oiling. The extra pump (comprising a pair of narrow, delivery-type, gears in a shallow body) was let into the inner face of the magneto-drive case and driven by the shaft of the mag-drive gear.

When Henry Teage finally asked about the engine's performance he was told that it developed 27bhp at 6,500rpm, could be run indefinitely at 7,000 and safely up to 7,500 for short periods. It *would* run, he was told, up to 8,000rpm, but that was considered to be beyond the limit of reasonable safety.

Representing some 77bhp/litre and 12bhp/litre/1,000rpm, that power claim seemed somewhat conservative, at least by comparison with rival makers' claims. Anyway, even before the K17/11 cam and the larger carburettor and inlet valve were available to give a useful power boost, it was difficult to accept that power started to wane appreciably from 6,500rpm. For, on the tallest gearing available, the engine would readily romp up to 7,000 — and beyond with the least encouragement from wind or gradient.

Whatever the dynamometer showed, however, the 1939 Mark 8 engine quickly established a reputation as the most competitive in its class — and smooth and dependable with it. In road racing everywhere, the latest KTT was the bike to beat. And at Brooklands my own machine — handicapped by the obligatory silencer in place of the open megaphone — was the only three-fifty to win a Gold Star (for lapping at 100mph or more during a race) without resorting to alcohol fuel.

Alas, there was a deplorable drop in the quality of some of the production engines built after the war, as there was also in the calibre of the factory's development work.

Whether from worn-out machine tools or waning pride, the workmanship in my 1950 model was disgraceful. For example, instead of being square to the crankcase mouth, the four long cylinder studs emulated the leaning tower of Pisa. Power and torque were noticeably down, so that top speed was 12mph short despite the K17/11 cam and the larger carburettor and inlet valve. Worst of

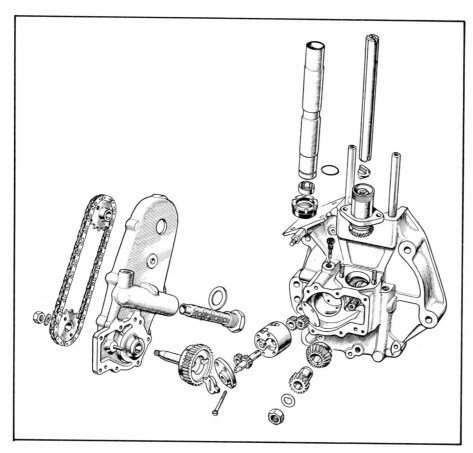

Left: The duplex oil pump was driven by a slotted coupling in the half-speed magneto-drive gear. Right: I-section valve rockers pivoted on fully floating bronze bushes; the spindles were eccentric for clearance adjustment. With the standard rocker radius (13/32in) uninterrupted contact with the cam was necessary, hence the rocker return springs. Increasing the radius to $\frac{5}{8}$in made the springs superfluous besides improving performance markedly.

Note the tall piston crown (with pockets) required to achieve the highest safe compression ratio with the deep head form necessary to accommodate large valves spaced at 70 degrees. A more compact combustion space gave better results. The massive Y-alloy head casting completely enclosed the camshaft, rockers, valves and springs.

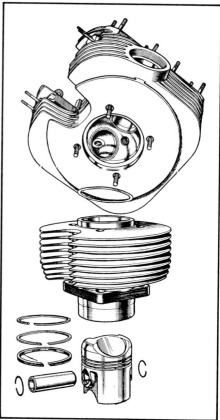

all, the valves floated noisily at only 6,400rpm, whereas those in the prewar engine had never got out of control, even beyond 7,500. It needed only one race with the new engine for the closing flanks of the cam lobes to be hammered hollow where the floating rockers suddenly caught up with them.

In my case, however, the cloud had a silver lining. For, if the engine had been anything like so well machined and built as its predecessor, there would have been much less incentive to embark on engine developments that not only restored reliability to the prewar level, but pushed power and torque well up the scale too.

The tragedy so far as racing development at the factory was concerned was, first, that Harold Willis had died of meningitis in June 1939; and second, that his understudy, Charles Udall, who took over, was ousted a few years after the war by Percy Goodman's son Bertram, whose well-cultivated charm and diplomacy were regrettably not matched by a comparable flair for development.

The factory's response to the cam problem, for example, was chromium plating — with the predictable result that flakes of plating broke off the closing flanks under impact and jammed the oil pump, so shear-

ing the drive with catastrophic results. My preference (advocated by Phil Irving in his book *Tuning for Speed*) was to build-up the Stellite-faced rocker heels and regrind them to the substantially larger radius of $\frac{5}{8}$in.

The makers were aghast at the idea, insisting that the standard radius of $\frac{13}{32}$in should on no account be changed since that gave constant valve acceleration. In effect, that meant that the valves accelerated steadily up to half lift, then decelerated at the same steady rate from half to full lift. The effect of the larger radius was to make initial valve acceleration much fiercer and to compress it into a considerably shorter period; thus deceleration up to full lift was at a lower rate and spread over a longer period. Similarly, valve acceleration (under spring pressure) from full lift towards closure was at the same reduced rate and spread over an equally extended period. The net result was that the springs had a much easier task in preventing loss of contact at the peak of the cam.

The improvement seemed magical. First, the engine would romp beyond 8,000rpm (too fast for bottom-end longevity) without a trace of valve float. Second, the rocker return springs could be discarded (a boon when assembling the engine) and weaker valve springs used. Third, there was an appreciable

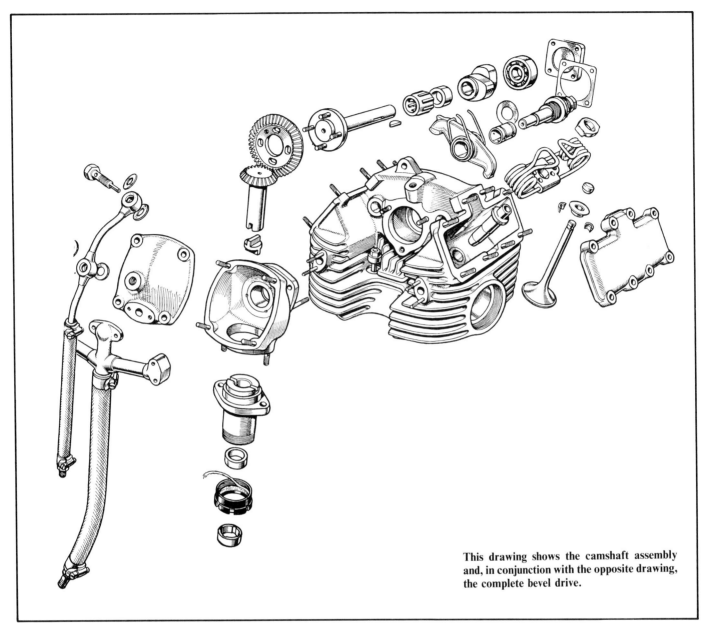

This drawing shows the camshaft assembly and, in conjunction with the opposite drawing, the complete bevel drive.

power bonus as a result of more effective overlap and deeper breathing.

To prevent the valves from kissing during overlap (owing to their higher lift during that period) all surplus metal was removed from the periphery. However, care had to be taken not to narrow the seats too much because the larger rocker radius resulted in a higher seat impact on closure.

Some years later, I was interested to learn that NSU (on their world championship-winning Rennmax 250cc twin and 125cc Rennfox single) and AJS (on the famous 350cc single-knocker 7R) had both exploited fierce initial valve acceleration with considerable benefit to high-speed valve control in their development programmes. In the Rennfox engine, NSU were even able to make the remarkable switch from double-ohc to single-ohc as a result.

Another contribution to the performance deficiency in my 1950 KTT, it seemed, was an alteration to the shape of the inlet port. In the 1939 engine the business end of the tract was curved downward so as to run parallel to the valve stem for a short distance before entering the combustion chamber. In my postwar engine the port had an old-fashioned flat layout, entering the combustion chamber at an angle that must have increased any loss of fresh charge to the exhaust — and for no better reason than to allow more metal between the roof of the tract and the valve-spring well. (Some riders' attempts to open out the earlier ports had broken into the well.)

After making a cutter of throat diameter, with a hemispherical end and a pilot for the valve guide, it was a simple matter to restore the business end of the port to the prewar shape, then blend it into the rest of the tract by hand grinding, taking care not to break through the roof. Once more the modification was rewarded by a welcome gain in power.

By then, the cumulative improvement brought about by the rocker and port modifications, plus the correction of machining errors, was such that, during practice for the 1950 Ulster Grand Prix, my KTT was so much faster on the straights than Bob

31

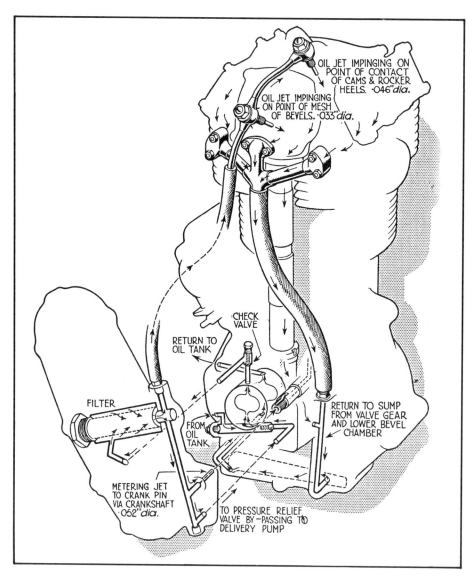

OIL JET IMPINGING ON POINT OF CONTACT OF CAMS & ROCKER HEELS. ·046″ dia.

OIL JET IMPINGING ON POINT OF MESH OF BEVELS. ·033″ dia.

CHECK VALVE

RETURN TO OIL TANK

FILTER

FROM OIL TANK

RETURN TO SUMP FROM VALVE GEAR AND LOWER BEVEL CHAMBER

METERING JET TO CRANK PIN VIA CRANKSHAFT ·052″ dia.

TO PRESSURE RELIEF VALVE BY-PASSING TO DELIVERY PUMP

In the lubrication system three calibrated jets controlled the flow of oil to vital parts. The biggest jet fed the big-end bearing (hence cylinder, piston and mains); the smallest was aimed at the meshing teeth of the upper bevels, while the third took care of the cam/rocker rubbing faces. A worthwhile modification was to blank off the drain from the lower bevel box to the sump and fit an extra, slim scavenge pump in the box. Purpose of the check valve was to prevent drainage from tank to crankcase while the engine was stationary.

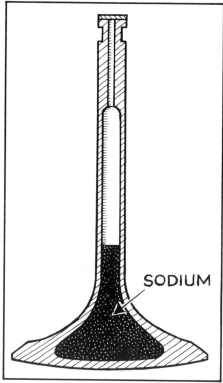

SODIUM

In a sodium-cooled valve the filling melts at running temperature and transfers heat from head to stem by splash. Thus heat is dissipated through the guide as well as the seat.

Foster's winning double-knocker works bike that I was repeatedly rolling the throttle back and hoping to spring a surprise on race day. Indeed, the engine was consistently over-revving in top gear and the bike would have been faster still had a larger (25-tooth) final-drive sprocket been available for the gearbox.

My hopes were dashed, however, when, early in practice, a pair of special brake cables (front and rear), freshly supplied by the cable makers, shed their nipples on the

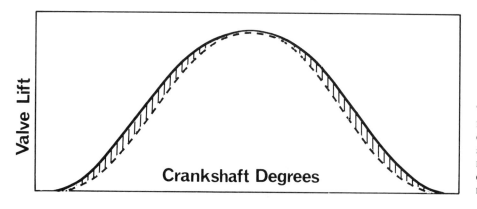

Valve Lift

Crankshaft Degrees

The shaded area in this valve-lift curve represents the deeper breathing obtained by increasing the rocker radius (solid line). This also increases the valve's initial acceleration rate, so extending the deceleration period; the effect is to maintain valve control at higher rpm with weaker springs.

The Mark 8 KTT Velocette as it appeared at the 1938 Earls Court Show.

approach to the Muckamore hairpin bend. The ensuing crash left the bike a charred wreck and put me on the sidelines until full-time journalism brought my development programme to an end with one important experiment still incomplete.

This had nothing to do with falling standards at the factory. It concerned combustion-chamber shape and was prompted some time earlier, on the prewar engine, by the need to lower the compression ratio drastically to suit the appallingly low octane rating of the fuel (Pool petrol) stipulated by the FIM shortly after the war.

Two pistons were available — the high-crown Mark 8 and the low-crown Mark 7; and although the ratio with either could be varied by altering the effective length of the cylinder, this alteration was limited by the vertical shaft assembly, for which only two thicknesses of coupling were available.

Some riders, who tried to obtain a low-enough ratio with the high-crown piston by stacking up the cylinder on compression plates, found that detonation (not necessarily audible) burned not only the piston crown but àlso the much more expensive cylinder head. In any case, that arrangement combined the defects of the high piston

crown (*ie,* large surface area and 'orange-peel' clearance volume) with the inevitable loss of power from the lower compression.

For a comparable ratio, the low-crown piston offered the benefits of a smaller surface area and a more compact clearance volume to offset some of the power loss — and there was the incidental advantage of a slight reduction in reciprocating weight. Experiments confirmed the wisdom of this approach.

The makers recommended the Mark 7 piston with the cylinder raised to give a ratio of 7.8:1 (51cc clearance volume); but I found this ratio could be exceeded — possibly

33

The author in action on the Brooklands Mountain Circuit in 1939 on the first of his two Mark 8 KTTs. Note the obligatory use of a Brooklands silencer instead of a megaphone exhaust.

because I had cut back the ignition advance to 28 degrees and removed all sharp edges from the combustion chamber, notably by reducing the diameters of the valve heads to the safe limit and putting a large radius all round the new periphery.

Progressively the cylinder was shortened until brief pinking could be heard as the engine accelerated through 5,500rpm (showing that to be the peak-torque speed), then putting a thin shim under the barrel to eliminate the noise. The next move was to make a candle-wax cast of the combustion chamber. This showed a long pocket at each side where the top edge of the piston land fell nearly an eighth of an inch short of the line where the parallel bore in the head met the part-spherical curvature.

The radius of the piston crown was found to be 3in and some simple drawing showed that the pockets could be eliminated if it was increased to 4in, with the same height in the centre. The further reduction in surface area would be negligible, but the combustion chamber would be much more compact and consequently might well take the increased compression ratio in its stride without pinking.

Unfortunately, by the time a raw piston casting had been obtained with sufficient metal in the crown to accommodate the larger radius, my plans had gone up in the Muckamore smoke. So the piston casting, with machining instructions, was passed to 'Sandy' Sandys-Winsch, who had recently bought my first (1939) Mark 8. An RAF man

stationed in Germany, he eventually completed the experiment and reported such an improvement that the Velo (still with the original rocker radius) easily outstripped rival five-hundreds as well as three-fifties in his Continental races.

Sadly, Sandys-Winsch was fatally injured at The Highlander in the 1954 Senior TT. But I remain convinced that the Mark 8 engine could comfortably have held its own with the AJS 7R engine, so admirably developed by Jack Williams, given continued development on the lines indicated, plus a change to square cylinder dimensions to accommodate a $1\frac{3}{4}$in-throat inlet valve, and slightly more robust mainshafts and main bearings. It was a great pity Harold Willis didn't survive to have the chance.

CHAPTER 4

Postwar Vincent Rapide

Legendary and versatile big V-twin from a courageous and highly talented partnership

Alone among the British factories that survived the Hitler war, the small Vincent-HRD company at Stevenage (later simply Vincent) had the courage to embark immediately on a radical new design. While rival managements for the most part took advantage of the sellers' market to rehash prewar models with cosmetic changes (and maybe a tentative move towards more sophisticated suspension) the highly talented Vincent team invested in reams of blank drawing paper and set out to offer the connoisseur an unprecedented blend of high speed, surging acceleration, effortless endurance, good handling and comfort.

Proudly advertised as the world's fastest standard production machine, the resulting 998cc (84 × 90mm), 50-degree V-twin Series B Rapide was a logical successor to the prewar Series A — itself a starkly functional roadburner that had earned deep affection and respect in the late 1930s for its outstanding speed and versatility.

A brainchild of Australian Phil Irving (later awarded the MBE for his wide-ranging contribution to the automobile industry) the engine of the Series A Rapide was virtually a brace of 499cc Meteor cylinders carried on a common crankcase. And the Meteor engine — with its distinctive high camshaft, splayed pushrods and straight, transverse rockers actuating valve-stem collars situated between upper and lower valve guides — was an earlier Irving design prompted by the wish to be done with proprietary engines following a spate of JAP failures in the 1934 Senior TT.

For all its irresistible fascination, compounded of punch, smoothness and a delightfully lilting exhaust note, the A Rapide had its weaknesses. First and foremost, the toughest available proprietary transmission — the heavyweight Burman four-speed gearbox and clutch — was way out of its depth when subjected to the massive torque of the engine. Then, lengthening the frame to house the engine had stretched the wheelbase to an unfashionable 59in.

As to the engine itself, the four small-bore curly pipes taking oil from the timing chest to the valve gear (besides the main feed and scavenge pipes) earned it the affectionate nickname of the plumber's nightmare. The 47-degree cylinder spacing (which permitted the use of existing drilling jigs in manufacture) didn't precisely suit any standard V-twin magneto. And, to obtain clearance under the tank, the front Amal carburettor had a horizontal mixing chamber, which was sensitive to precise alignment.

Following a committee decision on the general concept of the postwar model, with particular reference to the use of the engine as a structural frame member, Irving undertook the detail design, in which all these points were taken care of. The transmission was uprated by means of an ingenious self-servo clutch and integral construction of the massive crankcase and four-speed gearbox (a feature then almost unheard-of in British designs). Elimination of the conventional front down tube took 3in off the wheelbase. Plumbing was simplified by bleeding the feeds to the valve gear off the scavenge return pipe. To suit the standard Lucas V-twin magneto, the cylinders were spaced at 50 degrees; and the inlet stubs were shaped to accommodate vertical mixing chambers for both carburettors.

Throughout its nine years of production — in touring, sporting and racing guises for the Series B, C and D Rapides, Black Shadows and Black Lightnings, respectively — Irving's engine remained fundamentally unchanged. And although the machine was conceived as a whole rather than an assemblage of components designed in isolation, it was the power unit that *The Motor Cycle*'s technical editor Alan Baker analyzed in a straightforward question-and-answer interview with managing director Phil Vincent in the summer of 1953.

By that time Irving had been back in Australia for four years and the end of production at Stevenage was only two years off. Vincent's long, propaganda-like answers

struck me as too narrowly subjective, as though he possessed a patent on perfection. Hence — since the design unquestionably ranks as one of motor cycling's all-time greats — I was delighted many years later by the opportunity to discuss it, in both detail and philosophy, with the much more objective Irving.

Alan Baker's starting point was the absence of a conventional tubular frame and Vincent offered two justifications besides the wheelbase reduction. First, correctly designed as a frame member, the engine-gearbox unit provided a better strength/rigidity/weight ratio than any combination of engine and separate frame. Second, accessibility for major engine servicing was enhanced, since removal of the rear suspension and the box-section oil tank spanning the cylinder heads (complete with front suspension) left the engine completely exposed.

Remarking that the engine originally had hollow cylinder-head bolts embracing solid frame bolts, Baker asked why that arrangement had been superseded by single solid bolts taking both head and frame stresses through separate threads. The answer was that, in the absence of previous experience of using the engine as a structural member, slung by the heads, it was felt safer to use separate bolts lest frame stresses should tend to release the head joints. But the fear proved groundless and the simpler, cheaper arrangement of single high-tensile bolts was introduced at the end of 1948. Also, unskilled mechanics tended to overtighten the hollow bolts, sometimes causing one or more to break.

On crankshaft construction, Phil Vincent revealed that the finish-machined, 1in-diameter mainshafts (in En24 nickel-chrome steel) were pressed into the flywheels, and located by pins, before the wheels were finished on the periphery and side flange or bored and recessed for the crankpin. Since the periphery and flange were next ground off the mainshaft centres, they then formed

Phil Irving (Vincent) with the author.

Phil Vincent (Vincent).

suitable location surfaces for machining the crankpin holes and recesses true to the shafts, thereby ensuring 'astonishingly close' limits of accuracy in the interests of smooth running and main-bearing longevity.

For the crankpin, En36 case-hardening nickel-chrome steel was preferred to the more usual (and cheaper) case-hardening mild steel for its tougher, more homogeneous core, which enabled the hard case to withstand heavier loads without flaking. Because the big-end bearing design required a tolerance of no more than 0.002in in the

spacing of the flywheels, the pin was a parallel fit in the wheels and pulled up against ground shoulders with hardened steel side plates interposed; with a taper fit, that tolerance would have been difficult to maintain in production and impossible in servicing.

Despite the extreme accuracy required in manufacture, two spaced bearings for each mainshaft were preferred to single bearings as a means of preventing flexure of the flywheel assembly. Single bearings of equal load capacity would not only have been

heavier, but also larger in diameter, so having a higher rolling speed. Indeed, said Vincent, the double main bearings had twice the load capacity needed on the Rapide, so contributing further to long life.

Alan Baker next asked why the rollers in the big-end bearing were crowded rather than caged, and whether inter-roller pressure from centrifugal force didn't stop them from rolling properly at high rpm.

Vincent replied that prewar experiments by SKF had shown that small-diameter

36

rollers could be successfully guided off their ends without a cage, provided their length was little more than their diameter and precise control was maintained over the lengths of all the bearing's components, hence the small side clearances. In the Rapide big end, there were three rows of 3mm-diameter rollers in each connecting rod, making a total of 135 rollers per rod — 270 in the complete bearing. Thus individual roller loads were very low and bearing life was unusually long, provided the engine was not run habitually at excessive rpm.

At high engine speeds, he pointed out, all big-end rollers (caged or otherwise) tended to skid as a result of rapid fluctuations in effective rolling speed as the connecting rod swung back and forth on the gudgeon pin. With crowded rollers, sustained high rpm generated additional heat through inter-roller friction, so expanding the rollers and generating heat more quickly. For normal road use, Vincent concluded, the Rapide big end was as good as any for hard riding and superior at more modest speeds. For racing, however, he had reservations — good touring and good racing practice were at variance there.

I felt this remark was made with benefit of hindsight. For three years earlier, it was Vincent himself who insisted on using the standard bearing, in preference to a caged-roller alternative, when a small party of us went to Montlhéry in search of long-distance world records. And it was I who was at the helm when the bearing proved his subsequent point by locking solid at more than two miles a minute on the steep banking with but a quarter-hour to go before the first record (six hours) was due to fall. (Subsequently, several records were broken at a slower schedule, though not without another big-end failure.)

From experience, I was well aware of the virtues of the standard bearing for high-speed road use. I knew, too, of its numerous successes in the Isle of Man Clubman's TT races (150 miles). But in open racing both George Brown and Ted Davis (Stevenage staffmen) had found its useful life to be little more than 10 hours. At Montlhéry, conditions were even more exacting, for there was no respite from maximum revs so long as there was fuel in the tank. Hence my eventual delight in getting the full story of the bearing's evolution from Irving — you'll find it later in the chapter.

Back now to Alan Baker's analysis, which quoted Vincent as saying that the 40-ton forged steel flywheels were drilled to balance 45 per cent of the total reciprocating mass.

Irving's notes show a much more probable 35 per cent (equivalent to 70 per cent for each cylinder). But both men agreed that the precise balance factor was less important than rigidity in design and accuracy in manufacture. Indeed, Irving assured me there was no need for rebalancing when changing from 6.8:1 pistons to 12.5:1, although the high-compression pistons added 3½ ounces to the total reciprocating weight.

Justifying the use of high camshafts and short (6in) pushrods in preference to over-head camshafts, Vincent conceded the ohc's superiority for high-revving grand-prix engines. For a broader range of performance, however, the Rapide arrangement had several advantages, including simplicity, accessibility, lower height, fewer joints and less obstruction to the airflow over the hottest part of the cylinder head.

Three different materials were used in the timing gear: En24W nickel-chrome-molybdenum steel for the crankshaft pinion, camwheels and breather-valve pinion; forged Hiduminium RR77 light alloy for the large idler; and Tufnol for the magneto-drive pinion. For the highly stressed gears, said Vincent, En24 was chosen for its resistance to impact, excellent machinability, 70 tons/sq in tensile strength and good Brinell hardness. For the idler, however, RR77 gave

Basically a supremely effortless long-legged tourer, the postwar Vincent twin was so capable as to take world records and races of all sorts in its stride. This versatility was all the more remarkable considering the choice of materials was so restricted, both by commercial circumstances and by Government decree — a factor little appreciated outside the company. This 1951 Series C Black Shadow was a 125mph roadster.

longer life to the meshing steel gears, was quieter than steel and virtually prevented any increase in tooth backlash by virtue of its high expansion rate. For driving the magneto, which imposed a low but fluctuating load, Tufnol (as specified by Lucas) was particularly suitable on account of its quietness and light weight.

Alan Baker remarked on the difference in construction between Series A and B light-alloy cylinder heads. Whereas the Series B twins had valve seats of different materials shrunk in place and no separate boss for the plug thread, the first few Series A twins had their valve seats cast in place. Beyond that, there is a divergence of opinion as to the precise technique employed, though an early reversion to cast iron indicates problems in production or servicing in either case. Baker's analysis specifically mentioned 'a bronze casting in the head embracing inserts and plug boss' (as did *The Motor Cycle*'s original announcement of the new twin on October 15, 1936); this was the so-called pair-of-spectacles construction and seemingly was not challenged by Phil Vincent. Phil Irving, on the other hand, was adamant that this method was not used. Separate seats, he insisted, were cast in and there was at first no plug boss; but when the plug thread gave trouble a bronze sleeve was screwed in, which tended to screw out with the plug.

However, the issue is irrelevant to Vincent's justification of the Series B arrangement which, he explained, was cheaper, lighter, more reliable and provided better heat conductivity. For the inlet seats, austenitic iron was chosen for its resistance to wear by ingoing grit particles. Since the exhaust seats ran much hotter, the high expansion rate of aluminium bronze was necessary to ensure security.

Asked whether the 30-degree valve-seat angle was superior to the more common 45 degrees, Vincent simply claimed they had found the flatter angle highly satisfactory, particularly for resistance to hammering, distortion and wear. Similarly, it was baldly claimed that the rather shallow combustion-chamber recess and flattish piston dome were a very satisfactory compromise of such factors as surface/volume ratio, depth of clearance volume at top dead centre, and valve size, lift and included angle (65 degrees).

It was noted that the pivoted cam followers, made in En36 (the crankpin material), had flat rather than curved bases. Given the appropriate contour (asymmetrical in this case), the cams were said to be equally easy to make for either follower type; but the flat-base follower was easier both to manufacture and to regrind during servicing. The particular stainless-steel alloy used

for the pushrods gave a very stiff material which work-hardened rapidly. Hence the rods could be light and fitted as machined, since the ball ends would harden in the first few revs of the engine.

Unusually, each KE805 steel rocker had a press-fit spindle running in a separate Hiduminium L28 bearing in a tunnel in the cylinder head; Alan Baker queried the reason for such an unusual layout. After pointing out that the Hiduminium was an excellent bearing material for the spindle and expanded at a similar rate to the head, Phil Vincent explained that the whole assembly of rocker, spindle and bearing could be withdrawn from the head (through the large inspection hole) after slackening the hollow oil-feed bolt that located it, taking out the valve-clearance adjuster and removing the pushrod.

Conceding the better valve-stem support afforded by the two spaced guides, and the cooler conditions for the springs (above the upper guide), Alan Baker wondered whether the valves weren't too heavy as a result of their extra length. The increase in weight was minimal, Vincent said, because the upper half of the stem was considerably reduced in diameter. The advantage of putting the rocker between the guides was that its side thrust was resisted by the entire length of the guides, with none of the usual tilting. Thus wear rate was greatly reduced and alignment of valve and seat maintained more precisely.

While the Hiduminium 4L25 of the upper guide and the aluminium bronze of the lower one were both excellent bearing materials at appropriate temperatures, the bronze was necessary in the lower position because of its higher heat resistance. Since the front inlet valve was nearly vertical, drainage slots were provided in the rocker bearing to keep oil from rising above the top of the lower guide.

Alan Baker considered silchrome steel was an obvious choice for the inlet valves, but asked what type of steel was the DTD49B of the exhausts and why it was adopted. He was told that it was a standard aircraft specification for high-duty exhaust valves. Containing a large proportion of nickel and chromium, together with some manganese, tungsten and other elements, it had the essential quality of high tensile strength at high temperatures — 16 tons/sq in at 800 degrees C.

Oil was fed to the crankpin, camshaft bearings and cylinder walls at just over a gallon an hour per 1,000rpm. Except when the oil was cold, pressure was low because of the free escape from the big-end bearing. The relief valve was set at 35psi.

As to the reason for lubricating the valve

Engine of a 1948 Series B Black Shadow, showing the widely spread pushrod tubes — a characteristic of this design.

gear from the scavenge line, this was to obtain a low-pressure delivery — equivalent only to the 6in head below the scavenge outlet in the tank. As a result, large feed holes could be used, reducing the risk of blockage. Indeed, this risk was further reduced by making the holes larger than necessary and reducing their effective area by fitting loose joggle wires to keep them clear. Since scavenge oil was warm, proper rocker lubrication was achieved much sooner than if the oil came from the cold tank.

The unusual use of 18 double-coil springs instead of a single spring in the mainshaft shock absorber was claimed by Vincent to be more responsive to minor transmission shocks. (Total poundage was 400 unloaded, 900 fully compressed.) In this connection, Irving's later observations seemed much more relevant — there was a desperate shortage of spring steel in the aftermath of the war and the multi-spring layout was much lighter than a single spring.

Vincent considered that gear primary drive would have been too noisy, heavy and expensive — hence the triplex chain with the ingenious arrangement of the outer strands driving the clutch and the middle strand the dynamo. He discounted Baker's suggestion that the spring blade tensioner under the lower chain run might be unsuitable in overrun conditions: the blade, although adjustable, was rigidly anchored at both ends.

Where did the Black Shadow's extra power come from? Larger carburettors and inlet tracts; highly polished cylinder heads and ports; higher-compression pistons; and extra care in assembly. Power outputs? Forty-five bhp at 5,300rpm for the Rapide; 55 at 5,700 for the Shadow.

To Baker, the Rapide's 53.5lb-ft of torque at 3,900rpm suggested a deliberate attempt to put the accent on lusty pulling at low and medium engine speeds. Vincent concurred, deploring any sacrifice of widely useful low-end performance for a little-used gain at the top, and extolling the delights of effortless acceleration and hill-climbing, sweet running, tall gearing, fuel economy, easy maintenance and mechanical longevity. Were he starting again to market a machine for the connoisseur, he insisted, he would work along the same lines.

It is characteristic of great engineers that their designs reflect an unerring assessment of all the relevant contemporary circumstances. These include the availability of materials and technology, market demands (both immediate and near-future), fiscal or sporting regulations, even fashion. Given the objective and the circumstances, design proceeds by fundamental engineering principles,

George Brown sets off to break the Shelsley Walsh hill-climb record on Nero in 1954.

among which simplicity outranks complexity.

Phil Irving's conviction of the basic soundness of the Series B concept (and the Series A before it) was utterly unshakable. Indeed, it was most surprisingly vindicated by Japanese near-copies some 40 years later. Astronomical revs and peaky power curves were an inevitable by-product of the FIM's fixed-capacity grand-prix formula. For the connoisseur the priorities are entirely different.

Irving's reaction to my question as to how he would proceed with several decades of hindsight was similar to Giulio Carcano's when I posed the same question in relation to the various Moto Guzzi racers — ie, that the question was well-nigh impossible to answer. Experience and new technologies might dictate detail changes. But any new design would still be a product of the chosen objective, the relevant circumstances at the time and fundamental engineering.

In our discussion of specific features I was fascinated most by the evolution of the big-end bearing. It had its origin in the design of the Comet single (sporting sister of the Meteor) in 1934. No cages were then available commercially and there were no facilities for making them at Stevenage. Irving thought the split bronze cage used by Rudge too heavy and disliked the JAP practice of drilling the roller holes from one side of the cage, thus leaving only the other side continuous. Velocette had just intro-

duced their aluminium cage, with $\frac{3}{16} \times \frac{9}{16}$in rollers, but wouldn't supply outsiders.

SKF produced a lot of Swedish information about their new cageless bearing, with the small rollers guided from the sides, and agreed to prepare a design having three rows of rollers on a 40mm pin. This propounded a crankpin with three grooves, ground to a width tolerance of 0.001in each and having tiny undercuts in the corners to clear the grinding wheel — a very tricky proposition, especially to ensure that all three grooves had the same bottom diameter. So Irving suggested a plain parallel pin with two loose separators selected for width to give a total end clearance of 0.002 to 0.006in.

The snag there was that if the middle row worked over to one side, one outer row would have no clearance and the other too much. But SKF thought the idea might work, which it did at first. They also calculated that inter-roller pressure would become dangerously high by 5,800rpm, hence the factory's recommendation not to exceed that engine speed.

In the racing version of the engine, however, the outer two rows tended to skew, because their outer ends bore against the relatively stationary hardened side plates and their inner ends against the freely rotating separators. The solution was to fit four narrower loose separators, so that all roller ends bore against them and there was little

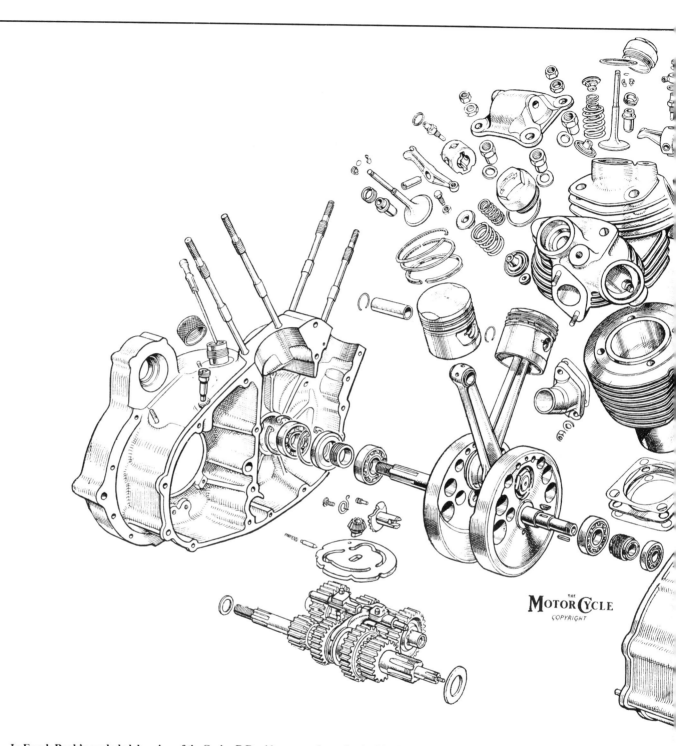

In Frank Beak's exploded drawing of the Series B Rapide power plant, the double threads at the top of the long cylinder studs are the only indication of its role as a frame member. Integral construction of crankcase and gearbox enhanced rigidity and neatness, saved weight and maintained correct alignment between the crankshaft and gearbox shafts. With both exhausts facing forward, the rear cylinder was offset $1\frac{1}{4}$ in to the right for better cooling; the consequent use of separate carburettors gave high volumetric efficiency. Unusual features include transverse rockers and double valve guides. Note the sensibly large size of all inspection caps.

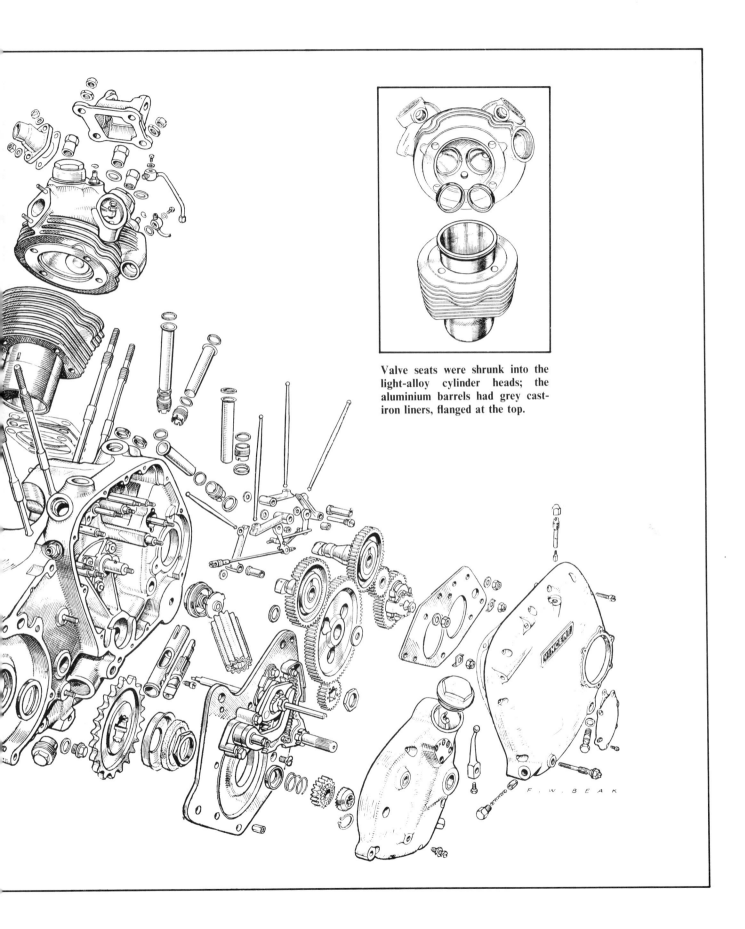

Valve seats were shrunk into the light-alloy cylinder heads; the aluminium barrels had grey cast-iron liners, flanged at the top.

F. W. BEAK

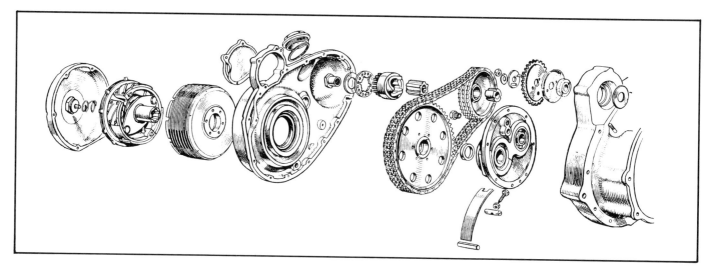

tendency to skew. Another improvement was the omission of one roller from each row (34 instead of 35) to allow for roller expansion.

Fitted in the Comet Special and TT engines, that bearing gave no trouble even when run up to 7,000rpm for short periods. Hence, when the Series A Rapide was designed, the TT big end was simply doubled-up, with a thick spacer between the rods to allow for the $1\frac{1}{4}$in cylinder offset.

Unfortunately, this incurred even more difficulty with end clearance because, if one rod worked over, it could take up all the clearance in the other set of rollers unless the con-rod sleeve on that side was wider than its four separators and three rows combined. Although feasible, this called for tighter tolerances than on the single-cylinder crankpin — and it might have been better to make the spacer integral with the pin, except for the extra inspection and assembly time involved.

However, the experimental A Rapide worked so well with a loose spacer that all the production versions were built that way and Irving could recall no premature big-end failure being reported prior to the war.

In the Series B engine, a Pilgrim rotary-plunger oil pump — worm-driven at 1/15th engine speed and giving an intermittent feed — superseded the A's continuous-delivery gear pump, which was characteristically prone to allow drainage from tank to sump. Nevertheless, the Series A's big end was carried over in the belief that it would still be satisfactory, as indeed it was for high-speed touring and Clubman's TT racing.

When Irving started to replace big ends after a couple of seasons on Australian speedway sidecar outfits in 1950, he tackled

There was nothing conventional about the finger-light pivoted-shoe self-servo clutch, multi-spring transmission shock absorber and triplex primary chain; the dynamo sprocket engaged the middle strand. Adjuster for the slipper-type chain tensioner was readily accessible.

the problem by fitting Velocette rollers in cages he made himself. Had he still been at Stevenage at that time, he would have made the same modification in production, for the $\frac{3}{16} \times \frac{9}{16}$in rollers gave better results than the $\frac{1}{4} \times \frac{1}{4}$in caged bearing eventually fitted to Black Lightning and Picador (target-towing) engines in his absence. What a happier time we might have had at Montlhéry . . . .

In a new design Irving would consider INA needle rollers in steel cages for both the big-end and inner main bearings; and he would probably fit a two-start worm to double the pump's pulse frequency. An alternative consideration would be plain bearings, although that would involve high-pressure oiling.

Switching attention from the bottom of the engine to the top, I found Irving would be in no great hurry to jump on the four-valve bandwagon, since the simpler two-valve arrangement had proved so successful for normal purposes. Nevertheless, in the event that more power might be required (or that the change might be a powerful sales stimulant) he had already drawn a four-valve layout involving no increase in engine size and little alteration in appearance.

In this, the paired valves oscillated in conventional single guides, with the included angle reduced to 30 degrees. The rockers moved in the normal fore-and-aft plane (not

transverse) but in a 'back-to-front' fashion, with the splayed pushrods actuating the outer arms and the double inner arms operating the valves. To facilitate cam design (with symmetrical lobes) the followers would no longer be pivoted and would have flat or slightly curved feet.

For a two-valve head, the original layout would be retained; but the rocker bearings would either be locked in position or chromium plated to avoid similar metals being in contact.

With the accent on long-distance fast touring rather than a seldom-used 150mph top speed, the standard compression ratio would be about 8.5:1.

Replacing the obsolete dynamo, the alternator would be on the mainshaft, with provision for keeping the magnets free of steel particles. Although electric starting might be a necessary selling point, the ignition system would incorporate an emergency-start device (even if it meant pushing) in the event of a discharged battery.

Having finalized the design of the multi-spring transmission shock absorber in the straitened circumstances following the war, Irving had no incentive to change; but he would do so today. Also, since riders seem content to struggle with heavy clutch operation on many Japanese bikes, he would use a diaphragm-spring clutch to tame the engine's torque, rather than the original self-servo clutch, which tended to slow the gear change because of its high spinning weight.

As a rider long-since enraptured by the charms of the Vincent big twins for devouring distance, I was delighted to find Phil Irving sticking so firmly to his conceptual guns. More than that, I had gained a fascinating insight into the mind of a true engineer.

CHAPTER 5

500cc Speedway JAP

Starkly simple engine whose bottom-end torque paid dividends on the short tracks for several decades

Thirty-five years' dominance of any branch of the sport is a phenomenal achievement. To the uninitiated it might suggest an inspired and sophisticated design, far ahead of its time. Yet the London-built 500cc JAP single that ruled speedway racing (and the short grass tracks) from the early 1930s to the late 1960s, with no major change in design, ranks as one of the plainest overhead-valve engines ever conceived. Such inspiration as it evinced lay in designer Stan Greening's particularly shrewd assessment of the basic requirements of the thrilling new sport, imported into the UK from Australia in 1928.

For a while, with no specially adapted machines on the market, the tracks were alive with a hotch-potch of stripped sports models, many of them highly incongruous. Quickly, a ruthless process of evolution eliminated all but a few dirt-track specials — notably the spectacular flat-twin Douglas, the four-valve Rudge and the Harley Pea-shooter; then within little more than three years since the sport had taken root in Britain, ambitious riders were faced with Hobson's choice: the Speedway JAP.

Both for the crucial sprint from the starting gate to the first corner, and for power-sliding the rear wheel through a deep carpet of cinders in the turns, its trump card was a broad spread of lusty torque from next door to zero rpm up to the 5,000 mark. No matter if the engine was getting a little short of breath by the end of the brief straights. It seldom had to exceed 6,000rpm on the speedway and its power peaked at 6,500rpm with a healthy 40bhp or more.

This all-important get-up-and-go was achieved by the old-fashioned recipe of long-stroke cylinder dimensions (80 × 99mm), modest valve timing with only 80 degrees of overlap, a compression ratio between 13.5 and 16:1 (on methanol) and a twin-float Track Amal carburettor giving an unobstructed fairway on full throttle. (When the Track Amal was no longer available, it was substituted by the Concentric, with the air slide removed.)

Since no race was as much as a mile in length and methanol burns much cooler than petrol, the iron cylinder and head had the shallowest of finning. For the same reasons, and because most of the heavily loaded bearings were of the low-friction roller variety, a copious oil circulation was unnecessary. A gravity-fed Pilgrim duplex-plunger pump supplied the big-end and rocker bearings with their meagre ration; drain oil collected in a box on the right-hand side of the crankcase (beneath the timing chest), from which it was blown down on to the track.

Those features — plus the option of light alloy for the connecting rod, the use of steel tubing for the pushrods (which bore directly on the roller-type cam followers, so saving the weight of tappets and their guides) and a subsequent change from aluminium to magnesium for the crankcase — helped to make the engine pretty light and contributed to a high overall power/weight ratio when it was installed in any of the available variety of spindly frames, with featherweight forks and brakeless wheels to match.

Equally important, the simplicity of the layout facilitated quick maintenance in the field, where full enclosure of the valve gear (by no means a universal feature in those days) kept out the grit-laden atmosphere. (Incidentally, pushrod valve operation, rather than overhead camshaft, not only simplified maintenance, but also kept the engine's centre of gravity low — a useful point when broadsiding.)

In detail there was nothing remotely adventurous in the design. The crankpin and both mainshafts were a taper fit in the flywheels and secured by nuts. Renewal of the pin and its caged rollers was advisable every 25 meetings (to forestall the break-up of the hard surface); and since repeated stripping and reassembly gradually pulled the pin farther into the wheels, it was supplied in $\frac{1}{32}$ and $\frac{1}{16}$in oversize lengths so that the necessary minimum of 0.015in side float could be maintained at the big end.

The main bearings, too, were of caged-roller type; and crankshaft endfloat was adjusted to a minimum of 0.020in by means of mainshaft shims. Balance factor was 70 per cent and unlikely to need correction unless the connecting-rod material (hence weight) had been changed.

The small end of the con-rod was bronze-bushed for the gudgeon pin, which was retained in the full-skirt Specialloid piston by wire circlips. Total-loss oiling made a scraper ring unnecessary; only two $\frac{1}{16}$in-wide compression rings were fitted, with a few drain holes just below the lower groove.

Pockets for valve clearance were machined on the domed piston crown. When, after the war, higher valve lifts became the vogue (through a rocker-pad modification) and this clearance had to be increased, a diecast Mahle piston (to JAP pattern and weight) was a worthwhile investment, since its thicker crown gave more scope for deepening the pockets. Even with the standard valve lift, however, the German piston was still preferable for its longer life; whereas the standard piston needed renewing every time the cylinder bore reached its wear limit, a Mahle piston would see out three or four bores.

Five long studs clamped both the cylinder head and barrel to the crankcase mouth. Compression ratio was adjusted by shims under the cylinder-base flange. Without shims, the combustion-chamber volume at top dead centre measured $33\frac{1}{4}$cc (giving a ratio of 16:1); but successful tuners might stack the barrel up by as much as 0.050in, so increasing the clearance volume to $39\frac{3}{4}$cc and lowering the ratio to 13.5:1.

Diameter of the inlet port was $1\frac{1}{4}$in. Both valves reciprocated in bronze guides and were closed by duplex coil springs; throat diameters were 43mm inlet, 36mm exhaust. Each valve rocker oscillated in a spaced-out pair of crowded needle-roller bearings clamped between the upper and lower halves of the rocker box.

Stan Greening (JAP).

Both cams were fitted on the same half-speed shaft, which was supported in bushes in the crankcase and timing cover. Outboard of the timing cover, the shaft carried a 15-tooth sprocket for the chain drive to the BTH magneto (substituted by other makes when supplies dried up); and outboard of the chain cover the half-speed shaft drove the oil pump.

To permit fine adjustment of the valve timing, the 22-tooth crankshaft pinion driving the camwheel had five evenly spaced keyways. More surprising, it was available in four diameters — standard; 0.006in under-size; 0.006 and 0.010in oversize — so that backlash could be minimized, short of tight meshing.

Clearly, any wear in the camshaft bushes had an adverse effect not only on the mesh of the teeth, but also, more seriously, on valve timing and lift. For that reason, some meticulous tuners removed the bushes and substituted Torrington needle-roller bearings.

As time went by, minor alterations were made to the engine in addition to the unavoidable carburettor and ignition changes and the switch to Elektron for the crankcase. For example, to lower the engine's rather ungainly height the cylinder barrel and connecting rod were shortened independently of subsequent slight shortening of the stroke and corresponding fattening of the bore. The pushrod return springs were omitted too — a move some users regarded as retrograde.

But once New Zealander Barry Briggs underlined the JAP's age (in Gothenburg in 1966) by switching to the Czechoslovak two-valve Jawa Eso for the last of his four world individual speedway titles, it was Don Godden — a talented rider/engineer who eventually won 13 British grass-track titles and the 1969 European long-track championship with JAP power — who took up the cudgels on behalf of the British engine.

With its higher premium on top-end power and a consequent sacrifice in bottom-end torque, the Jawa engine was considerably more robust than the JAP. That, and its oversquare cylinder dimensions (88 × 82mm), 3mm bigger carburettor, larger valves and 'hairy' cams giving 20 to 30 degrees more overlap, gave it an emphatic edge in power with 54bhp at 7,000rpm.

There was little Godden could do to improve the JAP's robustness or radically alter its bore and stroke. But, in his Gold Top version, which sold for £170 against £140 for the standard engine, he transformed the breathing characteristics by drastic cam modifications and associated changes. His methods were initially aimed at bringing long-track honours within the engine's reach. But the Gold Top specification duly filtered back to speedway, where track surfaces had become slicker, so reducing the importance of bottom-end torque at any price and giving scope for the considerable boost available from 3,000 to 6,000rpm. Indeed, the 4B cams soon fitted by JAP may well have been inspired by the Gold Top conversion.

To modify the original cams, Godden made a jig on which he ground the base circles to extend the opening and closing points and slightly increase the lift. Whereas the standard valve timing was inlet opens 45 degrees early, closes 62 late, exhaust opens 65 early, closes 35 late — the Gold Top figures were 60, 85, 90 and 55 respectively, giving a 35-degree increase in overlap (to 115 degrees).

Since the standard inlet-port shape was rather flat, that exaggerated overlap would have resulted in an excessive loss of fresh charge to the exhaust around top dead centre. To prevent this, the inlet port was carefully reshaped to deflect the ingoing charge away from the exhaust valve.

Valve float at high revs was avoided by changing the material of the tubular pushrods from steel to light alloy and by scrapping the standard return springs in favour of progressive-rate springs. None of these changes could be detected externally; hence the valve and rocker covers were anodized yellow to justify the Gold Top tag.

Although modified engines could safely be run up to 7,000rpm, riders were discouraged from lowering their gearing. With the standard cams, persistent overrevving might result in nothing worse than a bent exhaust valve (through valve float); but similar abuse of a Gold Top engine could have the much more dire consequence of a broken connecting rod. Consequently, duralumin rods were considered due for renewal every year.

Godden's personal preference, in his own 1,000-metre engine, was emphatically for the steel rod because competition at European championship level had forced him to push the power peak so far up the rev range that even the Gold Top modifications were inadequate.

The brutal cams in the 1,000-metre engine not only increased valve lift by about 50 per cent (to 11mm inlet, 12mm exhaust); also, despite the use of hairpin springs, they called for flats to be filed on both valve heads to prevent their tangling during overlap! Naturally, that precluded the fitting of oversize valves, but the inlet port was bored out to 1⅜in and fitted with an Amal GP carburettor.

Those radical changes — plus shortening the exhaust pipe from 52 to 35in and fitting a reverse-cone megaphone — completely transformed the power characteristics. Gone was not only the low-speed punch so necessary on ultra-short tracks, but also every vestige of useful power below 4,000rpm. But the pay-off was a real power boost from that speed to beyond 7,000. For short British tracks the engine would have been hopeless;

Don Godden (D V Godden Engineering).

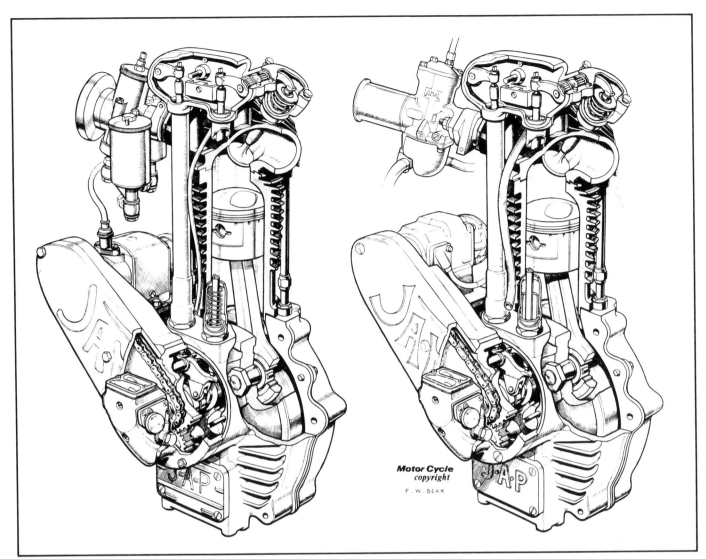

The drawing on the left — made by *The Motor Cycle* artist Frank Beak in the early 1930s — was updated in 1968 to show the intervening modifications. When original supplies dried up the Track Amal carburettor (with no throttle needle) was replaced by the 932 Concentric model (with the standard needle but the air slide removed) and the BTH magneto by an AEI or Marelli instrument. Overall engine height was lowered by two changes to the bore and stroke — from 80 x 99mm through 82 x 94 to 84 x 90 — and by shortening of the con-rod and cylinder barrel. The pushrod springs were discarded; also, undetectable from the drawings, the crankcase was cast in magnesium instead of aluminium and the cams were given much fiercer contours.

but in Godden's case it made the vast difference between barely qualifying when he first raced on the long German tracks with a standard engine in 1965 and getting to the top four years later.

When you are scratching that deep for power, every little counts; and the most ingenious modification on the 1,000-metre engine was driving the magneto at a quarter engine speed, instead of a half, to save half of the fraction of a bhp the mag normally absorbed.

In place of the standard pair of 15-tooth chain sprockets, Godden used 10 teeth at the bottom and 20 at the top. Next, to persuade the mag to deliver a spark every half turn

instead of every full turn, he replaced the single-lobe cam ring with a two-lobe ring from a twin-cylinder instrument. But since neither lobe on the new ring was in the same position as that on the original ring, the mag's internal timing had to be altered so that the points still separated when the armature was in the maximum-flux position. Nor was that all, for the two lobes didn't give identical timing and the leading edge of the 'earlier' lobe had to be stoned until they matched precisely.

The exact power of the Gold Top and 1,000-metre versions of the Speedway JAP is unknown. There was a time when Godden tried to keep tabs on development by testing

his engines on a dynamometer. But, like many engineers before and since, he found it impossible to equate bench and track performance and settled for assessing progress solely on the track.

The reign of the two-valve Jawa was much briefer than the JAP's, for 1975 ushered in the era of the four-valver. With a much broader spread of torque, that type of engine bypassed the two-valver's uneasy compromise between bottom- and top-end punch. First to prove the point was the Weslake (which Godden helped put on the map), followed by a four-valve Jawa, Godden's own GR500 and the Italian GM — but that's another story or two.

45

Don Godden in action at Lydden in 1969. He extended the Speedway JAP's competitive life not only by dynamic riding on British grass tracks and European long tracks but also by drastic engine development.

CHAPTER 6

Works BMW flat-twin

Immaculate and dependable, the last grand-prix four-stroke to succumb
to a two-stroke — after 19 world sidecar titles

BMW's achievements in classic road racing, both before and after the Hitler war, constitute one of the most scintillating chapters in the sport's history. Before the war, Karl Gall, Otto Ley and Jock West rode their blown 500cc flat-twins to an impressive string of grand-prix victories before Georg ('Schorsch') Meier snatched the European championship from Norton's firm grasp in 1938, then made history the following year as the first foreigner to win the Senior TT.

Shorn of their blowers after the war, the illustrious twins from Munich nevertheless soon reasserted themselves by putting a virtual stranglehold on the world sidecar championship for a scarcely credible period of 20 years. ('Virtual' because there were two brief hiccups: in 1968, when the resolute Helmut Fath — a former world champion on a private BMW — took the title again on his home-built Urs four; and in 1971, when Horst Owesle drove the same outfit to its second championship.)

Yet there is an ironical twist to the BMW saga. For both their rapid rise to solo stardom in the late 1930s and their eventual fall from sidecar supremacy in the middle 1970s had their seeds in a built-in bias in the international formula governing the championships. The prewar formula favoured supercharging which, though it made nonsense of classification by engine capacity, was not specifically forbidden by the rules; and BMW were among the first to exploit the possibilities.

To plug the loophole the formula was changed in 1946. But, although it was not generally realized at the time, the new formula (banning supercharging) also had a bias. It favoured, first, the engine with most cylinders; then (when the number of cylinders was limited to four) the two-stroke with crankcase induction. It was just such a two-stroke engine (the König flat-four) that eventually brought BMW's long classic reign to a close.

Technical architect of BMW's phenomenal run of sidecar championships was the highly talented Dipl-Ing Alex von Falkenhausen who, following a postwar spell designing and building his own AFM sports and racing cars, was invited to rejoin BMW as motorcycle race chief late in 1954.

By that time the Rennsport engine — the subject of this chapter — was already in production; indeed, it had just powered Willi Noll and his passenger Fritz Cron to the first of those championships. But, as Falkenhausen told me some years after his retirement at the end of 1975, the design incorporated several features that he would dearly have liked to change. In retrospect, four-stroke progress as a whole and some promising BMW experiments that never came to fruition leave no doubt that those changes could have enhanced BMW's superiority and extended their reign.

It has to be remembered that, in the aftermath of the war, Germany was excluded from the world championships until 1951. (Meanwhile, racing there was strictly national and the old supercharged machines of various makes predominated.)

'Once our country was back in the FIM,' Falkenhausen explained, 'BMW built the RS (Rennsport) model to promote racing and to give German riders a competitive machine at an affordable price.' Indeed, there seemed to be an element of altruism in the move, for the factory lost as much money on each sale as the customer paid for his machine (some DM6,000) so production was limited to 50.

Designed by Alfred Boening in 1952, the Rennsport engine inherited many basic features of the prewar engine — eg, a bore and stroke of 66 × 72mm, two valves per head with the wide included angle of 82 degrees, only two main bearings (except for a small outrigger in the timing cover) and the highly unusual combination of close-coupled double overhead camshafts and rockers.

'That valve-gear layout was crazy,' said Falkenhausen. However, it was easy to see the thinking behind it. Since both ohc drives came off the same half-speed bevel gear above the crankshaft, whereas the cylinders were necessarily slightly offset, the drives lined up naturally with the exhaust camshaft on the right and the inlet shaft on the left.

Seemingly to minimize the number of spur gears, the other camshafts (right inlet, left exhaust) were coupled directly to the driven shafts. Thus the cams were much too close together to actuate the valves directly (as is usual in double-ohc engines), while the use of rockers spread the valve angle too wide for a really compact combustion chamber. (An incidental advantage of the layout, however, was simple valve-clearance adjustment, for the rocker spindles were eccentric.)

In conjunction with a narrower valve angle, Falkenhausen would have liked to change to four valves per head with all the proven advantages — ie, deeper breathing; a more compact combustion chamber, with shorter flame travel from a central plug; and better valve control, hence the opportunity to raise peak rpm safely for increased power. (The RS engine peaked at 9,000rpm, with 58bhp on carburettors, and was safe to 9,500.)

Another restriction on safe revs was the absence of a bearing in the middle of the crankshaft. 'Two main bearings were sufficient for speeds up to 8,500-9,000rpm,' Falkenhausen told me. 'With a middle bearing to steady the shaft, the engine could have peaked at 10,500.'

An obvious route to greater power — four cylinders instead of two — was never seriously considered. 'A flat-four,' Falkenhausen, explained, 'with the front cylinders masking the rear pair, would have needed water cooling, which I considered too heavy for racing.'

Why, though, were the other design changes not made during the model's brief production run? Falkenhausen gave three reasons: 'First,' he said, 'the RS had reached the target it was aimed at. It was not too bad for solo racing, unbeatable for sidecar use and very reliable too.' (Tyres in those days

Alex von Falkenhausen (BMW).

did not permit the extreme cornering angles that were later to rule out wide transverse twins for solo grands prix; and for sidecar racing the low centre of gravity facilitated safe drifting, while the cylinders were well out in the cooling airstream and shaft drive was a boon for such arduous duty.)

'Second, we did not want to disappoint existing customers, who would have had to scrap their original models if we had made a substantially new engine. Third, BMW's financial situation at that time didn't allow much money for racing. So I used the small allocation to develop and prepare the RS for the world sidecar championship and world speed records.

'Later, in 1958-59, we built a 250cc flat-twin with a middle crankshaft bearing and it revved easily to 11,500. We also made a new cylinder head for the 500cc twin with desmodromic valve gear (giving freedom from valve float, whatever the revs, without resor-

ting to four valves). After short tests, however, both experiments had to be abandoned through lack of money; indeed, that shortage put an end to all our racing activities.

'At that time nobody foresaw the ultimate invincibility of the two-stroke; but in the early 1970s, when our financial situation was healthier and we would have liked to return to racing, the superiority of the two-stroke made it impossible, for BMW would never make a two-stroke. So our financial and engineering resources were put into car racing instead, with very satisfactory results.'

There is no need, however, to dwell on what might have been to appreciate the superb engineering that brought BMW so many sidecar titles. Indeed, when Alan Baker visited the race department in 1955 to analyze the Rennsport engine for *The Motor*

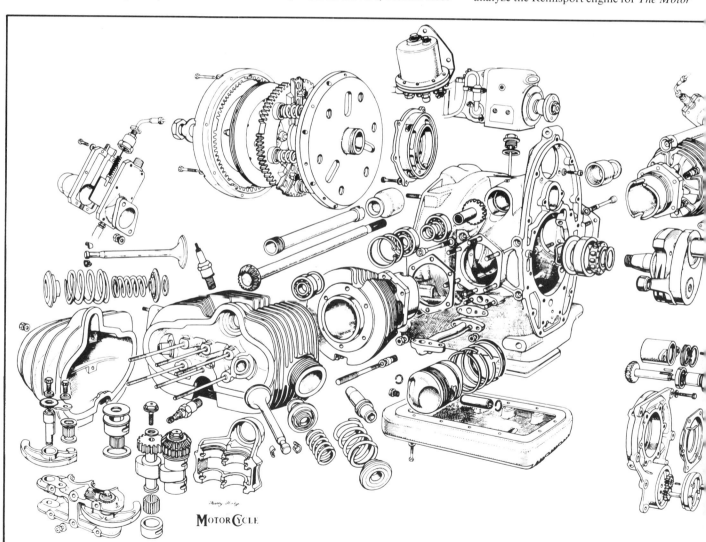

MOTORCYCLE

BMW's most successful postwar solo exponent, Walter Zeller was German 500cc champion in 1951, '54 and '55, then runner-up to John Surtees (MV Agusta) in the 1956 world championship.

1954 engine with which Willi Noll won the first of BMW's 19 world individual sidecar championships. Fed by a plunger-type pump on the front cover, the injector nozzles were screwed in the underside of the cylinder heads. Note the close-coupled, needle-bearing camshafts and straight valve rockers, four rings per piston, single-plate flywheel clutch and revmeter drive below fuel pump. To minimize cylinder offset, the middle web of the crank assembly was counterbored to accept the big-end eyes of the flat-section con-rods. The train of spur gears behind the front cover distributed the drive to the oil pump, cam-drive bevels and magneto.

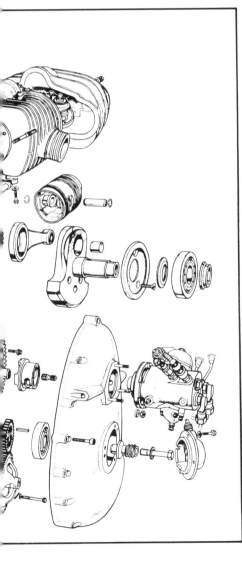

Cycle, Falkenhausen had not long taken charge and any thoughts of fundamental improvements lay in the future.

The engine laid bare for Baker's inspection was one of the 1954 works units, fitted with the third stage in an early Bosch fuel-injection programme, which eventually boosted power by 3bhp (to 61) at the same crankshaft speed. (In the first stage, fuel was sprayed at an angle through the sides of the induction tracts, between the flat throttle slides and the valve heads. The second experiment, in 1953, featured axial sprays into the air trumpets, upstream of the throttles. In the final stage, shown here in Harry Hodges' exploded drawing, fuel was pumped directly into the cylinder heads at about 570psi, through nozzles opposite the spark-

ing plugs. Eventually, however, carburettors were preferred for their more tractable throttle response on give-and-take circuits.)

A pressed-up construction was used for the sturdy 180-degree crankshaft. Both front and rear mainshafts and their two plain crankpins were hollow and of 35mm bearing diameter; the shafts were integral with their webs, which incorporated the balance weights. To shorten the assembly (and minimize the rocking couple), the two crankpin holes in the oval middle web had large-diameter counterbores adjacent to the big-end eyes, so reducing the offset of the connecting rods (hence the cylinders).

To lock the crankpins in the webs, solid expander plugs were driven into the ends of the pins — middle web first, then the outer

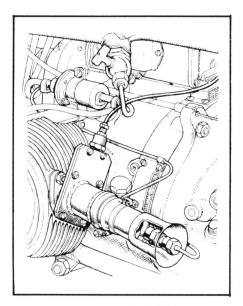

In the second stage of fuel-injection experiments petrol was sprayed into the intake bellmouths. Guillotine throttle slides were used with all three injection layouts.

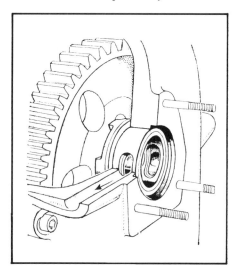

Crankcase breathing was timed by a ported sleeve driven by the half-speed timing gear.

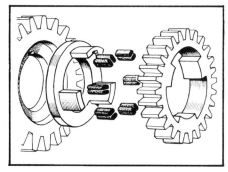

Segment-type shock absorber in the oil-pump drive.

webs following con-rod assembly. The outer expander plugs were drilled to lead oil from annular traps on the outer crank cheeks into the hollow crankpins and thence through radial holes to the single-row caged-roller big-end bearings. Fed with oil overflowing from the main bearings, the traps (thin discs with the periphery rolled over through 180 degrees) were screwed in place and also served as centrifugal filters.

Supporting the crankshaft were a self-aligning roller bearing (with slightly barrel-shape rollers) at the rear and a ball bearing at the front. To prevent the bearings from loosening in the Elektron (magnesium alloy) crankcase, they were pressed into flanged housings (steel rear, cast-iron front) which, in turn, were spigoted and bolted into the case. As mentioned earlier, the small ball bearing on the nose of the shaft was housed in the timing cover.

Bolted on the front face of a downward extension of the front main-bearing housing was the light-alloy body of the oil pump, in which two pairs of delivery gears fed different circuits; one took care of the main and big-end bearings, the other the cam gear.

Capacity of the finned Elektron sump was 2.8 litres (5 pints) and the SAE40 oil was drawn through a gauze strainer. Naturally the oil pushed through the main bearings to the big ends was then flung off to lubricate the pistons, cylinders and cam-drive bevel gears. In the other circuit, small-bore external pipes under the cylinder barrels took oil to metering jets (one each side) which sprayed it on to the cam/rocker rubbing faces, while larger-bore pipes alongside drained the oil back to the sump. There was, of course, no need for a scavenge pump.

Unusually for a four-stroke (and contributing further to a short, rigid crankshaft), the connecting rods had flat, rather than I-section, shanks. Since any bending stresses were predominantly in the planes of the $\frac{1}{4}$in-thick shanks, the absence of flanges caused no problem. Indeed, flanged rods had been found more prone to fatigue failure — from cracks starting at the joint of flange and web, where it was less easy to ensure a perfectly polished finish. To obviate unnecessary engine width, the rods were relatively short, measuring only 1.8 times the stroke between centres (rather than the more usual double stroke length).

Each big-end bearing had 14 10 × 7mm rollers running directly on the hardened surfaces of both crankpin and connecting-rod eye. To prevent contact with the roller tracks in the rods, the bars of the duralumin cages were relieved slightly on the outside. On their inner faces and sides, too, the bars were grooved to assist the spread of oil through the bearings.

The full-skirt pistons were unusual in having three compression rings above the taper-bored gudgeon pin and a slotted scraper below it. The bottom compression ring also helped in oil control, having a taper-ground face and small drain holes below the groove. Plain wire circlips retained the gudgeon pins and their piston bosses were particularly well reinforced at both ends.

This ghosted drawing of Fritz Scheidegger's 1962 kneeler outfit emphasizes how well the BMW engine facilitated the achievement of a low centre of gravity and a small frontal area. A very strong contender for the world championship for several years, Scheidegger built his first kneeler in 1960 and eventually took the title in 1965 and '66.

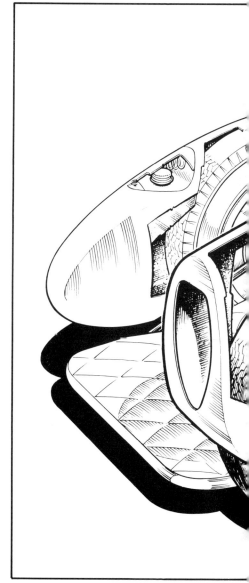

The relatively wide valve angle required high-dome piston crowns to achieve the compression ratio of 10.2:1 and the crown sides closely fitted the cylinder heads to promote squish turbulence. Clearance between piston crowns and valve heads was necessarily small and so the piston cutaways were shaped to match the valve contours — *ie,* a convex recess for the inlet valve and concave for the exhaust.

Because the die-cast light-alloy cylinders were so well placed for direct air cooling, their finning was relatively shallow. On the engine examined, the muffs were fitted with shrunk-in liners, their spigots protruding 1½in into the crankcase, with cutaways for con-rod clearance; but the later (and lighter) technique of chromium plating the light-alloy bores was already in use and gave

better heat dissipation. In both cases each base flange was clamped to the crankcase by six nuts.

In the part-spherical combustion chambers the valve-seat rings — manganese-steel inlet, bronze exhaust — were shrunk in place, while the sparking plugs were slightly canted (rearward on the right, forward on the left) to clear the cam-drive bevel shafts). Valve-guide material was bronze with a high tin content and valve diameters were 40mm (head) × 8½mm (stem) for the inlet and 36 × 11mm for the sodium-cooled exhaust. Duplex valve springs gave a seat pressure of 97lb and were retained by light-alloy top collars and stepped split collets.

With a 32mm bore at the flange, the inlet tracts had a downdraught angle of 15 degrees. Bolted to the flanges were flat boxes

housing the guillotine throttle slides; and rubber-mounted on stubs on the boxes were long, shallow-taper air trumpets. From trumpet mouth to throttle slide measured 8in and from slide to valve head a further 4½in.

The cylinder-head joints were made by lapping with abrasive paste and the subsequent method of assembly was unusual. First the six studs were screwed firmly into each head. Then the studs were threaded through their bosses in the barrels, after which sleeve nuts were screwed on to their inner ends. Instead of the customary hexagons, the nuts had external splines, permitting finer spannerwork.

Keyed to the front of the crankshaft were two adjacent steel spur gears. The smaller of them (close against the outrigger bearing in the front cover) drove the light-alloy oil-

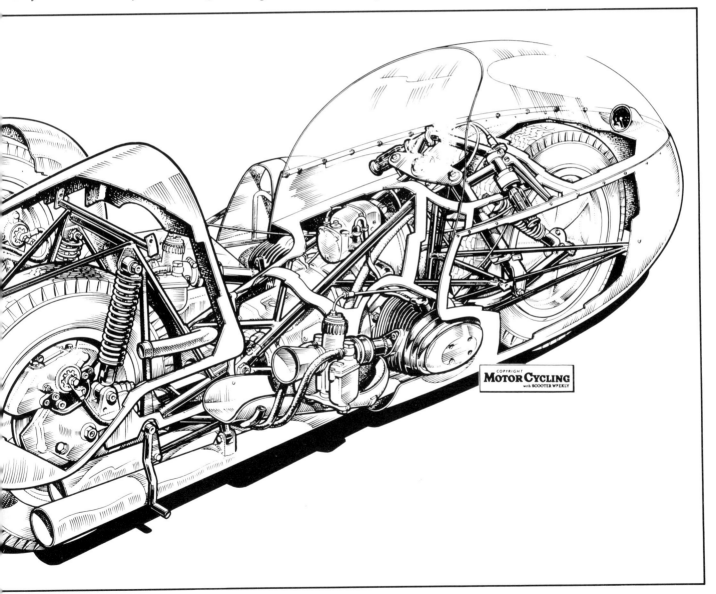

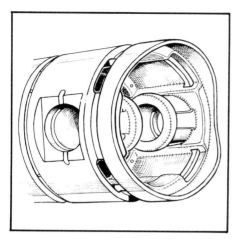

Reinforced gudgeon-pin bosses and oil-drain slots in the four-ring full-skirt piston.

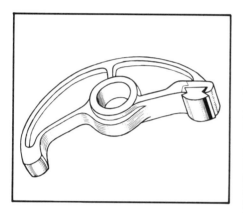

The straight valve rockers had chilled-cast-iron rubbing pads dovetailed into the cam-contact ends.

In each cylinder head, a split cast-iron housing accommodated not only the ball bearing supporting the bevel gear on the long shaft, but also the two needle-roller bearings flanking each cam and the needle bearings for the eccentric rocker spindles. Altogether, a commendably rigid layout. (In the prewar engine, the camshaft and rocker bearings were cast integrally with the cylinder heads but that led to distortion.)

Enclosing the long shafts, steel cover tubes screwed into the cylinder heads and were sealed at the inner ends by spring-loaded synthetic-rubber grommets in the crankcase.

A vernier-type coupling between each camshaft and its driving gear provided for precise valve timing. Unusually, this was symmetrical about the dead-centre positions, the valves opening and closing 60 degrees each side of tdc and 80 degrees each side of bdc. Adjustment of running clearances was facilitated by a serrated washer located by flats on the top end of each rocker spindle, which could thus be turned forward or backward by as little as one serration at a time in a meshing lock-plate. I-section steel forgings, hardened in the bores, the rockers had radiused chilled-cast-iron cam-follower pads dovetailed and shrunk into their inner ends to resist wear.

Clamped to the back of the timing chest, the magneto was driven by a steel gear on the half-speed shaft meshing with a light-alloy gear on the mag spindle. Thus all three driven gears in the chest were in light alloy; the one on the magneto spindle had its fixing holes elongated for precise adjustment of the fixed ignition timing.

Driven by two pegs on the front of the half-speed gear, the timed crankcase

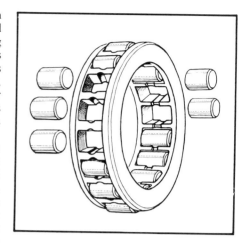

Bars of the duralumin big-end cage were relieved on the outside, to prevent contact with the con-rod eye, and grooved to promote the spread of oil.

breather took the form of a ported sleeve venting the case to atmosphere via two horizontal passages in the timing cover. Within the sleeve, a small coupling took the drive from the front of the half-speed shaft to the plunger-type fuel pump, which was mounted on the front of the cover and fed by gravity from the tank via a paper-cartridge filter.

Pipes from the bottom of the throttle boxes communicated induction-tract depression to one side of a diaphragm in the pump;

Spring-loaded synthetic-rubber grommets sealed the cam-drive cover tubes in the crankcase.

pump gear beneath it and incorporated a cush drive to reduce the shock loading on the meshing light-alloy teeth and so prevent breakage.

The larger of the crankshaft gears also drove a light-alloy gear (above it); tooth lubrication was taken care of by a piped bleed from the main-bearing housing aimed at the point where the teeth came out of mesh.

Running at half engine speed, the upper light-alloy gear was keyed to the front end of a horizontal shaft supported in a well-spaced pair of ball bearings in a duralumin housing let into the front crankcase wall. Formed at the rear of this shaft was the first bevel gear in the cam-drive train. Meshing with this gear were left and right bevels, each with its short hollow shaft supported in two closely spaced ball bearings; and splined into the outer ends of these shafts were the long solid shafts with integral bevels that drove the camshafts.

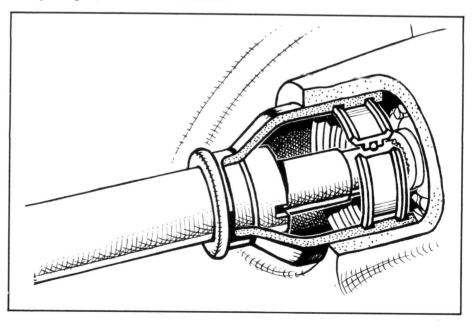

and movement of the diaphragm in response to varying throttle position partially rotated the plungers through a rack and two pinions. This rotation varied the effective porting in the pump, hence the amount of fuel injected into the cylinder heads; surplus fuel was returned to the tank.

To allow ample time for mixing, injection was timed appreciably before the completion of the inlet stroke, but was not critical to within 10 degrees; timing adjustment was provided by slots for the pump-mounting studs. An adjusting screw permitted basic setting of mixture strength. A half-litre oil container took care of pump lubrication.

Besides the 3bhp bonus conferred by the complete lack of obstruction in the inlet tracts and better atomization, direct injection reduced specific fuel consumption by 15 per cent (to a highly creditable 0.44lb/bhp/hour on full load) by preventing fuel loss to the exhaust during valve overlap.

The single-plate dry clutch was incorporated in a flywheel of 22½cm (approximately 9in) diameter carried on a substantial taper at the rear of the crankshaft. Six non-adjustable coil springs provided the pressure, while ducts in the housing admitted cooling air. The driven plate was splined on to the gearbox input shaft.

In the transmission examined there were five ratios, with top gear providing a reduction of 1.3:1, although at that time a four-speed gear cluster was still preferred for some circuits.

As mentioned earlier, peak power (whether with carburettors or fuel injection) was produced at 9,000rpm, while the engine was mechanically reliable for a further 500rpm. Only below 4,000rpm was there any misfiring (so-called megaphonitis) on full load; above that speed the engine surged lustily up the rev scale, getting into its full championship-winning stride at about 6,500rpm.

Under the terms of the FIM grand-prix formula in force during BMW's postwar heyday, the two-stroke's eventual power superiority was as inevitable as tomorrow's

On the way to the first of their six world titles, Klaus Enders and passenger Rolf Engelhardt negotiate Keppel Gate in the 1967 Sidecar TT, won by 'Siggi' Schauzu (BMW).

dawn; moreover, radical advances in tyres and chassis ensured that power would ultimately be the name of the sidecar game. For four-stroke fans, however, there remains a tantalizing conjecture: given peak revs of 10,500rpm, four-valve heads or desmo-

dromics, and Alex von Falkenhausen at the helm without crippling financial constraints, how much longer might BMW have successfully defended their sidecar stronghold — the last bastion of the grand-prix four-stroke?

CHAPTER 7

NSU Rennmax twin

Harbinger of the scientific approach to specific power — the high-revving two-fifty that left its rivals floundering

The international ban on supercharging for road racing (effective from 1947, four years before Germany's readmission to the FIM) not only put an end to the widespread use of brute force in the pursuit of engine power; it also sounded the death-knell for the sort of conservatism exemplified by Joe Craig's obstinate adherence to the upright two-valve big single for the Norton team. Within the new formula, engine design required a more scientific approach and it was the German NSU team, under the guidance of Dr Walter Froede, that pointed the way with the phenomenal 249cc Rennmax twin.

Since total piston displacement in each class was still limited, significant power gains in the absence of supercharging could come only from making the engine breathe and burn its fill more often — that is, pushing the power peak farther up the rpm scale. Shorter strokes, with correspondingly bigger bores, were an early step in the right direction, but only a small one so long as the engine had only one cylinder. At that time, the four-stroke was still supreme in classic racing; and, with inertia forces rocketing as the square of engine speed, peak revs were severely curtailed by the mechanical safety limits of the valve gear and connecting rod.

The obvious way round that obstacle was to use smaller cylinders (hence more of them for a given total displacement) for the lighter valves and con-rods could operate much faster within their safety limits. The problem then resolved itself into filling the cylinders adequately in the much shorter time available, which led to extended valve timings.

Conceived in the winter preceding the 1952 racing season, the original Rennmax twin had, for convenience, the bottom half of a shelved sports twin — with pressed-up, three-bearing crankshaft and integral chain-driven four-speed transmission — separate splayed bevel drives to the two overhead camshafts, and two cylinders from a failed 500cc racing four. At the time it was the only serious contender in its class with more than one cylinder — an inexplicable situation,

Dr Walter Froede (NSU).

except in the case of Moto Guzzi, whose whole racing philosophy was based on an ultra-low, ultra-slim, featherweight flat-single engine.

The wisdom of the twin-cylinder approach began to show when the new NSU engine gave 27bhp at 9,000rpm during pre-season bench tests. More to the point, it acquired a further 4bhp (at 10,000rpm) as the season progressed, gave sterling performances at Hockenheim, Nürburgring and the Berlin Avus track, and finally shook the confidence of the top-dog Moto Guzzi team during the 1952 Italian Grand Prix at Monza. There the up-and-coming Werner Haas took second place only inches behind the established Italian star Enrico Lorenzetti and ahead of his equally talented Moto Guzzi team-mate Fergus Anderson.

Convinced though he was of further gains to come, however, Dr Froede was well aware that the rewards to be won from higher peak revs were subject to the law of diminishing returns as mounting internal losses swall-

owed an ever-increasing proportion of dwindling power gains. So, while continuing to develop the Rennmax within the constraints of its original basic layout — for Haas to dominate the 1953 world 250cc championship — Froede made a systematic investigation into friction and pumping losses. His method was to use an external power source to motor a 125cc Rennfox engine round on the bench at about 10 stages of progressive assembly and to measure the power required at each stage. (For this purpose the Rennfox single, which preceded the Rennmax, could be regarded as virtually half the twin.)

The results (published in an ATZ paper in October 1953) were remarkable. In total the losses were found to increase as the square of engine speed (quoted as mean piston speed); and on full power some 34 per cent of the power produced in the combustion chamber (known as indicated horsepower) was dissipated in overcoming friction and pumping losses before the remainder was available (as brake horsepower) at the crankshaft.

The biggest thief was piston friction at 36.7 per cent (rings an extra 13.2 per cent); next were pumping losses (15.8 per cent); then, in descending order, main bearings and oil drag (9.2 per cent), connecting-rod bearings and timing gear (6.6 per cent each), valve actuation (4.6 per cent), magneto (4 per cent) and oil pump (3.3 per cent).

Even more interesting, Froede extrapolated his results to show that, for a cylinder size of 125cc, there would be no point in pushing peak revs beyond 14,000rpm; for even if breathing and combustion efficiency could be maintained at that speed any power gains in the combustion chamber would be completely cancelled within the engine. In view of the FIM's much later restriction on cylinder numbers (two for 250cc, four for 500cc) this meant that even the most sophisticated four-strokes in those classes would be theoretically limited to 14,000rpm. The fact that no conventional four-stroke with 125cc cylinders ever peaked

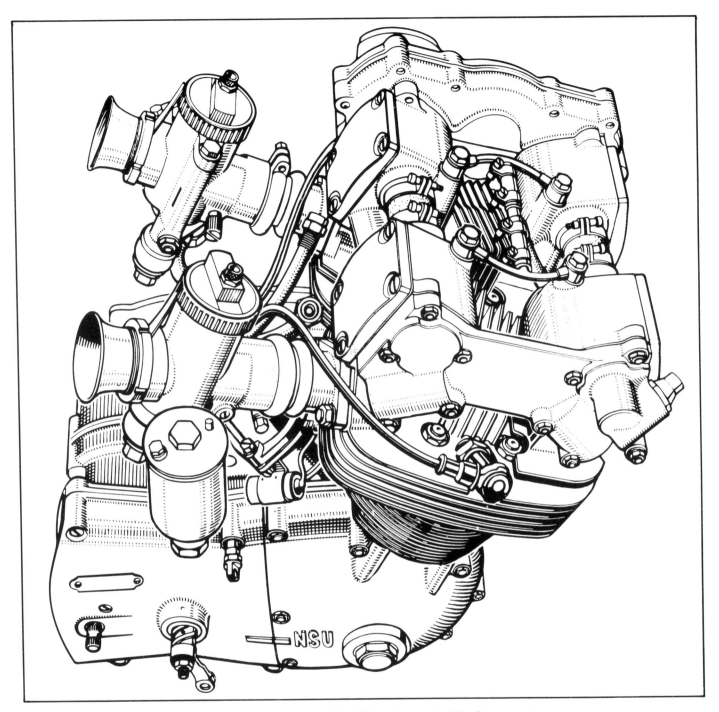

An NSU works drawing (as are the two exploded drawings) of the 1954 engine emphasizing its compactness.

so high (even with four-valve heads) under-lined the inevitability of impaired breathing and burning at ultra-high revs.

By experimenting with different inlet-port angles, Froede also investigated the effect of increasing the spiral-swirl rate of the gas stream entering the cylinder. Surprisingly, it was found possible to promote much too fast a swirl rate — and subsequent research

suggests three likely reasons for any adverse effects: (1) loss of heat to the combustion-chamber walls would be increased; (2) centrifugal force pushing the fuel droplets to the outside of the chamber might result in too rich a mixture at the plug points (in the side of the head); (3) the excessive gas speed might 'blow out the spark' (ie, inhibit flame propagation).

The second of these effects (too great a

concentration of liquid fuel around the out-side of the chamber, hence an unduly weak mixture at the core) is supported by Phil Irving's tale of an experimental Repco car-racing engine of the 1960s — a 3-litre, 90-degree V8 with a bore size of $3\frac{1}{2}$in. Of pent-roof shape, the combustion chambers had central plugs and four valves arranged in parallel pairs (with an included angle of about 30 degrees).

Unusually, however, induction was through diametrically opposed valves, not adjacent ones. And since the planes of the two inlet ports were spaced about $1\frac{1}{2}$in apart, the ingoing charge was given a 'two-start' spiral swirl. Moreover, the swirl rate was uncommonly fast because, compared with the single inlet port in a conventional two-valve head, each Repco inlet port had a very large offset angle (relative to the bore diameter).

Although starting and low-speed running were satisfactory, chronic misfiring occurred at high rpm, when so much of the fuel was thrown outwards that the core of the mixture at the plug points was too weak for efficient combustion. (Incidentally, Irving has quoted the critical swirl rate as six times crank speed.)

Actually, charge stratification of this sort is an important feature of modern lean-burn combustion techniques; but there is a limit to the difference between the richest and weakest strata (with the richest at the plug points)

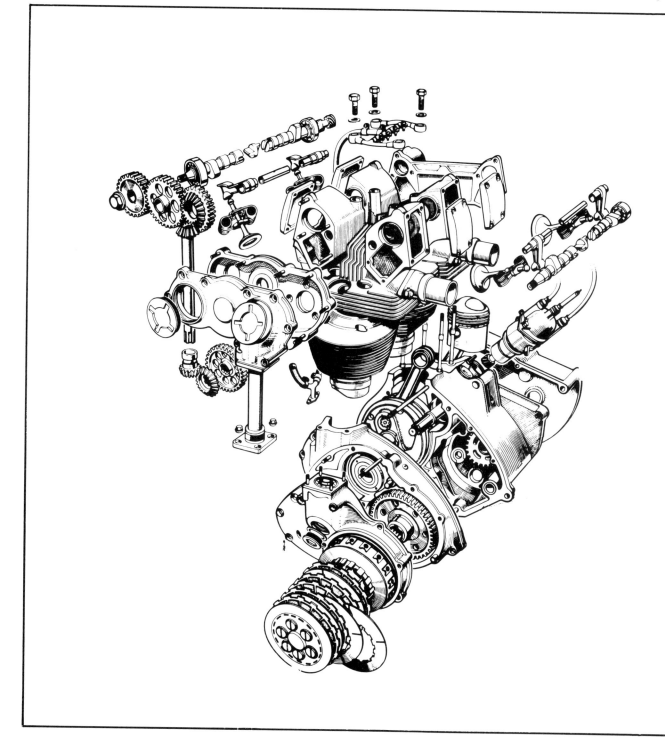

56

Final (1954) version of NSU's double-knocker, six-speed Rennmax engine. Supported in a total of eight roller bearings, the camshafts were in coupled right and left halves. The jackshaft above the flywheels was gear-driven from the middle of the crankshaft and itself transmitted the drive to the clutch, camshafts and ignition distributor.

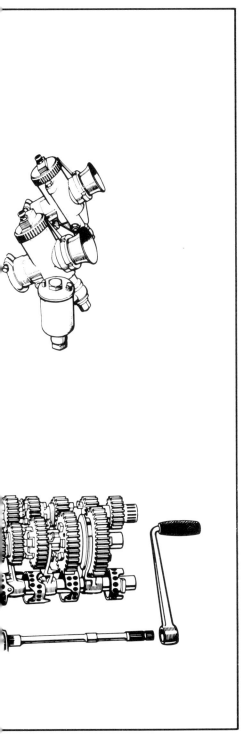

and much more sophisticated turbulence is required than can be generated by spiral swirl alone.

Froede put his research to brilliant use. In a wholesale redesign that eventually raised peak power to 39bhp at 11,500rpm, invested the word reliability with a new meaning and gave Haas a shattering superiority throughout the 1954 world championship, he concentrated on the obvious fundamentals — improving breathing and burning and minimizing the losses he had measured, together with any due to shaft flexure, distortion and overheating.

No part of the 1954 engine was more impressive than the new five-piece crankshaft, built up very rigidly by Hirth couplings and supported on four roller bearings. The middle portion comprised a straight-cut spur gear formed in the middle

of a short hollow shaft of 35mm journal diameter (approximately $1\frac{3}{8}$in); all drives were taken from this gear — transmission and ancillaries alike. On each end face of the short shaft was machined a fan-shape series of radial serrations to mate with similar serrations on the inner face of the adjacent 5in-diameter flywheel disc with its integral hollow crankpin.

The three parts were united by a double-ended bolt passing through the middle, with a different-pitch thread at each end. Since the female threads in the flywheel discs had correspondingly different pitches, turning the bolt clamped the assembly securely together. That is a Hirth coupling.

Left-hand cylinder head, showing the ample finning, bonded-rubber carburettor adaptor, alignment dowel and oil drain pipe.

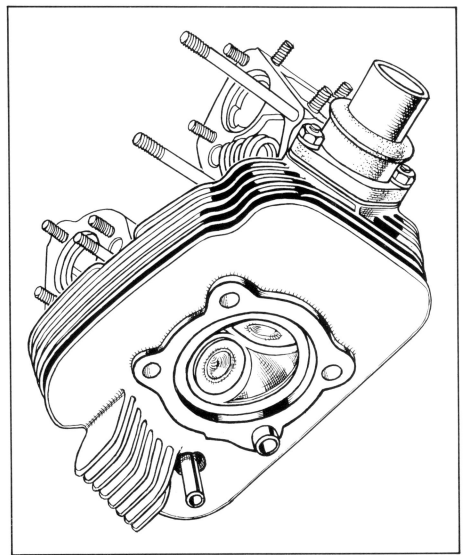

Above: The 1953 Rennmax twin that first dethroned Moto Guzzi from the world 250cc championship and (right) its engine. They are readily recognizable by the exposure of the hairpin valve springs and the prewar all-bevel cam-drive layout with splayed shaft tubes on the right.

Similarly, the outer faces of the crankpins and their mating faces on the remaining two flywheel discs were radially serrated and secured by two more differentially threaded bolts. Diameter of the integral hollow mainshafts was 25mm (approximately an inch) — reduced outboard of the bearings and ported to provide crankcase breathing through corresponding ports in the castings. Overall shaft length was a mere 10in.

All five crankshaft components were forged in nickel-chrome steel, heat treated then machined and polished all over. Final machining was carried out after assembly of the Hirth couplings, whose mating serrations were then marked for consistent assembly; thus crankshaft alignment could be guaranteed during servicing. The assembly was, of course, built up from the middle outward. The inner main bearings, flanking the spur gear, were of lipped pattern to locate the crankshaft laterally.

The forged-steel connecting rods were of I-section and highly polished all over as an insurance against fatigue cracks. To stiffen the big-end eyes against distortion at high rpm, each had a deep rib around the outside; two shallower ribs stiffened each small-end eye. Both ends of the rods were hardened. At the big end a single row of 5 × 10mm rollers ran directly in the rod; following failure in some early engines, the roller cages were made in high-duty aluminium alloy and anodized on the rubbing surfaces. Experiments with needle rollers at the small end were unsuccessful and fully floating bronze bushes were substituted.

Cast in high-duty aluminium alloy and heat treated, the crankcase was in four parts and incorporated a separate compartment for the transmission, which had been increased to six speeds. Removal of a partition gave access to the gear cluster without disturbing the engine; both gear shafts ran on needle-roller bearings. The main portion of the case was webbed internally to support the housing for the inner main bearings; it also formed the inner half of the openings for the cylinder liners.

Bolted to the sides of the main casting were the portions housing the outer main bearings and completing the cylinder openings. The remaining casting, on the left, housed the gear drive to the fabric-faced, multi-plate clutch, the clutch itself in a separate dry compartment, and the lower pair of bevel gears for the revised camshaft drive. A weight-saving experiment of casting the crankcase in Elektron (a magnesium-base alloy) was abandoned because of a tendency for the bearings to work loose.

Separate cylinder barrels and heads were retained for optimum cooling. Deeply spigoted into the crankcase mouths, the barrels were of bonded construction, made under an American Al-Fin licence; the jackets, with their 8mm-pitch cooling fins, were machined from solid aluminium-alloy billets. Bore and stroke dimensions were changed from square (54 × 54mm) to over-square (55.9 × 50.8mm); while the 3.2mm shortening of the stroke lessened piston speed, hence friction, the 1.9mm increase in bore diameter permitted the use of larger inlet valves and ports in the interest of high-speed breathing. At the same time, connecting-rod length was increased by 10mm for a twofold benefit. By curtailing the maximum values of piston acceleration and deceleration, the longer rods reduced the high-frequency vibration due to secondary inertia forces; they also gave the big-end bearings an easier life by reducing the cyclic fluctuations in their rotational speed that stem from the angular swing of the rods at top and bottom dead centres.

Light-alloy forgings, the full-skirt pistons

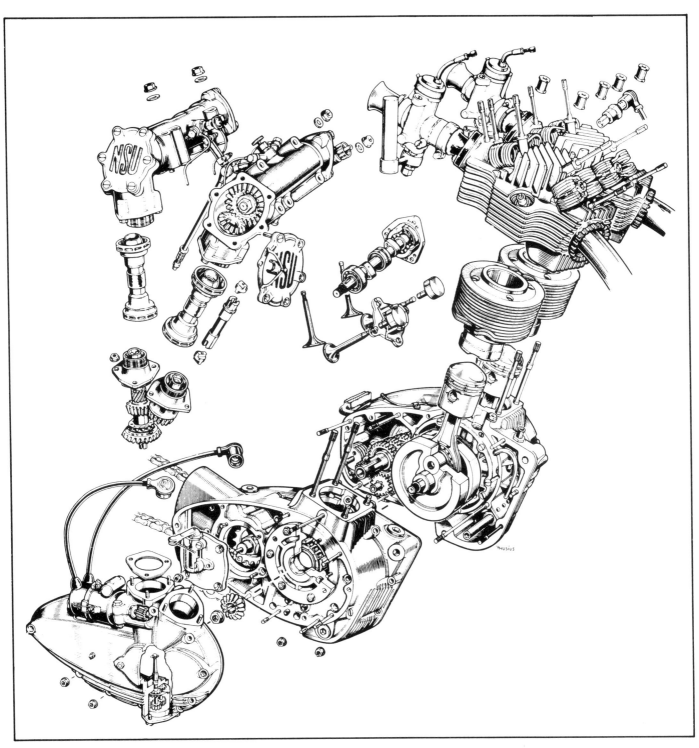

were ground oval externally to achieve true circularity at running temperatures; surplus weight was removed by internal milling. Diameter of the fully floating gudgeon pins, which were located by circlips, was practically $\frac{3}{4}$in. Above the pins were the customary slotted oil scraper and two compression rings.

Experiments were conducted with asymmetrical piston crowns designed to concentrate the combustion space as close as possible to the sparking plug, but the uneven mass distribution at first led to breakage. During the experiments, compression ratios ranged from 8:1 to 11:1; and although the breakages responded to careful graduation

of the metal thickness, crown shape finished up symmetrical, with cutaways for valve clearance, and gave a compression ratio of 9.8:1.

The aluminium-alloy cylinder heads, with their integral cam boxes and full valve enclosure, were characterized by massive

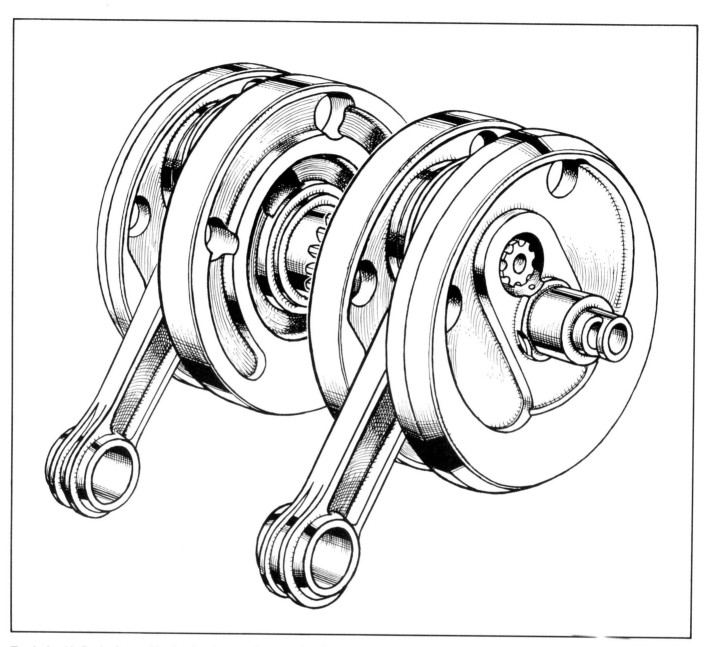

Ten-inch-wide flywheel assembly, showing the central power take-off, con-rod stiffening, left-side crankcase breather port and the end of one outer Hirth coupling bolt.

finning which was put to good use by an air deflector beneath the fuel tank. There were not only roughly square fins (in plan view) rooted on the combustion chambers, but also deep, slightly angled transverse fins between the inlet and exhaust cam boxes and a further cluster of deep fins below each exhaust port. A bronze alloy was used for the shrunk-in valve guides and seat rings, also for the screwed-and-pegged bosses for the 14mm sparking plugs. Combustion-chamber shape was part-spherical and the angle included by the valve stems was narrow for

the time at 50 degrees. The exhaust valves were hollow and sodium-cooled.

No cylinder-head gasket was used, the joints being ground, metal-to-metal. Eight long, waisted studs and sleeve nuts clamped the barrels and heads to the crankcase. Bonded rubber-and-steel mounting flanges insulated the Amal GP carburettors from engine vibration. With engine development, choke size increased progressively from 22 to 28mm.

For optimum rigidity four separate camshafts were used, each supported in two

roller bearings, one each side of the cam. Left and right camshafts were joined by tongued (Oldham-type) couplings enclosed in short rubber sleeves clipped to spigots on the cambox faces. Drive to the revmeter was taken from the outer end of the right-hand exhaust shaft.

Cam motion was transmitted to the valves by radiused levers pivoted on hollow spindles. Ball-end stem caps, seating in sockets in the underside of the levers, were made in different thicknesses for valve-clearance adjustment. Valve lift was 8mm (a shade

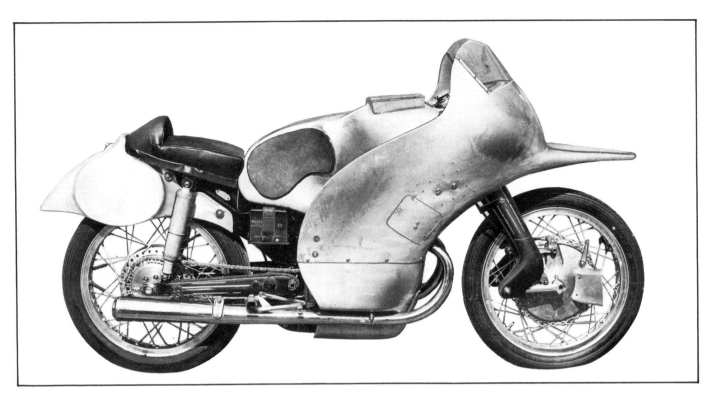

The despair of the opposition — final (1954) version of the pretty NSU Rennmax twin that set unprecedented standards of performance and reliability in the world 250cc championship that year.

Teutonic thoroughness. A typical grand-prix paddock scene during NSU's 1953-54 heyday, as the team's Rennmax engines are pre-heated with hot air while shrouded by tarpaulin sheets.

over $\frac{5}{16}$in) and NSU claimed that the optimum timing achieved, in conjunction with the resonant characteristics of 30in-long, shallow-taper exhaust megaphones, gave a breathing efficiency of 130 per cent, as measured by an airflow meter.

With neither paired valves nor desmodromics, Froede assured me that valve float had been pushed beyond 15,000rpm. To achieve this he was one of the first engineers to use a cam form that completed valve acceleration within the first quarter-lift, thus giving the overlapping hairpin springs appreciably more time to contain the inertia forces and reverse the motion; even so, spring poundage at full lift finished up at well over 200.

The cam drive started at the crankshaft spur gear, which meshed with a similar gear in the middle of an intermediate shaft supported in ball and roller bearings and lying above and to the rear of the flywheel assembly. Splined to the left-hand end of the intermediate shaft were, first, the clutch-drive pinion and then the first cam-drive bevel. This in turn drove a hollow vertical bevel running in ball bearings and splined internally to accept the bottom end of a long shaft. At the top end, a bevel gear formed on this shaft turned a crownwheel on the left-hand inlet camshaft. Dowelled to the back of the crownwheel, with provision for vernier adjustment, was a pinion that took the drive forward to the exhaust camshafts via an idler running on a hardened shaft. Unequal numbers of teeth on the vertical bevels distributed the cam loads evenly throughout the drive except, of course, for the first bevel and the gears on the camshafts.

Rennmax ignition was by battery and coil — not so much from a desire to save the small amount of power absorbed in driving a magneto, but because of repeated magneto trouble in the early stages of Rennfox development. As a bonus, the battery-and-coil set-up was lighter.

Driven by a skew gear on the right-hand end of the jackshaft, the distributor had two sets of contact points, each with a radial adjustment for gap setting and a circumferential adjustment for individual timing. Inevitably, the engine's high peak revs led to a fairly large ignition advance (40 degrees), which in turn made automatic advance and retard desirable — a most unusual feature in a grand-prix engine. It paid off in particularly docile starting; and the centrifugal mechanism ensured full advance by 5,000rpm — comfortably below the normal operating range. An overriding manual control enabled the rider to move the entire timing range if necessary. A special racing ignition coil, with comparatively few turns of heavy-gauge wire in the primary winding, was energized by two rubber-mounted 6-volt batteries connected in parallel to give a useful life of about five hours.

The oil pump was driven at a quarter engine speed from the crankshaft gear and circulated SAE20 racing oil at a rate of some 26 gallons an hour. To suit the unusual crankshaft construction a simple and effective system of big-end lubrication was adopted. In this, oil was forced through passages in the main crankcase casting and its main-bearing outer rings to squirt into annular channels in the adjacent faces of the inner flywheel discs, from where it centrifuged into the big-end bearings. Oil for the valve gear was fed through the hollow cam-lever spindles and the levers themselves to the rubbing faces.

Before being poured into the tank, the oil was heated to 90-100 degrees C and it settled to a running temperature of about 60 degrees. To get the maximum benefit from this preheating, the whole engine was heated in the paddock through massive hot-air trunking. Regarded by some as an amusing pantomime, this was really nothing more than a logical extension of the ultra-thorough racing philosophy that put the Rennmax way beyond the reach of its rivals. Indeed, Haas' winning speed in the 1954 French 250cc GP bettered Pierre Monneret's 350cc winning speed on a works AJS by more than 5mph; and in the German 250cc GP Haas was again faster (by 1mph) than the 350cc winner — Ray Amm on a works Norton.

Fitted, late that year, with one of the first full-frontal fairings (the dustbin type, to quote Fergus Anderson) a Rennmax was timed at Hockenheim at 135mph. Even with the less-slippery dolphin-type fairing used in that year's Lightweight TT, Haas' winning machine topped 125mph. But in no way was the excellence of NSU engineering better shown than by his fuel consumption of 42mpg in averaging more than 90mph throughout the TT when the Mountain course was much slower than it subsequently became. This was a convincing demonstration of fuel-efficiency.

NSU quit postwar grand-prix racing as suddenly and spectacularly as they took it up. It was many years before other teams, led by the Japanese, took the multi-cylinder route to power and followed it so far that the FIM eventually stepped in to limit cylinder numbers. The wonder is that it took the other engineers so long to recognize the inevitability of Dr Froede's scientific approach.

CHAPTER 8

Moto Guzzi flat-single

Winner of five consecutive world 350cc titles — a stretched 250cc engine overshadowed by its chassis

From 1953 to 1957 inclusive Giulio Carcano's Moto Guzzi flat singles made monkeys of the opposition as his riders won five world 350cc championships on the trot despite a power deficit of some 15 per cent or more compared with the rival German and Italian multis. Indeed, this audacious sequence of titles (the first two going to Fergus Anderson, the next two to Bill Lomas and the last to Keith Campbell) was halted not by Moto Guzzi's rivals, but by its management, which pulled the rug from under Carcano's feet without warning by withdrawing from racing at the end of 1957.

To the trackside observer the Moto Guzzi single's trump card was its ultra-low build, extremely light weight and superior penetration — a combination that gave the rider a considerable advantage in cornering speed, ease of handling and late braking, besides offsetting much of the power deficit in terms of straight-line performance. Correct though that assessment was, it tended to imply that Carcano's flair was confined to chassis development at the expense of engine development. Nothing could be farther from the truth.

As single-cylinder engines went, there was none better than the world-championship Moto Guzzi. Carcano's shrewd sense of priorities, his uncanny ability to pinpoint any source of trouble and rectify it in a trice, his imaginative experimentation and his willingness to change and, if necessary, change back again — all these were hallmarks not just of an open-minded development engineer but of a genius with the clearest and most penetrating intellect in the business.

Never for a moment did he dispute that the single was completely outclassed for sheer power. But he recognized more clearly than his rivals that races were won on the track, not on the dynamometer. No engineer had a shrewder appreciation that a road-racing machine is much more than a mobile engine — that high power is only one of several requirements.

The multis, he reasoned, traded their power bonus for a higher centre of gravity and extra bulk and weight — thus impairing handling and braking and partially offsetting their theoretical advantage in acceleration, climb and speed. But although the low-slung flat-single engine (with its inevitable power sacrifice) was crucial to the 350cc Moto Guzzi's dynamic superiority, Carcano never underrated the importance of engine performance.

Nor did the pursuit of that performance imply a worship of bhp at all costs. For tortuous circuits in particular — indeed for some of the faster laps too — he recognized that a narrow torque spread was too high a price to pay for an extra bhp on the peak of the power curve. And since no formula exists for relating dynamometer results directly to track performance, he determined the relative importance of different engine characteristics through private track testing linked to bench testing.

Following his engineering studies in Milan and a year's compulsory military service, Carcano joined Moto Guzzi in 1935. Officially his job was to liaise with the Italian army, but his enthusiasm took him also to race meetings where the works riders were competing — on the 250cc flat single (both unblown and blown), the unblown 500cc 120-degree twin and the blown 500cc three-abreast. By the time the war had come and gone he found himself in charge of the racing department, initially developing existing designs — with the exception of the outlawed blown models, of course. His team never exceeded 12 men including himself, two draughtsmen and eight or nine mechanics.

Boosting the flat single from 250 to 350cc was Fergus Anderson's inspiration, at the end of 1952, and the idea was soundly based for four good reasons. Only a few months earlier he had brought the little red bike's tally of Lightweight TT wins up to seven (a victory he was to repeat the following year); by the end of the season his partner Enrico Lorenzetti had clinched the team's third

world 250cc championship in four years; the chassis could obviously handle a lot more power; and finally a stretched two-fifty must always be more competitive in the 350cc class than a scaled-down five-hundred, which several rival three-fifties virtually were.

Tentatively, Carcano bored out a cylinder from 68 to 72mm and lengthened the stroke from 68 to 80mm by moving the crankpin as close to the edge of the crank webs as seemed safe. The capacity increase (from 247 to 326cc) pushed up peak power (measured at the rear wheel) from 28.5bhp at 8,400rpm to 31 at 7,700. Overall gearing was raised to suit; and since there was only a negligible increase on the machine's original 264lb weight, acceleration was considerably improved while top speed rose from about 125 to 130mph.

Almost immediately Anderson provided a significant pointer to future results when, in May 1953, he gave Moto Guzzi their first 350cc victory — in the German GP at Hockenheim, which was then a simple loop with the predominant emphasis on speed. The following month — again as a lone entry — he underlined the message by finishing third to the works Nortons of Ray Amm and Ken Kavanagh in the Junior TT, in those days a full seven-lap race. With confidence reinforced, Carcano quickly produced a full-size engine (75 × 79mm, 349cc) and Anderson romped to a fairytale world championship backed up by Lorenzetti, who relegated Amm to third place.

Besides the dynamic advantages mentioned earlier, Moto Guzzi's traditional single-cylinder layout had others. The cylinder head was well placed for direct cooling and lent itself to the use of a long induction tract (15in from carburettor mouth to valve head on the three-fifty) with the steep downdraught angle of 33 degrees, albeit no offset. In conjunction with a valve-stem included angle of less than 60 degrees (very narrow at the time) these features enhanced both cylinder filling and combustion.

Giulio Carcano (Moto Guzzi).

Use of an outside flywheel made for a compact and rigid union of crankcase and five-speed gearbox; and since there was only one pair of (straight-cut) gears in the primary drive, while the final drive was taken from a sleeve gear on the gearbox input shaft, power loss in the transmission was uncommonly low at 7 to 8 per cent.

The bored-and-stroked 326cc engine naturally inherited the guinea-pig two-fifty's bevel-driven single overhead camshaft, 10:1 compression ratio and single 14mm sparking plug. Contrary to popular rumour, the induction tract was parallel, not tapered; in common with the carburettor it had a bore of 35mm (about 1⅜in). Valve-head diameters were 35mm inlet and 30mm exhaust. Made in three pieces, the crankshaft had a caged-roller big-end bearing. A single oiling system served the engine, gear cluster and clutch, which had alternate steel and bronze plates.

Apart from the revised bore and stroke dimensions, the full-size engine incorporated only one major change from the 326cc specification — the crankshaft was made in one piece, with a split, uncaged needle-roller bearing at the big end to suit. Otherwise the differences were of a minor nature to suit the bigger bore — *ie,* a 2mm increase in the diameters of the two valve heads and the carburettor bore — while the compression ratio was lowered slightly, to 9.5:1. The 37mm carb proved to be too large, however, and the 35mm instrument was quickly reinstated.

Power went up a further 2.5bhp (to 33.5) at even lower rpm (7,500); and though subsequent engines revved a bit higher, Carcano always aimed by clever cam design to keep the power peak as far down the rev scale as possible in the interests of mechanical reliability and ease of handling.

Notwithstanding Anderson's 'hole-in-one' championship, however (an apt description

since he was a first-class golfer!) Moto Guzzi's 1953 season was not devoid of troubles. Chief of these was short big-end life — as already explained in the Vincent twin chapter, crowded rollers are unsuitable for high-speed big-end bearings. Also the second bore increase had left the iron cylinder liner too thin so that it distorted, as did the piston; consequently oil consumption was heavy, necessitating a very soft grade of sparking plug to prevent fouling.

In good time for the 1954 title chase Carcano had these problems licked. Reverting to a built-up crankshaft enabled him to reinstate the caged-roller con-rod bearing and so banish the big-end trouble. Thickening the cylinder liner and fitting a stiffer piston slashed oil consumption. All that was then required was Anderson's continuing trackcraft and the second 350cc title was in the bag.

In a riding sense, however, Anderson had finally come to terms with the fact that he was a veteran and accepted the responsibility of team management. And while he remained prepared, if necessary, to defend his title in 1955, he kept a shrewd lookout for a younger rider with the potential to fill his boots. His search was rewarded during TT practice when he learned that the talented Bill Lomas, 20 years his junior, was unhappy with the strings attached to a provisional ride on a works 7R AJS and enlisted him in the Moto Guzzi team with no such strings.

Meanwhile Carcano had designed a spaceframe specifically to suit his latest (full frontal) fairing; and since the new frame necessitated different mounting lugs on the engine he took the opportunity for an extensive rehash. Out went the cylinder liner (of whatever thickness) in favour of chromium plating of the light-alloy bore in conjunction with a full-skirt piston having a much reduced working clearance. Initially the piston crown was of pent-roof shape, giving a compression ratio of 9.4:1; but later on the shape was changed to a shallow part-spherical dome in the middle blending into a flat surrounding squish band. Primarily to improve valve control in the event of overrevving, but also in the hope of a mite more power, the bevel-driven camshaft and rockers gave way to two shafts and hollow bucket-type followers.

To reduce piston speed and improve breathing at peak rpm, the cylinder bore was increased to 80mm (necessitating a stroke reduction to 69.5mm), while the carburettor choke went up to 37mm to suit and valve sizes to 41 and 36mm.

Because the 5mm bore increase lengthened flame travel Carcano decided to switch to dual ignition with a 10mm plug in each side

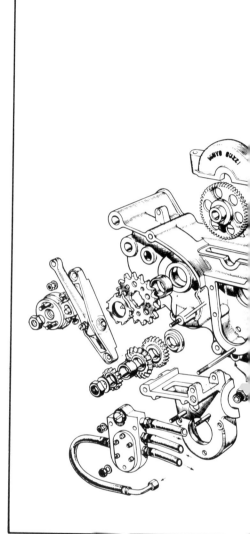

of the head (with differential timing) although teething troubles delayed final adoption of that plug size for two years. After an experiment with two independent magnetos, current was eventually supplied by a pair of batteries (each energizing a separate coil) since some magneto bothers had cropped up in 1954.

These revisions raised peak power to 35bhp at 7,800rpm, whereupon Lomas not only won his first Moto Guzzi race, the Junior TT, but followed up with an emphatic world championship before helping Anderson and Dickie Dale raise the world 12-hour record to 102.27mph at Montlhéry in the autumn.

Although most of the following winter's

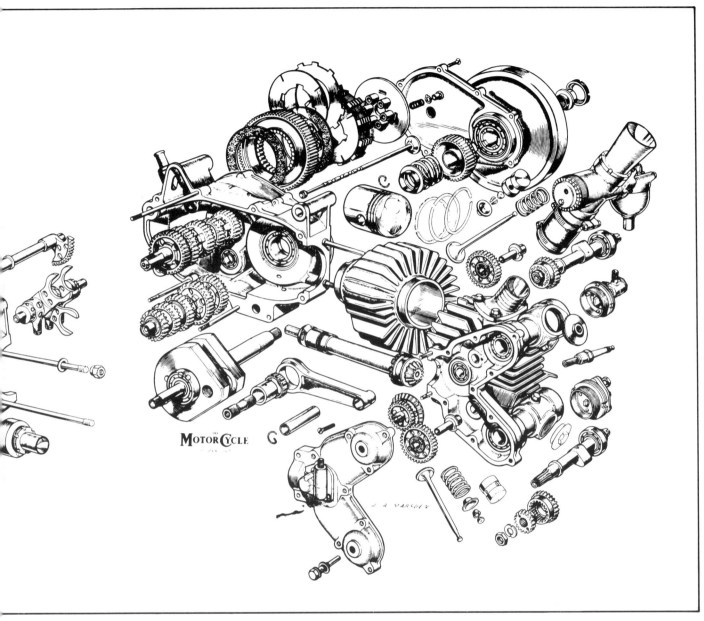

MOTORCYCLE

work was concentrated on the chassis, a modified cam form enhanced the torque curve while the spacing of the gear ratios was modified. Beating off a persistent challenge from August Hobl on the three-cylinder DKW two-stroke, Lomas managed to retain his title despite coming a cropper in the final round at Monza.

But misgivings were stirring in Carcano's mind. Both the Italian fours (the Gilera especially) had an edge in top speed while Helmut Görg had endowed the DKW with a highly competitive turn of acceleration from low and medium speeds. More to the point, Carcano had a shrewd suspicion that he himself had sacrificed too much bottom-end

punch for the speed increases of the past two years. A comparative test session on the twisty Modena circuit proved him right — despite its lower power, the 1954 long-stroke single-knocker lapped faster than Lomas' title winner simply because it accelerated more briskly out of the slow corners. (There is an obvious analogy here with drag racing, where 'getting out of the hole' first is crucial to success.)

So far as the engine was concerned, then, Carcano's priority for 1957 was to boost low-speed torque. His first move was to revert to the 1954 cylinder dimensions (75 × 79mm) while leaving carburettor size at 37mm (it was 2mm smaller in 1954). Similarly, although valve sizes were reduced to

Sound engineering with no frills — Keith Campbell's 1957 world championship-winning 349cc (75 x 79mm) engine was a product of five years' purposeful evolution. The prone cylinder installation allowed a long, 33 degree-downdraught induction tract. For maximum effect with minimum weight, the mass of the backward-rotating flywheel was concentrated in the rim. The absence of a cylinder liner and extensive use of magnesium and aluminium contributed to ultra-low weight. The all-metal clutch ran in oil and the transmission absorbed only 8 per cent of crankshaft power.

39mm (inlet) and 33mm (exhaust) they were still larger than in the 1954 engine.

Since the extra weight of two batteries, coils and contact breakers had hardly been justified in the 80-bore engine by the very slight gain in low-down power — and flame travel had now been shortened by the smaller bore anyway — magneto ignition was reinstated, which meant a return to single ignition (still with a 10mm plug). Had a twin-spark mag been available the second plug might well have been retained, although the sensitivity of 10mm plugs to fouling at that time would have been against it (dual ignition had required less spark advance and if one plug fouled, particularly the earlier-firing one, the timing on the surviving one was much too late for competitive performance).

To Carcano's delight these alterations produced not only the healthy boost in torque that he sought but also an extra 3bhp (to 38 at the rear wheel) — and very creditably at only marginally higher peak revs, 7,800 to 8,000rpm. Equally remarkable in view of a switch to single valve springs (to save weight!), valve float was banished beyond 8,400rpm.

The engine's enhanced tractability was a boon to mechanics and riders alike. No longer did the spannermen have to change internal gear ratios to suit different circuits, while maintenance requirements were negligible. On the track the machine was extraordinarily easy to ride — partly by virtue of the engine's high torque and partly because of the final reduction in overall weight to a phenomenal 216lb in Continental trim and only 224lb in TT trim, with fatter tyres and extra tankage for a non-stop 264-mile race.

With Bill Lomas one of several victims of oil spilt on the track during the 1957 Imola Easter meeting, it fell to Australian Keith Campbell to vindicate Carcano's philosophy by keeping the world 350cc championship in Moto Guzzi's hands for the fifth year running when he comfortably outpointed Gilera stars Bob McIntyre and Libero Liberati. Indeed, Carcano's theories could have had no better proof than in two of Campbell's victories over the 45bhp Gileras on vastly different tracks. First, in the Dutch TT on the twisty Assen circuit, he beat McIntyre — at that time the world's top rider and fresh from his TT double — simply because he was able to outbrake him and corner faster. Only eight days later he inflicted similar humiliation on Liberati in the Belgian GP on the ultra-fast Francorchamps circuit, with its premium on speed and three-figure ear'oling. Some years later Carcano assured me that,

except on circuits such as the old Hockenheim loop and the near flat-out Reims lap in France, Campbell's 140mph single was a better tool than the experimental 350cc version of his water-cooled V8 with 48bhp.

So much for development; now for the technical details. Underlying all the changes described was a constant watch on weight. Steel or iron was never used where aluminium would do — for example, the oil-pump body, banjo unions and many nuts were made in aluminium. Nor was aluminium used where the even lighter magnesium would do — eg, for all light-alloy castings except the cylinder barrel and head. Studs were waisted to root thread diameter, gears perforated and so forth.

Yet nowhere was stiffness or rigidity sacrificed. Forged integrally with their bob-weights, both mainshafts were 30mm in diameter — the right-hand one supported in a ball bearing, the other one in a roller bearing and those bearings only $2\frac{3}{8}$in apart. Clamping the two bobweights to the 36mm-diameter hollow crankpin was a double-ended, differentially threaded stud with internal splines at both ends for assembly and dismantling. The big-end cage housed 14 10 × 6mm rollers. Measuring approximately $6\frac{1}{2}$in between centres, the connecting rod was of I-section with a single web round the unsleeved big-end eye and a bronze-bushed small end.

The bobweights were $5\frac{1}{4} \times \frac{7}{8}$in discs with chords machined at an angle on both sides of the crankpin location and a small hole diametrically opposite for final balance. A plain taper fit on the end of the left-hand shaft, the 9in-diameter outside flywheel had a 50mm-diameter boss formed on its inner face by which it was supported in a massive roller bearing in the cover of the primary drive compartment. Maximum flywheel effect for minimum weight was achieved by using an I-section with most of the mass concentrated in the $\frac{5}{8}$in-wide rim (which was marked for dead-centre and timing positions).

On the inboard face of the flywheel boss, four dogs engaged with similar dogs on the 41-tooth primary drive gear, which was a sliding fit on the shaft and dished on the inside to accommodate a stiff spring that kept the dogs in engagement. Thus the gear was driven by the flywheel, not the shaft, and the shaft was relieved of a good deal of the torsional stresses arising from the trans-

In foul weather, Bill Lomas led from John Surtees (MV Agusta four) for 95 per cent of the 1956 Junior TT, until stopped by a split valve cap. Winner was Lomas' team mate Ken Kavanagh.

This picture of Bill Lomas' 1956 championship-winning engine emphasizes its low build and steep induction layout. This 80mm-bore engine had battery ignition and different mounting lugs from the later unit.

mission. Width of the gear teeth (and those on the meshing 72-tooth clutch pinion of course) was ⅝in.

Immediately outboard of the right-hand main bearing, the shaft was reduced to 19mm diameter and keyed into the magneto gear, the camshaft-drive bevel and the oil-pump pinion in that order. Surprisingly, the so-called hunting-tooth system (for distributing the cam loads evenly over all the teeth on the two coupling-shaft bevels) was not used: from crankshaft to cylinder head, the numbers of teeth on the four bevels were 19, 19, 14 and 28. Formed integrally with its 14-tooth bevel, the coupling shaft was

splined into the 19-tooth one to allow for cylinder expansion; both these bevels ran in ball bearings in the cover tube.

Supported in ball bearings in both the cylinder head and the V-shape gear-train cover, the crownwheel was riveted to a spur gear that drove the two intermediates; they had pressed-in ball bearings supported on hollow flanged spindles, pegged to prevent rotation. Vernier couplings in the camshaft gears allowed timing variations of 2.35 degrees.

Each camshaft ran in a roller bearing on the right and a ball bearing on the left, with a severe-looking harmonic cam formed integ-

rally nearer to the ball bearing. Both cams gave a lift of 12mm, but the inlet naturally had a considerably longer dwell. Both perforated and waisted, the followers slid in aluminium-bronze guides and closely surrounded the six-coil springs. Checked through plugged holes in the camshaft tunnels, valve clearances were adjusted by hardened end caps of different thicknesses on the stems.

All 29 cylinder fins were arranged longitudinally (to suit the horizontal installation) and the chromium bore was etched for oil retention. Both barrel and head were retained by four long studs. The cam boxes were cast integrally with the head, which had steel valve-seat rings, a part-spherical combustion surface, a two-stud fixing for the flanged exhaust pipe and three studs for the inlet stub.

Contrary to the usual Continental pattern of all-indirect drive, the gear cluster was of mainshaft/layshaft type, as favoured in most British transmissions but with crossover drive like that in the postwar Vincent twins. Ball and roller bearings supported both shafts in the two main castings, which incorporated four massive mounting lugs, one on the rear-fork pivot axis. In the top rear corner of the crankcase-cum-gearbox was a baffled compartment with a $\frac{5}{8}$in-bore breather pipe. Noteworthy features of the $5\frac{1}{4}$in-diameter clutch were four radial slots in each steel plate to prevent buckling and the use of four balls and four rollers, arranged alternately in the thrust rod for clutch withdrawal.

Oil from the large-diameter top tube of the frame was pumped to the big-end bearing and into the hollow camshafts, from which it exuded at the rubbing faces. It was scavenged not only from the sump (by the main pump) but also from the lower (exhaust) cambox — into which oil drained through drillways from the upper box — by an auxiliary pump on the end of the exhaust camshaft. The fuel pump was driven by the inlet camshaft and the valve gear breathed through the inlet-valve cap to the oil container.

Even allowing for the help of its elegant full-frontal fairing, the 350cc Moto Guzzi's phenomenal average of more than 60mpg in winning the Junior TT and other classic grands prix left no doubt as to the engine's intrinsic efficiency. Nine years after the factory quit racing, the lack of a worthy intellectual challenge eventually drove Carcano into

freelance yacht design, where he quickly matched his remarkable grand-prix racing achievements. Many years later still, he switched to management of the Italian national star-class yacht racing team only on the death of his draughtsman, who had served him loyally ever since 1935.

By coincidence, when I called at Carcano's humble Mandello home in September 1982 he had just returned from leading his team to victory over the Americans in the Sardinia Cup. After 25 years away from motorcycle racing, he confessed in answer to my question, it was impossible to say categorically whether he would do anything differently if he were starting all over again. Except that modern technology might enable him to take some short cuts, however, he doubted it since he had always worked from fundamental principles — as indeed any true professional must. No budding race engineer could wish for a more inspiring example.

On the way to his world title for Moto Guzzi, Keith Campbell passes John Hartle (Norton) on the inside during the 1957 Swedish 350cc Grand Prix.

CHAPTER 9

MZ disc-valve single

Mechanically simple, technologically phenomenal — first grand-prix
engine with 200bhp/litre and the model for countless Japanese track
successes

Despite its arbitrary nature (for a start it favours smaller cylinders) bhp/litre has long been used as a yardstick for comparing racing engines of different types and sizes. Shortly before the war, Joe Craig's claim of 50bhp for the 500cc twin-camshaft TT Norton (100bhp/litre) was a significant milestone in specific power from an unsupercharged petrol-burning engine, although blown engines of the same era (two-stroke as well as four-stroke) naturally bettered it. After the war, with supercharging banned for classic racing, engines with smaller cylinders improved on Craig's mark by leaps and bounds. With 156bhp/litre, the 250cc NSU Rennmax twin of 1954 made an enormous advance, which was almost matched by the 152bhp/litre of the 125cc desmodromic Ducati single soon afterwards, then quickly outdated by the 180bhp/litre of the 125cc desmo twin.

All those engines were four-strokes and the widespread assumption that the grand-prix two-stroke was doomed to failure without supercharging seemed to be reinforced when the exciting 350cc DKW three of the mid-1950s, with piston-controlled induction, withdrew its brave challenge to the all-conquering Moto Guzzis while its specific power was no higher than 130bhp/litre, competitive though that was on the track.

But any assumption of two-stroke ineptitude was utterly false because the next milestone in specific power — a stunning 200bhp/litre — was set by the East German 125cc MZ single, with disc-valve induction, in 1961. The seeming suddenness of that leap in two-stroke performance was an illusion. For whereas Helmut Görg's development work at DKW in Ingolstadt had received widespread press coverage, Walter Kaaden's simultaneous efforts in MZ's Zschopau race shop (ironically DKW's prewar home) were concealed from all but a perceptive few by the difficulties of communication across the Iron Curtain. In fact, the little MZ engine had topped 130bhp/litre about the same time as the DKW (1955-56).

By 1959, the bike's surging potential had attracted top Western stars despite serious currency problems. In that year's Lightweight 125cc TT — after breaking Tarquinio Provini's two-year-old lap record (set on a twin-camshaft FB Mondial) — Luigi Taveri led the dynamic Italian (then on a double-knocker MV Agusta) throughout the race until an overtight helmet blurred his vision and forced him to slow enough for the two-stroke's plug to jib and let Provini past to win. Three months later, Ernst Degner, MZ's home-bred star, removed any lingering doubt about the calibre of the East German challenge by narrowly beating MV Agusta's world champion Carlo Ubbiali on his home ground (Monza) to win the Italian GP.

With an unmatched 25bhp (the new milestone) at his disposal in 1961 — and with the East and West German and Italian GPs under his belt — Degner had the coveted world championship within his grasp. Despite a subsequent crankshaft failure in the Swedish GP, he still held a two-point lead over Tom Phillis (Honda) with only the Argentine GP remaining. Alas for MZ, Degner's long-planned defection to the West came to fruition in Sweden. As a result his competition licence was suspended for the Argentine race and Phillis gratefully accepted his gift of the world 125cc title, Honda's first.

The following winter, artist Lawrie Watts and I went to Zschopau, where Walter Kaaden spread out a dismantled engine for our inspection. Our immediate impression was of the meagre level of his resources and the engine's utter mechanical simplicity. The three-piece pressed-up flywheel assembly was supported in the vertically split crankcase by three main bearings (two left, one right) — one each side lipped for lateral location; running clearance for both flanks and rims of the flywheels was a bare half-millimetre (0.020in). On the left was the primary drive pinion for the bolted-on six-speed gearbox, also the revmeter drive. On

the right, the cutaway spring-steel inlet disc (about 0.016in thick × 4¾in diameter) was clamped to a hub splined to the mainshaft. This arrangement allowed the valve to float about half a millimetre in the tiny gap between the machined outer face of the crankcase and the inner face of the spigoted cover carrying the flat-slide BVF carburettor and half-speed gear-driven IKA magneto. Carburettor size at that time was 29mm where the emphasis was on maximum speed, 27mm where acceleration was top priority. The inlet tract was inclined upward to direct the charge into the space it had to fill (ie, above the flywheels); and the rim of the right-hand wheel was bevelled to prevent obstruction of the port. (The other rim was bevelled too, but only to simplify production.)

Both ends of the I-section connecting rod were fitted with caged needle-roller bearings and the silicon-aluminium alloy piston had only one ring (chromium-plated); shedding the second ring, though it may have impaired gas sealing below 6,000rpm, gave a bonus of 0.2bhp where the engine spent most of its working life, between 9,000 and 11,000rpm. The piston skirt was cut away on both sides to clear the main transfer passages and additionally on the right front corner to clear the inlet port. A window high in the front of the skirt fed the third transfer port, diametrically opposite the exhaust port.

Deeply finned, the iron-sleeved aluminium-alloy cylinder had square-cut exhaust and transfer ports — the exhaust port shortened by machining it well back to minimize heat absorption from the outgoing gases, and fitted with a double-wall quick-change adaptor for the 40mm-bore pipe. Equally well finned, the cylinder head had a half-moon squish band on the exhaust (rear) side, closely matching the shallow dome of the piston crown; the effect of this, besides enhancing turbulence at top dead centre, was to help deflect the looping transfer streams away from the exhaust port. In conjunction with the carefully designed resonant exhaust box and close control of both the direction

Walter Kaaden (MZ).

and speed of the three transfer streams, this feature contributed to a TT fuel consumption of 49mpg, remarkably low for such a high-performance two-stroke — although subsequent power increases inevitably increased the engine's thirst.

The mechanical simplicity of that 1961 engine concealed the more subtle reasons for its success — all of them based on Kaaden's recognition that an unsupercharged crankcase-induction two-stroke must be treated as a high-speed resonating engine rather than a relatively low-revving pumping engine such as the blown DKW split singles (and split twins) that dominated the European 250 and 350cc championships just before the war.

The basic problems facing two-stroke engineers both before and after the war stemmed from the symmetrical timing of piston-controlled ports. This symmetry first curtailed the length of the inlet phase unless port closure was so late that some of the fresh charge was blown back out of the crankcase by the descending piston. It then allowed some of the charge in the cylinder to escape through the exhaust port just after the transfer ports had closed. In the blown DKWs the inlet restriction was overcome by supercharging and the gas escape by the split-cylinder arrangement, in which out-of-phase pistons closed the exhaust port before the transfers. For Kaaden the first solution was outlawed by the supercharging ban, while the consequent need for much higher engine speeds ruled out the split-cylinder arrangement, both on account of the weight

In the 1961 German GP at Hockenheim Alan Shepherd makes his MZ debut with an experimental forward-facing exhaust port. Although the change took the crisp edge off the engine's torque, he finished second to Ernst Degner, similarly mounted.

of the articulated connecting rods and their pistons and the impossibility of filling a divided cylinder in the much shorter time available.

Instead, his use of a disc valve enabled inlet duration to be greatly lengthened by early opening without such late closure as to allow significant blowback through the carburettor. By experiment, too, the valve's timing was phased to match the natural resonant frequency of the inlet tract (including the crankcase); and its very rapid opening of the port helped strengthen the pressure pulse. Preventing a significant escape of fresh gas immediately following transfer was one of the functions of the resonant exhaust box. The first portion of this assisted transfer by accentuating the depression in the exhaust port around bottom dead centre; the reverse-cone portion (or baffle) then reflected a positive pressure pulse back to the port just before closure to resist any escape.

The extent of the engine's dependence on resonances rather than piston motion to control gas flow is shown by calculating the time available for the various phases. Even with the inlet period extended by use of a disc valve, no more than 1/300th of a second (0.0033s) was available to fill the crankcase at peak revs (10,800rpm). The cylinder had to be emptied and replenished with the fresh charge from the crankcase, with as little loss as possible, within an even briefer period. And of that concurrent exhaust/transfer phase, little more than a tenth — *ie,* 1/2,600th part of a second (0.00038s) — was available, between exhaust opening and

transfer opening (the so-called blowdown period), for cylinder pressure to drop low enough for transfer to be possible anyway. On the piston's upstroke, the success or otherwise of the designer's efforts to minimize gas loss (crucial for both power and consumption) was determined in an identical infinitesimal fraction of time.

Kaaden's first MZ racing engine (in 1953) was a three-speed 125cc two-stroke single with an engine-speed magneto, disc-controlled induction, only the conventional two transfer ports, and two rear exhaust pipes with open megaphones. The reason for exhausting the cylinder from the rear instead of the front was not so much to straighten or shorten the pipes as to seal the crankcase from the exhaust ports as effectively as possible. On the firing stroke, the forward swing of the con-rod resulted in the piston being thrust hard against the rear cylinder wall, so forming a good seal and transferring the running clearance to the front. (In a few races in 1961 this theory was vindicated when the exhaust pipe was transferred to the front — with a consequent slight blunting of torque, hence throttle response.) During the season, power of that original engine was raised from 9 to 11.75bhp (at 7,800rpm) by increasing the size of the exhaust and transfer ports, raising the compression ratio and modifying the length and taper angle of the exhaust pipes.

For 1954, a four-speed gear cluster was fitted, while further engine tuning raised peak power to 13bhp at 8,000rpm. During

In the first year of the third transfer port, Ernst Degner leads Mike Hailwood (desmodromic Ducati) in the Lightweight 125cc TT, which took place on the Clypse circuit.

the year two experimental engines were investigated — one a parallel twin, the other an opposed-piston layout with two chain-coupled crankshafts, in which the upper (exhaust) piston had a 15-degree lead over the lower (transfer) piston. Since both engines produced only 12bhp at 9,000rpm they were discarded.

For 1955, the two exhaust pipes were replaced by a single pipe with a baffled outlet and power climbed to 15bhp at 9,000rpm. That was the first step towards the subsequent complex exhaust system, in which calculations involving gas speed and temperature produced theoretical dimensions, which were then refined by dozens of painstaking experiments (leading to the quick-change exhaust adaptor). The induction and transfer layouts were equally critical for performance, but they were determined by experiment alone, not calculation. At that stage the little MZ was winning national races, though slightly overshadowed in world-championship events by the DKW single from Ingolstadt with its cylindrical rotary valve.

The MZ's mounting revs, however, were by then impairing the engine's tractability and stamina. To solve the first problem, a six-speed gearbox was introduced for 1956 to

compensate for the narrowing power band. At the same time, four measures were taken to restore stamina. First, caged needle rollers replaced the bronze small-end bush, which was particularly vulnerable to high revs because of its hot environment and scanty lubrication. Second, the caged big-end rollers were slimmed to 3mm diameter to reduce skidding. Third, more robust main bearings were fitted. Finally, the troublesome magneto gave way to battery-powered ignition, though still with an engine-speed contact breaker.

While those improvements boosted peak power to a reliable 16.5bhp at 9,200rpm, another offbeat engine layout was tried and discarded. The cylinder was horizontal and the disc, driven by skew gears, fed the crankcase at the top rear, plumb on the centre line, with the twin aims of symmetrical filling and better cooling and lubrication of the big end. (MZ lubrication was always by a 5-per-cent mix of SAE20 vegetable oil in the petrol.) Unfortunately, the masking of the crankcase raised its temperature sufficiently to reduce charge density and so limit maximum power to 14bhp. Worse still, piston seizures were frequent, as were failures of the skew gears.

The remaining steady climb of the regular

engine to 25bhp took five years of intensive all-round development, during which the biggest single gain (about 1½bhp) came in 1959 from the introduction of the auxiliary transfer port. Its primary object was to pass some cool, oily gas over the small-end bearing which — at speeds above 10,000rpm — had again reached the end of its tether. The ruse succeeded, while the extra power was an unexpected bonus stemming from the more complete transfer of the gas under the piston crown and the improved gas-flow pattern in the cylinder. To optimize the benefit, a manometer was used to check gas speed at various places in the cylinder. Best results were obtained from a gas speed of 25 metres per second (82ft/sec) through the third port (and an upward inclination of 30 degrees) in conjunction with an appreciably lower speed through the side ports, whose streams had little upward inclination and converged at an included angle of approximately 120 degrees.

Further contact-breaker trouble was beaten in 1960 by gearing it down to half speed and including two opposed sets of points, operating alternately — an arrangement that naturally doubled the time devoted to spark timing. Once the scheme was proved, a change to a half-speed rotating-magnet magneto saved a lot of wiring and the bother of charging and transporting batteries.

Besides the fundamental two-stroke problems of cylinder distortion, bearing lubrication, plug fouling, piston holing and suchlike, an overall difficulty arose in the late 1950s. At peak powers above about 20bhp, engines became increasingly temperamental and needed individual treatment. However carefully a star engine was copied, it was impossible to guarantee a duplicate performance. As a result, detailed specifications varied. Primary (crankcase) compression ratios ranged from 1.3 to 1.5:1, secondaries from 15 to 16:1. Disc timing might vary 5 degrees either side of the nominal figures, while the piston window could be as narrow as 18mm or as wide as 22mm.

This sensitivity made demands on the rider too. He had to judge the best position for the mixture-control lever while flat-out in practice, so that the carburettor could be correctly rejetted for the race with the lever wide open. Incorrect jetting could cause piston seizure (through weakness) or loss of power through port obstruction if the lever had to be closed appreciably. Werner Musiol was probably MZ's best rider in this respect — in 1963 he rode Mike Hailwood's bike in practice to find the best lever position for him.

Even worse for MZ than Degner's defection and the consequent loss of the 1961 world championship was the fact that he took with him to Suzuki (who had plotted his escape) vital engine parts, drawings and material specifications. Soon Suzuki were winning world championships galore with 'Oriental MZs' and the other Japanese two-stroke race teams quickly followed suit, as did various European teams. Indeed, engines built to Kaaden's basic formula took the vast majority of world championships in all classes for the next 30 years and more.

It was 1983 before the formula was effectively challenged. By then, despite phenomenal improvements in tyre grip, the sheer power of the leading five-hundreds (about 130bhp) had once more become an embarrassment for the riders. At the cost of some superfluous peak power, Honda achieved a worthwhile improvement in midrange flexibility by using compound-petal automatic reed valves (invented by a Norwegian, Eyvind Boyensen) rather than discs to control the induction in their three-cylinder two-stroke and Freddie Spencer scored their first world 500cc championship.

I recently asked Kaaden whether, during his early days at MZ, he ever foresaw the two-stroke's overwhelming dominance of grand-

prix racing — a superiority so great that the FIM eventually agreed to Honda's request for four-strokes to be allowed to use turbochargers (exhaust-driven superchargers). No, he never did.

'When I took up 125cc racing in 1949,' he told me, 'I had to make do with what was available locally — and that meant two-strokes with piston-controlled induction. I built and raced an ultra-low solo with 12in wheels and a 100cc three-speed engine (from an LT100 DKW) which I tuned and converted to foot change. At the end of 1952, after four years of reasonable success, I was approached by MZ (then known as IFA-DKW) to run their racing department.' Kaaden accepted the offer.

Meanwhile, his friend Daniel Zimmerman had been getting excellent results in Formula 3 car racing from disc inlet valves in the crank chambers of his 500cc twin-cylinder two-stroke engine. 'Zimmerman didn't invent the disc valve,' Kaaden said, 'it had been known for 50 to 60 years.' But so impressed was Kaaden by its simplicity and potential that he adopted it from the start at MZ — the first motorcycle race engineer to do so.

'What,' I asked next, 'was the highest power you ever extracted from the 125cc single?'

'By 1969, three years before we quit the grands prix for financial reasons,' I was told, 'peak power had risen to 31.2-31.4bhp at 11,600-11,800rpm.' That 25-per-cent increase in specific power since Degner's day was due partly to the power peak's migration up the rev scale but, even more creditably, to a substantial improvement in breathing and burning efficiency — that is, 21.6bhp/litre/ 1,000rpm against 18.5 for the 1961 engine. Indeed, some 10 years later, Suzuki's highly successful RG500 square four was producing no more power from each of its cylinders.

Naturally, the 1969 MZ's higher peak revs involved extended port timings, based as they are on time. The squish band was no longer half-moon but annular, since that shape was easier to machine precisely to a given compression ratio. For six years the small-end bearing had had crowded rollers (no cage) to increase its load-bearing capacity. A Krober electronic magneto had displaced the East German instrument for greater reliability. Carburation had long been simplified by a change to Mikuni (32mm) in 1965. And cooling was by water (from 1963) following an interim arrangement the previous year with an air-cooled head and water-cooled barrel.

If only a sparking plug had been available to withstand the heat, Kaaden would have liked to retain that interim system — and not

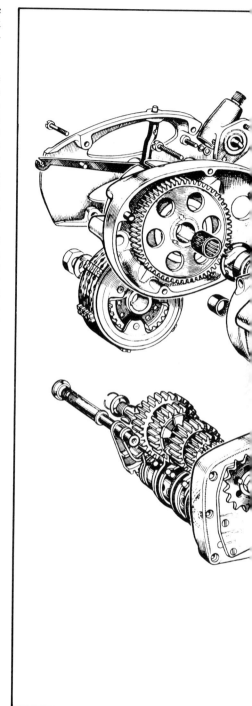

Simplicity itself and only 46lb in weight — 1961 version of the 125cc six-speed MZ single, first grand-prix engine to reach 200bhp/litre. Peak revs were 10,800rpm, maximum safe 11,500. Both con-rod bearings and all those in the gearbox were caged rollers.

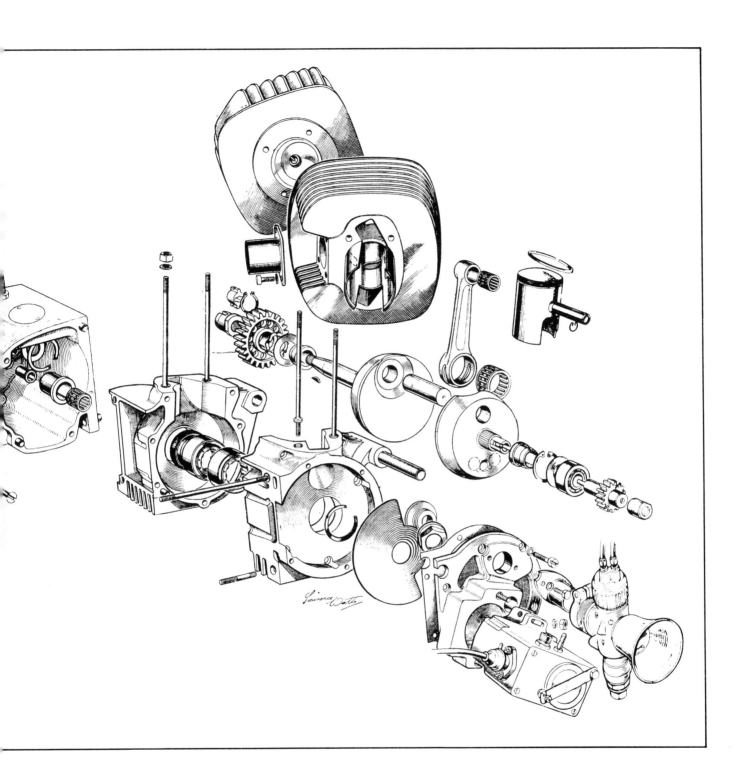

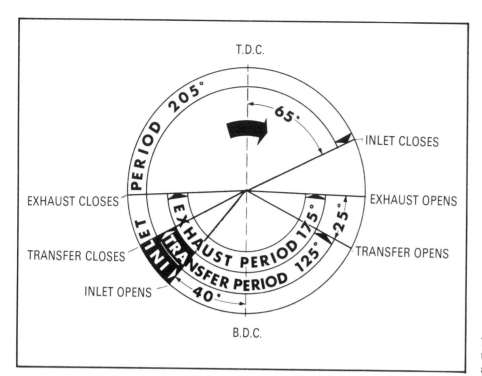

T.D.C.

PERIOD 205°

65°

INLET CLOSES

EXHAUST CLOSES

EXHAUST PERIOD 175°

25°

EXHAUST OPENS

TRANSFER CLOSES

TRANSFER PERIOD 125°

TRANSFER OPENS

INLET OPENS

INLET (TRANSFER)

40°

B.D.C.

This port-timing diagram shows the asymmetric inlet phase, 25-degree blowdown period and 22½-degree overlap of inlet and transfer. All three transfer ports opened together.

The half-speed rotating-magnet magneto had two sets of contact points, which operated alternately.

Below: The window in the front of the piston skirt fed the third transfer port. The skirt sides were cut away to clear the inlet and side transfer passages. Use of only one ring gave a 0.2bhp bonus from 9,000 to 11,000rpm!

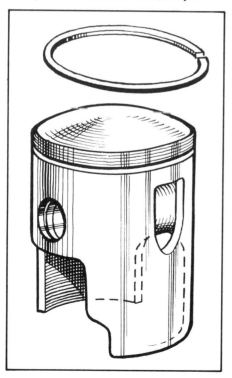

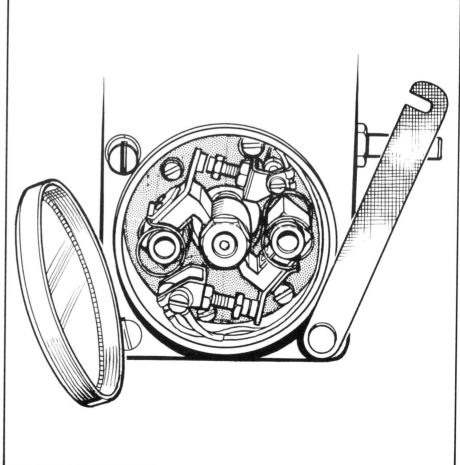

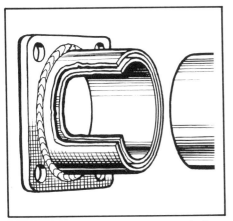

A double-wall adaptor permitted quick changes of the spring-retained exhaust box during exhaustive bench testing, besides reducing the risk of cracking.

just for the convenience of being able to slip the head off for a peep inside without first draining the water. Water cooling freed the cylinder from distortion, so improving stamina and permitting the piston clearance to be halved for crisper port control. At the same time the head ran hotter when air-cooled, so absorbing less combustion heat to the benefit of thermal efficiency and power. Unfortunately, the heat of the plug increased the risk of a holed piston crown. Wouldn't a ceramic coating have protected the crown from heat? According to Kaaden, a 1mm coating only delayed piston failure by a few seconds; although it prevented a hole, the complete crown collapsed soon afterwards. A piston made entirely of ceramics might have done the trick.

Why was the Mikuni carburettor so much better than the BVF or Amal? Chiefly because of its more precise mixture control on part-throttle. With any carburettor, main-jet size was determined during full-throttle, full-power bench testing. During a race, however, the engine spent some of its time on part-throttle and any slight weakness there quickly caused piston seizure. Only the Mikuni could be relied on to maintain the correct air/fuel ratio for complete combustion (known as stochiometric, approximately 15:1 by weight) throughout the whole throttle range.

Why were grand-prix two-strokes so acutely sensitive to ignition timing? Again, carburation was involved. The optimum spark timing was also determined during full-power bench testing to suit the correct mixture strength. It was essential to maintain that timing precisely on the track, otherwise carburation would be incorrect and seizure could result.

Couldn't the reduced incidence of piston seizures be ascribed also to the use of plated

1964 engine with thermo-siphon water cooling of cylinder and head; the consequent elimination of cylinder distortion permitted halving of the piston clearance.

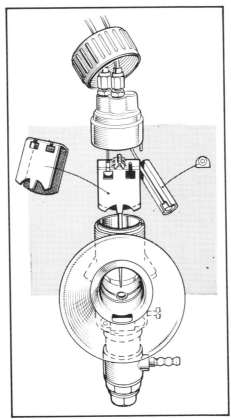

Despite the obstruction caused by the air slide and throttle needle, a flat-slide BVF carburettor was chosen to keep the inlet tract as short as possible.

Built in 1969, this experimental 125cc tandem twin was a guinea-pig for a two-fifty to supersede the excessively wide parallel twin. Some 250cc engines were built but never raced.

aluminium cylinder bores — *eg,* Nikasil (nickel, cadmium and silicon) — in which the risk of early seizure was lower because the initial expansion of the bore matched the piston's rapid growth more closely? Kaaden had tried plated bores but, in view of his shoestring budget, the cons outweighed the pros. For a start the cost of plating (by Mahle in West Germany) was more than that of the cylinder. Then, even a minor seizure with a plated bore meant the end of the race whereas an iron-sleeved cylinder might remain serviceable to the finish. Nor was there a compensating power bonus because the sharp port edges that ensured crisp opening in an iron sleeve caused the

plating to flake and had to be slightly rounded.

What about big-end reliability, which Suzuki had seemingly enhanced in the RG500 by transferring the lateral location of the con-rod from the bottom to the top to reduce the amount of heat fed into the bearing by rubbing friction? MZ rods were always located at the bottom and their big-end problems were solved by attention to cage material. When light alloy was substituted for steel the cage became unreliable at high temperatures. The final solution was to use a 25/4 chrome-molybdenum steel thinly plated with copper and silver.

Why did MZ retain square cylinder

dimensions rather than make them slightly oversquare, Japanese style? Simply because 54 × 54mm bore and stroke gave the best power (56 × 50.2mm was tried but never raced).

I reminded Kaaden of the 125cc (43 × 43mm) tandem twin he built in 1969 as a guinea-pig for a larger version to replace the overwide 250cc parallel twin. It followed established lines with thermo-siphon water cooling, two half-speed magnetos, annular squish bands and crowded-roller small ends; compression ratio was 18:1 and choke size of the carburettors 25mm. How did it compare with the single for width, weight and power?

On the credit side, Kaaden told me, the bike was 80mm (just over 3in) narrower across the fairing and the engine finished up with 10 per cent more power — 34.6bhp at 13,000 — 13,200rpm — a combination that raised top speed. On the debit side, however, the engine was 6kg (13lb) heavier and its power curve too peaky (it was designed before the FIM restricted transmissions to six speeds). 'It was a classic example,' he concluded, 'of the lack of agreement between bench tests and track performance. Even at Monza, in 1969, Günther Bartusch was slower on the twin (then giving 32bhp) than Laszlo Szabo, whose single had only 27bhp, but was much more flexible.'

Finally I asked Kaaden what (besides being able to retain top Western riders) he would have done differently if he'd had the sort of budget and resources enjoyed by his Japanese counterparts. With typical honesty he replied: 'I would simply have made progress more quickly. At MZ we were restricted to everyday materials rather than the high-duty alloys (and electrical insulation) readily available in the West. Whereas some Japanese engineers had access to eight test benches and were able to build their engines in batches of 50, I had only one dynamometer and had to make my engines in threes.'

To that modest reply I would add that — in such a hypothetical situation — Degner might well have lacked the incentive to defect. Japanese two-stroke progress would then have been much slower and MZ would have reaped the just reward of Kaaden's talents. As it was, there could be no better example of the triumph of talent over adversity. If there were any justice in such matters, Kaaden would long since have been awarded the freedom of Japan.

CHAPTER 10

Pushrod Jawa Eso

Last of the two-valve cinder-shifters — a robust but short-lived compliment to the Speedway JAP

Aficionados of the Speedway JAP (Chapter 5) consider it a compliment to the British design that the Czechoslovak Jawa that dethroned it after a phenomenal 35 years at the top was of similar basic layout. Both were high-compression two-valve singles with pushrod valve operation, magneto ignition and total-loss oiling. The Jawa scored by being more up-to-date in detail. It was stiffer in construction; its valve acceleration was fiercer and the timing more freakish; its cylinder bore was 8mm larger, so easing the way (through bigger ports and valves) to deeper high-speed breathing; and the stroke was 17mm shorter, so permitting considerably higher peak rpm for a similar mean piston speed. Inevitably, the different breathing characteristics involved some sacrifice of torque at rock-bottom revs — but not too much in the circumstances of the mid-1960s. (In general, speedway riders find higher-revving engines easier to handle because of their readier throttle response. Indeed, riders have been known to undergear for that reason, to the detriment of big-end life.)

It is true that some similarity in basic design was unavoidable under the FIM rules stipulating only one cylinder (maximum 500cc) and one carburettor. But, in flattering the JAP, Jawa revealed a shortsighted psychology. As the legendary Moto Guzzi wizard Giulio Carcano told me later (in connection with his second speciality, international yacht racing): 'If you simply copy yesterday's world beater you doom yourself to early failure. You must think afresh; you must progress.'

How does that apply to Jawa? By sticking to two valves they set a limit to their advance on the JAP. After a reign only a quarter as long as the JAP's, the new engine was itself outdated even more emphatically by the flood of four-valvers, spearheaded by the pushrod Weslake in 1975.

Back in the mid-1960s, the cinder-shifter with the keenest perception of the new Jawa's bright future on the short tracks was the great New Zealander Barry Briggs, whom no-one could accuse of an anti-British bias. Barry had not only campaigned JAPs for 10 years, he had won three world speedway championships on them — at Wembley in 1957 and '58 and at Gothenburg in 1964. But after his first season with a Jawa — during which he won his fourth and final world title (on the Swedish track again in 1966) — he was so convinced of its superiority in power, reliability and wear rate that he set up as sole importer in Southampton. It was there, in the summer of 1968, that he stripped an engine for me to examine and *Motor Cycle* artist Ira Epton to draw.

Already Barry's foresight had been vindicated, with 80 per cent of the world's speedway riders having switched to the Czech two-valver. The Jawa, he claimed, owed its power characteristics to its development for the longer European tracks, where full-throttle power at peak revs was decisive. But he contended that the pulling power so valuable on UK tracks was available provided you cleaned-up the bottom-end carburation. His simple recipe for this was to replace the standard 35mm Dellorto carb by an Amal GP for British tracks (though even abroad it paid to refine the Dellorto's mixture strength experimentally at low revs).

Why was it then, I asked, that Ove Fundin had deliberately changed from a Jawa to a JAP to win the world championship in 1967? 'Simply because the final that year was at Wembley,' Barry assured me.

'There and there alone,' he continued, 'the track is so tight and lacking in favourable camber that the only foolproof tactic is to beat your rivals to the first bend (a Fundin speciality), grab the inside line and hold it all through. For that, there is nothing to beat the JAP's typical long-stroke punch from rock-bottom revs.

'I would have done the same myself — but only for Wembley.' To reinforce his argument, Barry reminded me that Fundin then took his JAP to Belle Vue and was soundly beaten. Horses for courses.

Briggs' version of the pushrod Jawa's background was subsequently challenged by Don Godden, who amassed no fewer than 13 British grass-track titles and the 1969 European long-track championship on JAPs with drastically modified cams. Godden — whose track prowess was harnessed to considerable engineering talent, and who had been involved technically with Jawa — assured me that the Czech pushrod engine, originally called the Eso (Ace in English), was in fact designed initially for speedway racing and only later developed for the long tracks.

Be that as it may, Barry told me that, in short-track trim with a plain exhaust pipe, the Jawa was churning out 54bhp (on methanol) at just short of 7,000rpm and was mechanically safe up to 8,000. Tuned for the long German and Danish sand tracks, with a reverse-cone megaphone on the exhaust, the engine was good for an extra 4bhp.

In either trim, its robust construction ensured reliable running, while the makers' successful efforts to prevent dust and water from getting inside resulted in a low rate of wear.

Consequently, engines were often run for some 30 meetings without major attention. Even Barry himself would cheerfully do 10 meetings before stripping the engine — a task he used to perform every three meetings before changing makes.

One of the most striking features of the engine was its valve timing. Not so much the 57/61-degree inlet lead and 42/47-degree exhaust lag — exaggerations of that order are common in out-and-out racing two-valvers peaking around 7,000rpm. What surprised me was that the inlet valve closed as much as 80-88 degrees late and the exhaust opened a whopping 94-100 degrees before bottom dead centre. Since Jawa were known to experiment with many cam forms, I could only conclude that the timing resulted from trial and error. Indeed, the figures for God-

Jawas supreme — Barry Briggs, first to spot the Czech engine's potential, leads fellow-New Zealand legend Ivan Mauger in an international meeting in Britain in 1971.

den's ultimate long-track JAP cam were not much different from the Jawa's.

When I subsequently asked several experts for a theoretical justification of the extra early exhaust opening, the most plausible came from Doug Hele, renowned development engineer for Norton and Triumph. It was, he suggested, a corollary of the very high compression ratio (permitted by the use of alcohol fuel). This resulted in faster burning, so that combustion was completed sooner. Once the 'work was done' it was prudent to open the valve and let the burnt gas out, with no fear of overheating the valve. In turn, Doug reasoned, the early exhaust opening ought to allow the inlet valve to be opened earlier, so giving the column of fresh gas more time to get moving.

Incidentally, the timing figures given were not distorted by the use of special (positive or negative) clearances, specified in some engines to facilitate accurate setting. In the Jawa they were checked with running clearances (0.004in inlet, 0.006in exhaust) and a dial gauge on the valve stem registering 0.002in lift to simulate running conditions — *ie*, all backlash taken up.

The cam lobes had a brutal shape which, in conjunction with flat-base followers,

imparted fierce initial acceleration (and final deceleration) to the valves. The twofold effect was to give a large total opening area under the valve-motion curve (lift plotted against crank angle) while allowing the duplex coil springs ample time to arrest and reverse the motion (through compressing the initial acceleration and final deceleration periods). Thus both efficiency (through deep breathing) and mechanical safety (through relative freedom from valve float) were promoted by the same design feature.

Full advantage was taken of the 88mm bore diameter to accommodate valves of 44mm throat diameter (inlet) and 39mm (exhaust), which seated on cast-steel rings shrunk in the aluminium-alloy cylinder head. The inlet guide (like the exhaust) was full length — *ie*, not cut back flush with the port wall.

An immediate indication of the engine's sturdy construction was given by the appearance of the crankcase, the mouth of which was extended upward to embrace the 2½in-long spigot at the bottom of the cylinder. A detachable plug in the left-hand half of the case provided access to top-dead-centre and ignition-timing marks on the drive-side flywheel rim so there was no

excuse, even in the field, for hit-or-miss timing methods.

Jawa relied on a heavy press fit to secure the 1in-diameter mainshafts in the 7 × 1in flywheels — no tapers and nuts. Each shaft was supported directly in two rows of caged ¼ × ½in rollers (no inner race), with the flanged outer rings shrunk in the case and secured by screws. Unlike the mainshafts, the crankpin was a taper fit in the wheels, although the nuts also clamped them hard against the sides of the 39mm-diameter bearing ring pressed on the pin.

An unusual feature of the big-end bearing was the fact that each of the 14 slots in the light-alloy cage housed two rollers of different lengths — one 6mm, the other 8mm. On assembly, the rollers were staggered so as to prevent the formation of a ridge round the middle of the crankpin ring and connecting-rod eye. The rod itself was a steel forging with a stiffening rib round the big-end eye.

A surprisingly light die-casting, the full-skirt piston had three ring grooves of identical width, though the rings varied in type. The top one was chromium-plated and taper-faced, the second plain and the bottom one stepped for oil scraping (through holes in the land below the groove).

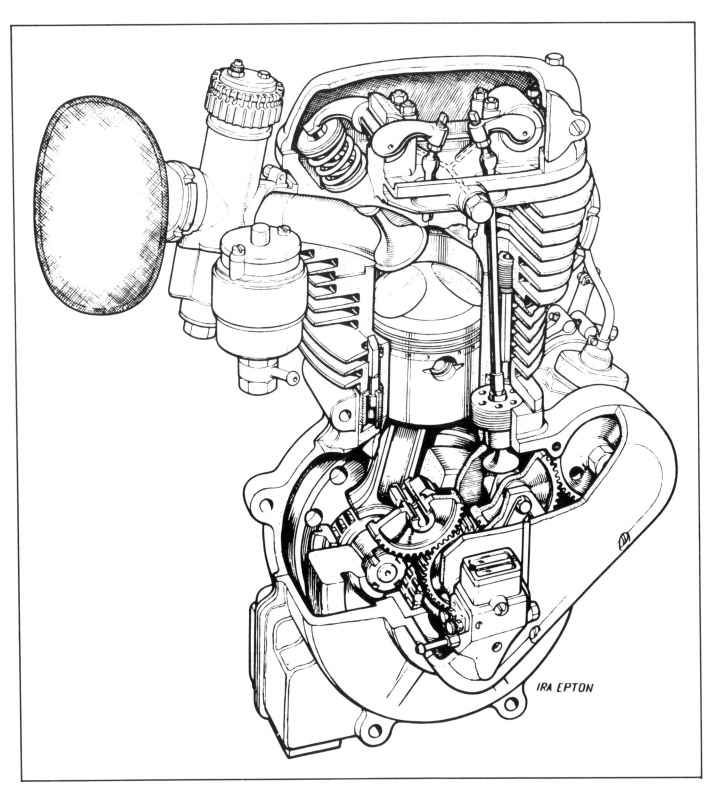

IRA EPTON

Conceptually similar to the two-valve Speedway JAP it dethroned, the Jawa Eso thereby set a limit to its reign, which was abruptly terminated by the four-valve Weslake. Noteworthy here is the sturdy construction, with the tall crankcase embracing a 2¼in-long cylinder spigot. Cylinder dimensions (88 x 82mm) were well oversquare; compression ratio was 14:1 and the standard carburettor a 35mm Dellorto. Interesting details include the staggered big-end rollers, double-row roller main bearings, split flanged rocker bushes, double fully floating flanged cam-wheel bushes and the light-alloy outrigger plate stabilizing the timing-gear train.

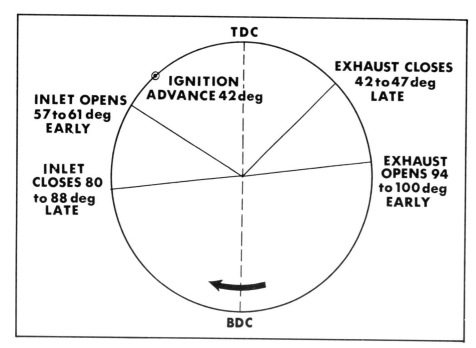

TDC

IGNITION ADVANCE 42 deg

EXHAUST CLOSES 42 to 47 deg LATE

INLET OPENS 57 to 61 deg EARLY

INLET CLOSES 80 to 88 deg LATE

EXHAUST OPENS 94 to 100 deg EARLY

BDC

Most striking feature of the exaggerated valve timing was the extremely early exhaust opening — reminiscent of grand-prix two-stroke practice.

Within the framework of the FIM's basic rules, no speedway engine could hope to match the sophistication of a grand-prix special, where the restrictions on design, albeit comprehensive, were much less severe. Nevertheless, as Weslake showed in 1975, paired valves offered scope for improvements in tractability, power and mechanical safety alike. And, since taming valve float only transferred an engine's Achilles heel to the roller-bearing big end, a plain bearing there (with pressure oiling to suit) was another advance just waiting to be made.

A few years after the Weslake takeover, Jawa themselves switched to four valves. But they followed grand-prix practice too closely for speedway conditions. Double overhead camshafts made the engine too top-heavy for easy handling on tight tracks and too complex for quick servicing in the field. Moreover, despite a smaller bore and longer stroke (85 × 87mm = 493cc), the engine needed a carburettor of 38 or 40mm to give of its best, so its competitiveness in speedway was particularly hard hit when the FIM misguidedly penalized four-valvers by limiting their carb size to 34mm while allowing 36mm for two-valvers. (Accepting the need to curb engine power — for which the justification was obscure, to say the least — then restricting carburettor size was a valid way to do it. But differentiating between the two valve arrangements showed a deplorable bias against shrewd design.)

Jawa's eventual response to the virtual knobbling of its double-knocker engine was to stay with four valves and the new cylinder dimensions, but change to a single-ohc layout with more tractable power. For speedway it was a considerable improvement; but, at the time of writing, it had shown no sign of restoring its makers to the top of the popularity poll, being handsomely outperformed by single-ohc four-valvers from GM (in Italy), Godden and Antig-Weslake (in Britain) in that order — and even by the evergreen Weslake pushrod four-valver that had dethroned the two-valve Jawa some 10 years earlier.

The flanged iron cylinder liner was shrunk in an aluminium-alloy jacket, the seven cooling fins of which embodied the two pushrod tunnels, sealed at the head joint by rubber rings. Both cylinder and head were clamped down by four studs anchored in the crankcase and screwed up into long bronze inserts, themselves screwed and pegged in the head.

The compression ratio was adjusted by selecting the thickness of copper head gaskets to give a clearance volume of 38 to 39cc (13.8 to 14.1:1). Usually this necessitated two gaskets — one 0.040in thick, the other 0.020in.

To prevent the valve springs from losing their temper, they were insulated from the heat of the head by special washers under the bottom spring cups; also trapped beneath the cups were steel shims to correct the installed length of the springs. The top spring collars were in light alloy and retained by split collets and wire circlips.

A detachable plate in the valve cover gave access to the ball-ended clearance adjusters at the pushrod ends of the highly polished rockers, whose $\frac{1}{2}$in-diameter shafts were supported in split, double-flanged bushes.

There were five gears in the timing train — the taper-bored crankshaft pinion with a

choice of five keyways, an idler with its spindle end slotted to drive the oil pump, the two camwheels and a magneto pinion, driven by the exhaust camwheel. (Ignition advance was fixed at 42 degrees.) Each camwheel had two fully floating flanged bushes supporting it on a fixed spindle.

To stabilize the gear train, a rectangular light-alloy outrigger plate was bolted to the cam spindles and two crankcase bosses; pressed in the plate was a bush for the outer end of the idler spindle.

The cam followers slid in light-alloy guides screwed into the crankcase. Duralumin rod was used for the pushrods, which had pressed-on steel ends.

As in the Speedway JAP, there were two deliveries from the oil pump. The first fed the big end through a spring-loaded quill in the timing side of the crankshaft, while the other went through an external pipe to the cylinder head, where it fed the rocker bushes before spilling out on to the valves.

Like most speedway engines, the Jawa featured a crude but effective means of accommodating misalignment of the primary drive sprockets. In this, the engine sprocket was free to move $\frac{5}{16}$in laterally between two robust circlips on a splined hub keyed and tapered to the crankshaft.

CHAPTER 11

125cc desmodromic Ducati

Unique triple-knocker giant-killer that presaged a range of sporting
twins which transformed the makers' image

Fabio Taglioni's contribution to motorcycle engineering was unique. The desmodromic valve gear he masterminded at Ducati in the 1950s first provided a sensationally successful solution to the stubborn problems of high-speed reliability and power in 125cc grand-prix racing. Subsequently, a simplified version translated neatly to the big V-twins (L-twins in Italian parlance) that spread those successes into other spheres of road racing in the 1970s and '80s. Overall, desmodromics provided the *cachet* that raised Ducati from a lowly position as just another producer of snappy tiddlers to a pinnacle as one of Europe's most prestigious manufacturers of high-performance sportsters — and, in Formula TT and endurance racing, a thorn in the flesh of the much wealthier Japanese teams.

For success in engineering there is no substitute for talent, and Taglioni gave early evidence of both his intellectual stature and his persistence. When a leg wound sustained in the 1939-45 war prevented him from attending Bologna University for the full five-year course, he acquired the necessary books, taught himself (often in hospital) and qualified as an *Ingeniere* at the university in only three years — in 1948.

Desmodromic valve control is simply a system in which the valves are not only opened positively (*ie,* by cams) but closed positively too, by other cams instead of by springs. During the 1950s the limitations of spring closure were becoming increasingly obvious in 125cc world-championship racing as the peak-power revs of the leading single-cylinder engines climbed to some 12,000rpm. The large valves, high lifts, extended opening periods and high compression ratios responsible for these power characteristics left precious little clearance between the valve heads themselves or between valves and piston crown. A brief bout of overrevving in the heat of battle found the valve springs no longer able to keep the cam followers in contact with the closing flanks of the cams, with the result that the floating

exhaust valve tangled either with the opening inlet valve or with the rising piston.

Taglioni's solution to valve float formed in his mind as early as 1948 and he foresaw that it would not only render an engine invulnerable to overrevving but open the way to more power, since the valves could be lifted even higher in safety, to the benefit of high-speed breathing. It was six years, however, before he joined Ducati and had the facilities to translate his dream into metal. Within a year his first triple-camshaft desmodromic engine was built; another year and it made its racing debut in the Swedish GP at Hedemora where — with peak power already boosted from 16bhp at 12,000rpm to 18 at 12,500 compared with the double-knocker valve-spring engine from which it was derived — Gianni degli Antoni won so convincingly as to lap every other finisher.

For a time the top-dog FB Mondial and MV Agusta teams weathered the storm, thanks in no small measure to the dynamic riding, especially on twisty circuits, of the fiery Italian Tarquinio Provini, his immaculate compatriot Carlo Ubbiali and the dapper little Swiss Luigi Taveri. But once Taveri recognized the desmo's potential and threw in his lot with the Bologna team the Ducati quickly came into its own.

In the 1958 TT, on the tortuous 10.79-mile Clypse circuit, Taveri put his erstwhile MV teammate Ubbiali in the shade until the desmo suffered one of its rare breakdowns. Even so the MV was chased home by three more Ducatis. Taglioni then produced an extra bhp by increasing the valve lift, whereupon Alberto Gandossi and Romolo Ferri promptly relegated Provini (who had switched to MV following Mondial's withdrawal) to third place in the Belgian GP on the ultra-fast Francorchamps circuit. The grand-prix scene then moved to Sweden where Gandossi and Taveri inflicted similar humiliation on Ubbiali.

Their very pride at stake, MV threw all their resources into a last-ditch stand in the Italian GP at Monza. On a circuit where

engine power outweighed cornering prowess, the Ducati team toyed with them. Bruno Spaggiari and Gandossi filled the first two places on singles. Franco Villa was third on a new triple-knocker parallel-twin with appreciably more power (22.5bhp at 14,000rpm) but a narrower useful rev band and a little more weight. Dave Chadwick and Taveri brought another brace of singles home fourth and fifth, leaving sixth place to the only works MV to finish, ridden by Enzo Vezzalini, who was lapped. Both Provini and Ubbiali had driven their engines to destruction in the forlorn chase.

In the 125cc class at least, valve springs seemed to be on the brink of extinction. But Ducati had a lean track season in 1959 as a result of an injury to Spaggiari — for although they engaged the up-and-coming Mike Hailwood he proved too bulky for the tiny machines. At the end of the year the company, whose state-controlled management never matched its engineering expertise, decided a little glory was enough and quit grand-prix racing, leaving Taglioni to concentrate on series production.

When he then spread out a dismantled single-cylinder engine for my inspection in Bologna I was struck not only by the novelty of its three camshafts and the queer-looking closing cams with their 'inverted' rockers, but also by obvious signs that the rest of the power unit was practically bog-standard — a tribute to the design quality of the bread-and-butter models as well as to Taglioni's skill in keeping down race-shop costs. The cylinder head (with integral cambox) was a direct replacement for those on the firm's two catalogue racers — the single-ohc Formula 3 and the double-ohc Grand Prix. Lower down there was a redundant kick-starter boss in the left-side crankcase casting and a vacant space on the same side of the crankshaft where the generator was fitted on the roadsters. Finally, the gear cluster had only the usual four pairs of pinions in the main compartment. The fifth pair was in the

Fabio Taglioni (Ducati).

primary drive case, sandwiched between the clutch and the gearbox wall, as was the sixth pair preferred by Ferri.

Even the cambox layout bore a strong family resemblance to those on the catalogue racers, with the opening cams on the front and rear shafts, *à la* Grand Prix engine, and the two closers in the middle where the Formula 3 had its camshaft. All cams were a taper fit and, for experimental purposes, only one of the closers was fixed relative to the middle shaft.

In contrast to most bevel cam drives, the Ducati had its crankshaft bevel gear facing inward because it was situated outboard of the spur gears driving the oil pump and contact breaker. Integral with its top and bottom bevel gears, the two-part vertical shaft was not joined by a separate coupling (British style) or by splines (German style). Instead, the mating ends were machined away to half-diameter (*ie,* D-section) and held together by a close-fitting steel sleeve. Two ball bearings, separated by a sleeve, supported the bottom vertical bevel, while the top one was carried in a double-row self-aligning ball bearing.

Vertical-shaft diameter was 15mm for the lower (shorter) portion, as it was for the ends of the upper portion, which was waisted for most of its length. Remarkably, the diameter of the waisted portion was varied to control the engine's torque characteristics. Minimum safe diameter was 11mm, which brought peak torque down to 8,000rpm for give-and-take circuits. Maximum diameter was 14.8mm, which raised the torque peak much closer to the power peak for circuits with a preponderance of flat-out going.

In the 1958 Lightweight 125cc TT Luigi Taveri keeps the triple-knocker Ducati ahead of MV Agusta's world champion Carlo Ubbiali on the 10.79-mile Clypse circuit.

Clearly, the greater degree of torsion in the slimmer shaft retarded valve actuation relative to piston position. Within limits it was an ingenious form of variable valve timing.

At the top, the crownwheel on the middle camshaft was at first pressed into the large-diameter, narrow spur gear that spread the drive to the front and rear camshafts. Later this press fit was supplemented by welding to prevent relative movement, but some of these integral gears broke. Taglioni's ultimate solution was to use what he called an elastic press fit, with a triangular nylon insert joining the two parts; this, he claimed, absorbed vibration without allowing relative angular movement that would interfere with the valve timing. To distribute the cam loadings among the vertical bevel teeth, the overall 2:1 reduction between crankshaft and camshafts was achieved through bevel sizes of 21, 30, 20 and 28 teeth, counting from the bottom upward.

All three camshafts were supported in ball bearings at the right-hand end while a roller bearing (for the middle shaft) and bronze bushes (for the others) coped with radial loading from the cams at the other end. Valve actuation was neatness itself. The followers for the opening cams were fingers pivoted inboard of the shafts and bearing on conventional hardened caps on the valve stems. The inner arms of the closing rockers bore on the underside of their cams while the outer ends were forked to embrace the valve stems and raise them through flanged collars located by split wire rings. Both fingers and rockers pivoted on fully floating bronze bushes.

The valve caps and collars were all available in different thicknesses for adjusting the running clearances. For, just as all poppet valves need a small clearance at the tip regardless of temperature if they are to seat fully and the cam base circle and follower are

Standard from the cylinder head down, the desmodromic engine gave few external clues to its special identity. Note the additional sparking plug behind the top bevel box.

not to suffer excessive rubbing loads, so do the valves in a desmo need some clearance at the closing contacts too if they are not to be stretched and the cams and rockers overloaded. In the 125cc single, collar thickness was selected so that the closing cams returned the valves to some 0.012in from their seats, leaving valve inertia and gas pressure to do the rest. Consequently, if the engine was turned slowly by hand, compression seemed to be poor; but when it was spun briskly, as in a pushstart, the valves seated firmly. Early on, indeed, light rocker return springs were fitted to ensure full compression at very low rpm; but they were soon discarded to obviate the risk of broken pieces causing damage and their omission made no difference to pushstarting or running. (On later roadsters, light rocker return springs were reinstated to improve idling and kickstarting and to prevent fretting of the circlip grooves.)

It is clear from the foregoing description (and from Frank Beak's drawing) that the reciprocating mass of the little desmo's valve gear was heavier than that in either the Formula 3 or Grand Prix engine, with their double hairpin valve springs. Since the inertia forces responsible for valve float are proportional to reciprocating mass, such added weight would be intolerable in a high-revving valve-spring engine. The saving grace of positive closure is that it prevents the inertia forces from causing the valves to fling. Incidentally, maximum safe revs — governed by big-end loads and exploited for extra engine braking — were 14,000rpm for the single and 17,000 for the twin. (Short big-end life was the price paid for outbraking the opposition.)

By the time of my first visit to Taglioni's race shop, valve lifts (compared to those in the Grand Prix engine and with identical timing) had been increased from 7.5mm (inlet) to 8.1mm (just over $\frac{5}{16}$in) and from 7mm (exhaust) to 7.4mm (just over $\frac{9}{32}$in). Also, the original 14mm sparking plug on the left had been joined by a 10mm plug almost opposite (just in front of the bevel box). This allowed the ignition advance to be cut from 42 to 36 degrees and the enhanced torque gave better throttle response. Ignition current came from a 6-volt battery feeding two 3-volt coils — one for each plug.

Each valve was inclined 40 degrees to the cylinder axis, giving an included angle of 80 degrees. They operated in bronze guides

(narrowed at the top to clear the forked rocker ends) and seated on shrunk-in rings of aluminium-bronze, a material usually reserved for exhaust-valve seats because of its high thermal conductivity; its relative softness compared with more usual inlet-seat materials caused no problem. Stem diameter was 7mm in both cases. As in the Grand Prix engine, valve-throat diameters were 31mm (approximately $1\frac{7}{32}$in) inlet and 27mm ($1\frac{1}{16}$in) exhaust — the overall diameters naturally being about 2mm larger.

At the carburettor end, the inlet port was 27mm in diameter, as was the choke of the Dellorto carburettor. For ultra-fast circuits, however (such as Monza, Francorchamps and the old Hockenheim loop), carburettor size was increased to 29mm, whereas it could be as small as 22 to 23mm for tricky national circuits. Overall, fuel consumption averaged about 45mpg. Ideally, of course, desmodromic valve operation called for an air filter to prevent a sizeable piece of grit from being trapped under the inlet valve, so damaging both the valve and the rubbing face of the rocker. But the filters available at the time would have restricted breathing, hence power, so Taglioni preferred to risk an unrestricted inlet. Determined experimentally for optimum turbulence, the layout of the tract itself is discussed later; at the time of

my visit it was quoted as 15 degrees offset and 12 degrees downdraught.

Comprising a cast-iron sleeve shrunk in a light-alloy jacket, with a ground joint at the top (no gasket), the cylinder was clamped between head and crankcase by four long, waisted bolts. The forged three-ring piston, with its full skirt profiled at the bottom to clear the flywheels, had several ribs under the part-spherical crown to stiffen the bosses for the 16mm taper-bored gudgeon pin. To match the valve heads, the cutaways in the crown were convex; compression ratio was 10:1. As in the Grand Prix and Formula 3 engines, bore and stroke measured 55.25 × 52mm.

Italian fashion, the robust castings housing the flywheel assembly and gear cluster incorporated an underslung oil compartment supplying the common lubrication system. Since the two ball bearings (25.52mm bore, 15mm wide) supporting the crankshaft were of axial-thrust type, the necessary end loading was provided by a large star washer between the drive-side bearing and flywheel. This arrangement eliminated the vibration experienced at peak revs with roller bearings, owing to the inevitable radial running clearance, however small. At the right-hand extremity, just out-

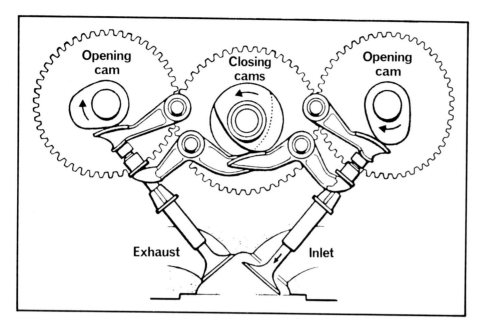

Opening cam

Closing cams

Opening cam

Exhaust

Inlet

Classic in the simplicity of its adaptation from the production single- and double-ohc valve-spring layouts, the desmo valve gear closed the valves positively by cams and rockers.

Interesting details are the self-aligning bearing at the upper end of the vertical bevel shaft; the D-section coupling of the two halves of the shaft; the revmeter drive at the end of the rear camshaft; the opposed sparking plugs; the drastic lightening of all four cam lobes; and the location of the fifth pair of transmission gears in the primary drive case. Note also the method of balancing the forged flywheels and the star washer providing the necessary end thrust for the ball-thrust main bearings.

board of the first bevel gear, the crankshaft was supported by a bronze bush in the timing cover.

Each flywheel disc was forged integrally with its mainshaft (drilled for lightness). An interference fit in the wheels (no nuts), the crankpin was 25mm in diameter at the ends and 30mm on the roller track; it too was hollowed, to feed oil to the big-end bearing, and sealed at the ends with light-alloy plugs. For balancing, the rims of the flywheels were machined to near-chords each side of the crankpin hole, then milled out edgeways to leave two webs.

A steel forging 107mm between centres, the connecting rod was unsleeved at the ends, both of which were stiffened by double webs. The cage for the 19 3.5mm-diameter big-end rollers was made of steel rather than light alloy to resist centrifugal distortion and consequent failure.

At the left-hand extremity, too, the crankshaft had outrigger support — in this case a ball bearing in the side cover. Just inboard of the bearing was the straight-cut spur gear that drove the six-plate clutch with its bonded-on friction pads. Unusually, the tongues on both driving and driven plates were part-circular in profile — a shape claimed to reduce indentation of the grooves in the clutch drum and hub. All gears were indirect, with crossover drive, and both shafts ran in ball bearings; selection was through a grooved drum and three forks.

Lubrication was simple: since gravity took care of oil return, the pump had only one pair of gears. These drew SAE20 castor-base oil from the 2-litre sump through a long cylindrical gauze strainer and fed it through crankshaft passages to the big-end bearing

and through an external pipe to the valve gear. Oil flung from the big end took care of the transmission as well as the piston and cylinder. The external pipe led, via a T-junction, to the left-hand ends of the hollow camshafts, from which oil exuded through holes in the rubbing faces of the cams before lubricating the rest of the valve gear by splash.

Although sharing the same principles, the tiny (42.5 × 44mm) twin naturally differed considerably in detail. The pistons moved in step and the two flywheel assemblies were clamped by Hirth (radially serrated) couplings to opposite ends of the middle portion of the crankshaft, on which was formed a spur gear. This drove a jackshaft which, from right to left, distributed the drive through a train of gears (in a case between the cylinders) to the camshafts and contact breakers, then through skew gears to the oil pump and finally, through a pair of spur gears, to the clutch and six-speed, all-indirect gear cluster. Both engine and clutch rotated backwards. The cam drive resulted in a 7-inch spacing of the cylinder axes; and, because of space restrictions, there was less induction offset and only one plug (10mm) in each combustion chamber. Compression ratio was 10.2:1.

When last I called on Taglioni he was working a three-day week in semi-retirement. His desmodromic technology had been vastly expanded and he'd had 26 years to reflect on that Monza massacre and its aftermath. Assuming the role of devil's advocate, I challenged him with questions designed to make him justify his unusual methods.

Following hard on Ducati's grand-prix withdrawal, I reminded him, Honda had chosen very light paired valves to cure valve float and boost power — with the bonus of a central plug position for the shortest possible flame path and squish segments fore and aft to squirt the compressed charge towards the advancing flame front. Wasn't that a better approach? Not in the early 1950s, I was told, when valve-spring materials and technology were inferior. In any case, Taglioni did not accept that a pent-roof combustion chamber with paired valves and squish segments necessarily had greater potential. With its inlet tract square to the valves (for optimum filling) its turbulence was uncontrolled, whereas a two-valver's turbulence could be perfected experimentally. It was usual to start by offsetting the inlet tract about 20 degrees for a centrifugal swirl and converting that to a spiral by using a similar degree of downdraught. Both angles were then modified independently until the best results were obtained. Squish areas were formed on both sides of the piston crown and the flame path could be shortened by the use of two plugs. In view of the foregoing, it was no surprise to learn that, although Taglioni had schemed a four-valve desmo head in his mind, he had never made it.

Which version of the 125cc triple-knocker was preferred on the track — the single or the twin? The single, largely because more time had gone into its development. Although its peak power was less, it was lighter and more tractable. Incidentally, Taglioni claimed that the highest power produced by the two versions was 23bhp at 12,500rpm (single) and 26 at 14,000 (twin). In terms of bhp/litre/1,000rpm, these figures represent 14.72 and 14.86, respectively — among the very best in racing four-strokes. Indeed, Honda never reached 26bhp with their 125cc grand-prix twin before abandoning it and taking the four- and five-cylinder route to more power.

Was the 125cc four-cylinder Ducati ever made? Yes, but not with desmodromic valve gear. Like the tiny Honda four (which it predated by several years) it had four-valve heads and valve springs. It, like the twin, never had the benefit of long-enough development.

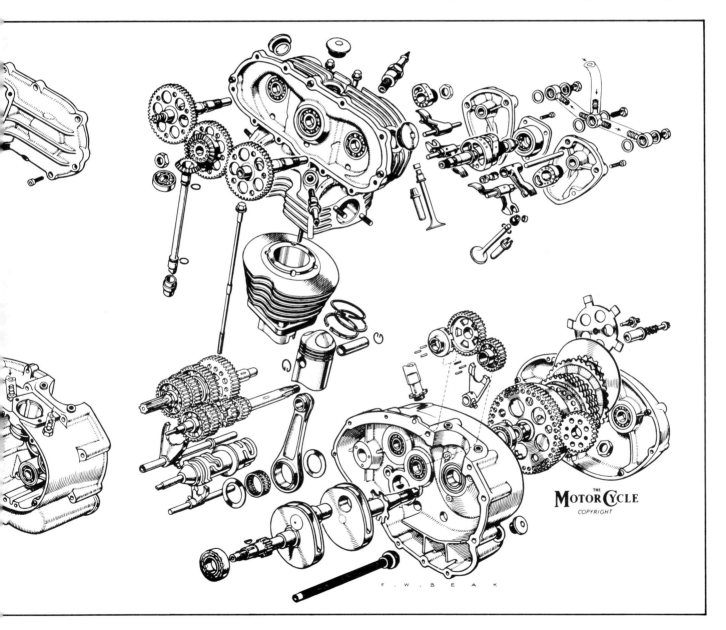

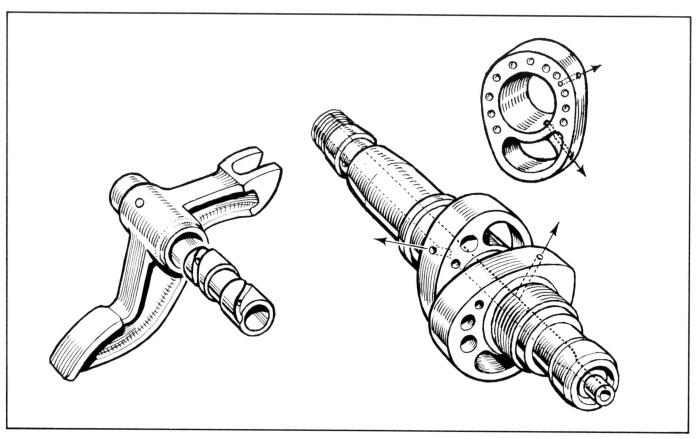

Valve rockers and levers pivoted on fully floating bushes. Oil pumped into the three camshafts reached the rubbing faces through drillways.

With hindsight, would Taglioni like to have done anything differently? No, he did the best he could within the limits of his experience. Indeed, if he had been designing a 125cc four-stroke grand-prix engine under the FIM formula current at the time (no more than two cylinders and six gears) his approach would have been fundamentally unchanged. (Later, with effect from 1987, the FIM would restrict 125cc engines to a single cylinder, which would only have reinforced his view.)

Finally, I asked if he had ever been tempted to switch to car racing. Smiling broadly, he said: 'Yes, but I was too stupid to grasp the opportunity!' For stupidity read loyalty — for which Ducati and motorcycle racing have much to be thankful.

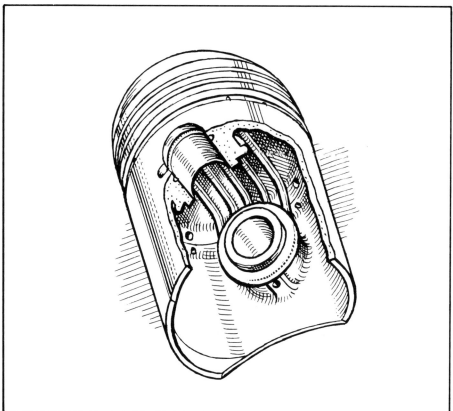

Ample stiffening ribs connected the gudgeon-pin bosses to the piston crown. There were oil drain holes in both the scraper-ring groove and the land below it — a requirement sometimes overlooked in piston design.

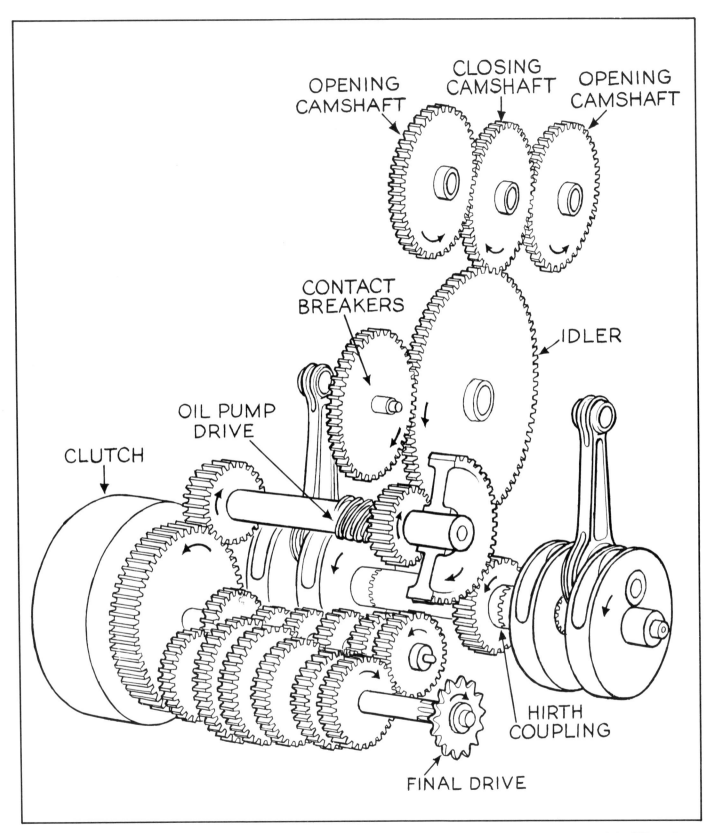

OPENING CAMSHAFT

CLOSING CAMSHAFT

OPENING CAMSHAFT

CONTACT BREAKERS

IDLER

OIL PUMP DRIVE

CLUTCH

HIRTH COUPLING

FINAL DRIVE

Cogs galore! Schematic drawing of the crankshaft assembly, six-speed transmission and camshaft and ancillary drives of the 125cc twin.

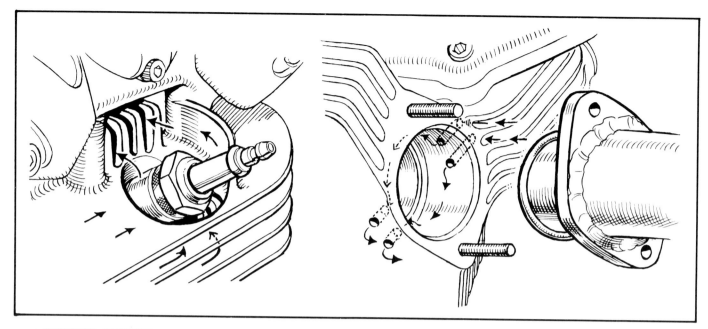

Two dubious cooling aids — a curved baffle to scoop air to the left-side plug and across the head; and holes to circulate air round the trapped end of the exhaust pipe.

Dave Chadwick, third in the 1958 Lightweight 125cc TT, on one of the three desmos that chased world champion Carlo Ubbiali home.

CHAPTER 12

Outside-flywheel Norton

In their final form the works singles belatedly copied Moto Guzzi's
crankshaft layout — but not closely enough

When, in the spring of 1955, technical editor Alan Baker and artist Lawrie Watts visited Norton's legendary race chief Joe Craig to analyse his first outside-flywheel engine for *The Motor Cycle,* they expected to see the 499cc version. After all, that was the engine the fearless Ray Amm had relied on to beat world champion Geoff Duke's Gilera four in the previous year's controversial Senior TT — the race that was suddenly shortened from seven laps to four in atrocious weather when Duke, but not Amm, had made a lengthy refuelling stop. Instead, *The Motor Cycle's* men were shown the 349cc version because, as Baker's story explained, the smaller engine 'was most readily to hand when the man arrived with the spanners'.

Subsequent investigation suggests that Craig's real reason for offering the smaller engine was simply that there was no five-hundred available without a broken crankshaft! Such was the long-standing reputation of his works engines for reliability that no ulterior motive was suspected. But Joe's worldwide reputation as a single-cylinder development engineer owed most to his painstaking work on the top half of the engine; crankshaft stress calculations were hardly his forte. And when he took a belated leaf out of Moto Guzzi's book and abandoned internal flywheels, he made the mistake of failing to increase the diameter of the five-hundred's drive-side mainshaft, which remained at 1.156in, as it was in the 1953 engine (probably the best he ever fielded).

In any 500cc single-cylinder racing engine — particularly one with the punch of a Craig-developed top half — the cyclic torque fluctuations throughout the 720 degrees of each four-stroke cycle are enormous. With Norton's conventional crankshaft layout (up to 1953) those fluctuations were damped by the considerable inertia of a hefty pair of 8in-diameter flywheels inside the crankcase, so that the torque loading in the drive-side mainshaft was fairly steady. In the 1954 engine, by contrast, the relatively light bob-weights in the case had nothing like enough

inertia to suppress the torque fluctuations; hence the drive-side mainshaft itself was continuously subjected to them and repeatedly sheared after only a few races. The fact that the 9in-diameter outside flywheel provided some additional inertia (albeit less than the previous internal pair) was irrelevant — the crucial fact was that its inertia was at the wrong end of the mainshaft.

Joe Craig's conversion to the outside-flywheel concept of the rival Moto Guzzi singles was part of a programme to reduce engine height (in both sizes he simultaneously shortened both the stroke and the connecting rod). In the absence of stress calculations, however, he would have done better to copy the crankshaft dimensions, too, for even the 350cc Moto Guzzi — for all its phenomenal lightness — had a fatter drive-side mainshaft (1.181in) than the bigger Norton — and beefier bobweights, too.

With its less-violent torque fluctuations, Craig's smaller outside-flywheel engine was free from crankshaft failure. But he heeded the lesson of the 1954 five-hundred when laying the big engine flat for 1955 (another concession to Moto Guzzi practice), for the new engine had a drive-side mainshaft of 1½in diameter. Alas, the flat Norton never showed its paces, for the factory quit racing during the close season.

Designed by Walter Moore, the progenitor of all the overhead-camshaft Nortons — a tall 490cc (79 × 100mm) thumper with an iron cylinder head and a single bevel-driven camshaft — got off to a flying start in 1927, when Alec Bennett won the Senior TT at record speed after Stanley Woods had established a lap record before retiring. The following year the factory introduced a 348cc version with the almost equally long-stroke cylinder dimensions of 71 × 88mm. But it was 1931 before the Norton singles began their virtual stranglehold on the Junior and Senior TT races (starting with Tim Hunt's double victory); and the fuse that

initiated that explosion was an engine rehash the previous year by Arthur Carroll in collaboration with Joe Craig, who had by then taken charge of development with the avowed aim of marrying reliability to performance.

From then onward the technical specification of the works engines was updated almost unobtrusively year by year: aluminium-bronze heads in 1932; bi-metal heads and barrels in 1933; hairpin valve springs and megaphone exhausts in 1934; double overhead camshafts tried tentatively in 1936, then adopted the following year along with the first stage in a progression of shorter strokes and fatter bores, culminating eventually in 90 × 78.4mm for the 499cc engine and 78 × 73mm for the other.

Before Norton withdrew from the TT at the end of 1954 their ohc engines had secured them 28 victories (including Eric Oliver's sidecar TT in 1954). And long after that, privately prepared models won the 1959 Formula 1 500cc race (Bob McIntyre) and the 1963 Junior and Senior TTs (Phil Read and Mike Hailwood, respectively). But the Manx machines sold over the counter bore much less resemblance to the works specials than was the case with the KTT Velocette and 7R AJS. Even in 1952, an analysis of the two Manx engines by *The Motor Cycle's* assistant editor George Wilson (also in conjunction with Joe Craig) showed not only that they retained the original long strokes of 100mm (Model 30) and 88mm (Model 40), but also that (notwithstanding their different capacities and engine speeds) their valve and ignition timings were identical, as were the diameters of their mainshafts, main bearings, crankpins and gudgeon pins. Clearly neither could breathe so freely at high rpm as the short-stroke works engines, while the Model 40's crankshaft must have been unnecessarily heavy, since its dimensions were adequate for the Model 30.

Notwithstanding its dimensional inadequacy on the drive side of the larger engine, the KE805-steel crankshaft for the 1954

89

Joe Craig (Norton).

Harry Weslake (Weslake).

was completed by pressing the timing-side crankweb on to the pin and securing it with a castellated nut, subsequently milled away to clear the main-bearing housing. The bore of the pin was filled by a solid aluminium plug, drilled for big-end lubrication.

Highly polished all over to remove any blemishes that might otherwise initiate fatigue failure, the I-section connecting rod was forged in heat-treated KE805. To stiffen the big-end eye there were two circumferential ribs (three in the larger engine) blending into the shank of the rod farther up. There was no separate outer race for the roller bearing, but a duralumin bush was fitted at the small end, with two holes and a helical groove to spread oil along the gudgeon pin.

To cope with the overhang of the taper-mounted flywheel and outboard chain drive, the left-side main bearing was no less than $1\frac{1}{4}$in wide, with a row of 13 $\frac{5}{16} \times \frac{5}{16}$in rollers at each end of a duralumin cage, which was closed by riveted-on end plates. The separate bearing races comprised a hardened sleeve shrunk on the mainshaft and a flanged ring pressed in the crankcase and clamped by a large bronze nut on the outside. A double-row ball bearing on the timing side located the crankshaft laterally. Again a flanged outer race was pressed in the case (and secured by six countersunk screws) but there

were two inner races — one for each row of balls.

As suggested by the elaborate precautions for preventing the main-bearing outer races from loosening, the crankcase castings were in Elektron (a magnesium alloy); the inner surfaces were highly polished to reduce oil drag. Each half had four circumferential stiffening ribs and accurate alignment was ensured by a spigot and two dowels. For rigidity the crankcase mouth extended more than halfway up the liner of the Al-Fin bonded cylinder barrel, leaving room for only six cooling fins on the smaller engine, eight on the five-hundred, all of them surrounding the cam-drive vertical-shaft tube.

Flywheel diameter was the same on both sizes of engine. Surprisingly, no attempt was made to concentrate the weight in the rim; the wheel was a plain disc of S82 steel, $\frac{21}{32}$in thick for the three-fifty, $\frac{3}{4}$in for the five-hundred. On its outboard face was an integral sleeve on which the chain sprocket was carried and driven through a shock absorber containing four pairs of spheroidal rubbers — a device first used in 1931 but shelved from 1950 to '53 when the transmission shock absorber was in the clutch.

Keyed to the timing-side mainshaft were, first, the bevel gear for the cam drive (with shim adjustment for depth of mesh), then a

works engines was obviously designed for maximum bending stiffness. Each of the mainshafts was forged integrally with its crankweb-cum-bobweight, while the hollow crankpin was also part of the drive-side forging. To achieve the desired balance factor blind holes were drilled in the outer faces of the bobweights for the three-fifty (illustrated here) whereas heavy-metal plugs were inserted in drillings for the five-hundred.

Flanged at both ends, the inner race of the big-end bearing was shrunk on the crankpin. The duralumin cage housed 14 $\frac{5}{8} \times \frac{5}{16}$in rollers (15 in the five-hundred). Assembly

Early morning practice shot of Ray Amm on the peculiarly streamlined Norton he later rode to victory in the abruptly shortened 1954 Senior TT.

90

Because of its plain section, the outside flywheel did not make the best use of its weight, which would have been better concentrated in the rim.

small spur pinion which meshed with a double-diameter gear behind it; that gear drove the oil pump through a tongued coupling and the magneto through a chain sprocket on the outer end of its integral shaft. (Two years earlier the mag had been changed from rotating-armature to rotating-magnet type).

In the cam drive the upper and lower vertical bevel gears were connected by the traditional long shaft with an Oldham (tongued) coupling at each end. In a finned housing bolted to the crankcase, the integral shaft of the lower bevel ran in a bronze bush, flanged at its bottom end to take the upward thrust from the bevel teeth. Above the bush was a small double-row self-aligning ball bearing for the bottom end of the connecting shaft. A similar bearing layout was used at the top, with the flanged bush in a housing bolted to the cambox and the ball bearing in the cylinder head itself (as from 1950).

A model of rigidity and minimum friction,

the cam-gear train comprised the bevel crownwheel and five spur gears. Both the crownwheel and the middle spur gear were carried on a flanged shaft (with vernier adjustment for basic valve timing); and the shaft was supported in a ball bearing in the main cambox casting and a roller bearing in an I-section light-alloy outrigger plate bolted inside the cambox. Fixed spindles, also located in the main casting and outrigger plate, supported the two idler gears through double-row caged roller bearings. The camshafts themselves ran in ball bearings in cambox and single-row caged rollers in detachable housings in the cover on the left. Vernier couplings between the cams and their gears provided for individual valve timing; and the nut clamping-up the inlet cam assembly was bevelled on its outer face to form a cam for the AC pump that lifted fuel from the pannier tanks to the top tank. A slot in the end of the crownwheel shaft accepted the tongue for the revmeter drive.

Side thrust from the cams was taken by hollow, cylindrical followers (tappets) interposed between them and the valve-stem caps. Since the followers were ground to a 1-inch radius on the rubbing surface, they were prevented from rotating by a flat formed on one side. Shims of various thicknesses under the stem caps provided for valve clearance adjustment. The hairpin return springs — surprisingly still exposed long after rival engines had switched to full enclosure to prevent oil leakage — exerted a pressure of 104lb with the valves seated.

Making a ground joint with the top of the spigoted cylinder, the head was cast in RR53b high-duty aluminium alloy. While the copper-alloy valve guides were a press fit, the valve-seat rings were shrunk in — a wear-resistant austenitic iron for the inlet and a high-conductivity copper alloy for the much hotter (albeit sodium-cooled) exhaust. In both sizes of engine the valve stems had an

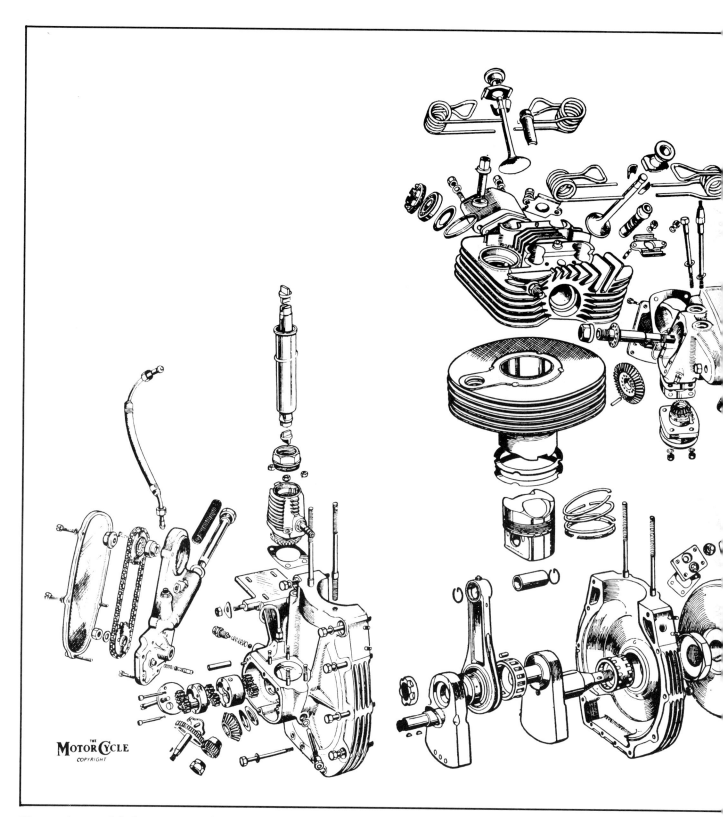

The two-piece crankshaft was supported in a double-row bearing on each side — caged balls on the timing side, caged rollers on the drive side. In the half-speed oil pump one pair of gears delivered the oil, the two other pairs scavenged it — one from the crankcase, the other from the lower bevel housing. From the overhead bevel shaft a train of five spur gears drove the twin camshafts, which actuated the valves through inverted buckets. Note the oil scroll cut in the outside of the exhaust-valve guide, and the large crankcase breather embodying two non-return valves.

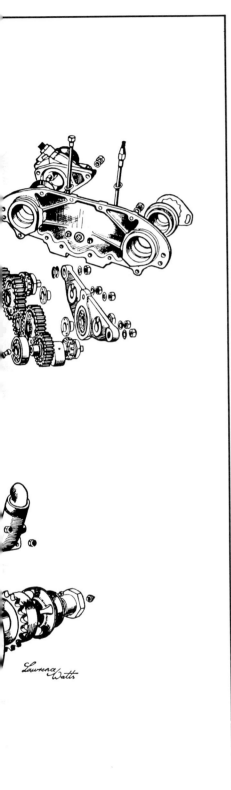

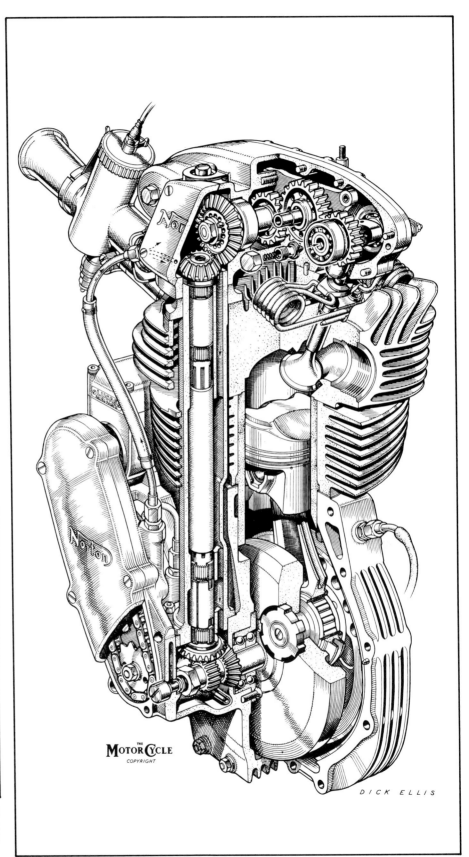

For comparison with the outside-flywheel works engine, here is a sectioned drawing of a standard Manx engine with its hefty internal flywheels (right).

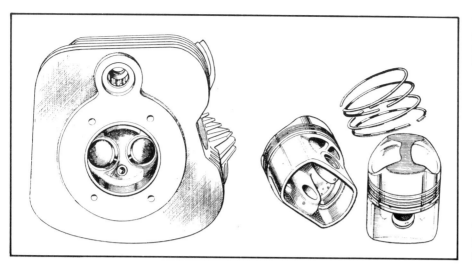

These drawings show the strong construction of the piston and the flat crown matching the squish bands on opposite sides of the cylinder head.

The outer race of the double-row main ball bearing was flanged for security in the timing-side half of the magnesium-alloy crankcase.

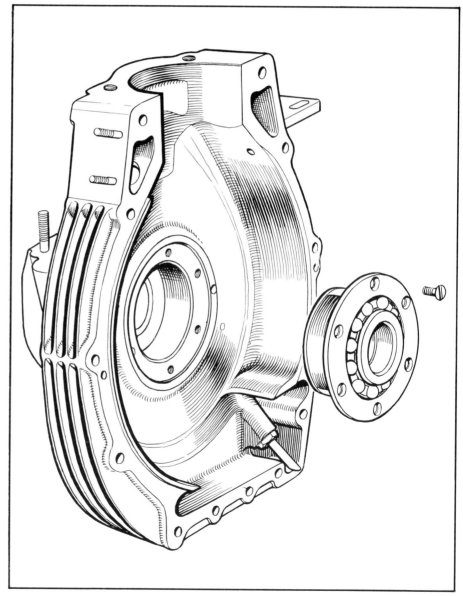

included angle of 64 degrees (32 degrees each side of the cylinder axis), which was fairly narrow at the time. Downdraught angle of the inlet tract was 20 degrees. Valve-head diameters were $1\frac{5}{8}$in (inlet) and $1\frac{1}{2}$in (exhaust) for the smaller engine, 2in and $1\frac{3}{4}$in respectively for the five-hundred.

The most interesting aspect of the head was the underside — the combustion space. In the middle, this was machined to a part-spherical shape, into which the valve seats intruded front and rear. Since the diameter of this middle recess was appreciably smaller than the cylinder bore there was a wide, flat squish band on each side extending from one valve seat to the other. To match these bands at top dead centre with as little clearance as was necessary to prevent metallic contact, the top of the high piston crown was machined flat, leaving a dumbell-shape surface. As a further contribution towards a compact combustion space and a high compression ratio (10.8:1, 349cc; 10.4, 499cc) the underhead shapes of the valves (concave inlet, convex exhaust) were closely followed in the piston-crown recesses.

Although the piston skirt was of slipper type, the side walls were of the same depth as the thrust faces and thickened along the bottom edge for stiffness. The taper-bored gudgeon pin was unusually short since its bosses (which extended right up to the piston crown) were entirely inboard of the side walls. To minimize piston friction there was very little skirt below gudgeon-pin level. Ring complement was the usual two narrow ones for compression plus an oil scraper.

At Monza the previous year (1953), the cylinder head of the bigger Norton had two sparking plugs — one at each side — fired simultaneously by battery and coil rather than magneto (bore and stroke at that time were 88 × 82mm). However, when the slight power increase on the dynamometer failed to

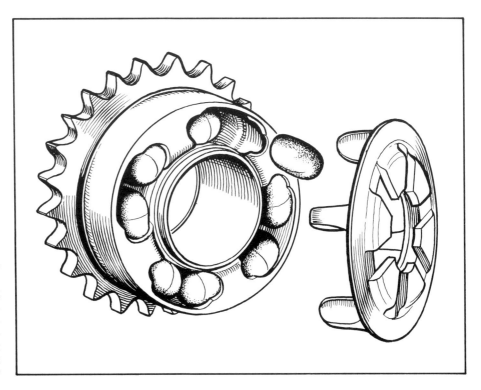

produce any improvement in lap times, the second (right-hand) plug was discarded and the magneto reinstated.

Carburettor choke size was $1\frac{3}{16}$in for the smaller engine, $1\frac{13}{32}$in for the larger. To insulate the instrument from cylinder-head heat, a Tufnol washer was sandwiched between the head and the carb spacer — which was 2in long on the three-fifty, $1\frac{7}{8}$in on the five-hundred. Joe Craig specified a few changes from the standard Amal GP layout — a large intake trumpet, a better internal shape and a so-called 'piped' pilot system designed to prevent fuel from flooding the engine when the bike was leaned over.

To stabilize the fuel supply to the mixing chamber, a weir-type carburettor had been adopted in 1953, with surplus fuel pumped back to the tank. For simplicity on the 1954 engines the scavenge pump was discarded; and while the weir was retained to govern fuel level in the jet, a float controlled the flow rate from the tank.

There were three pairs of gears in the oil pump — one for delivery (30 gallons an hour at an engine speed of 6,000rpm), the others for scavenging. The delivery gears forced the oil through a cylindrical gauze filter in the back of the magneto chaincase and thence into two circuits. One !ed through the timing-side mainshaft to the big-end bearing whence the oil was flung on to the piston and cylinder; this oil was scavenged from the crankcase sump. The other circuit went via an external pipe to the cambox, where it fed the lift flanks of both cams through drillings before splashing on to the gear train. Oil from the inlet end of the cambox lubricated all the bevel gears as it drained via the vertical-shaft tube to the bottom bevel chamber. Oil from the front end of the cambox took a less orthodox path to the bevel chamber — draining through a scroll turned on the outside of the exhaust-valve guide (where it picked up heat) then through a small radiator mounted on a frame tube. All the oil in the bevel chamber was returned to the tank by the other scavenge pump. Since oil temperature did not normally exceed 60 degrees C, a relatively thin (SAE20) racing grade was chosen to reduce fluid friction.

Peak power was 38bhp at 8,250rpm for the three-fifty, 54 at 7,500 for the five-hundred. With these figures in mind I was fascinated to learn some years later that Joe Craig had had the opportunity of a 10 to 12-per-cent power increase for 1953 and had turned it down!

Early in 1976, while I was visiting Harry Weslake's little factory at Rye, Sussex, he showed me the graph reproduced here, which he had unearthed while searching through his records for a biography. The graph shows the results of airflow tests carried out in the winter of 1952-53 on an 88mm-bore works Norton two-valve cylinder head, supplied by Craig for evaluation, and a four-valve Weslake mock-up that could have been a direct replacement for it.

Flow rate was measured at seven progressive valve lifts from $\frac{1}{8}$in to the $\frac{1}{2}$in full lift of the Norton inlet cam. The benefit of the four-valver's freer breathing was greatest (no less than 50 per cent) at the smallest lift, reducing to 17 per cent at full lift, and might well have been greater with the subsequent 90mm

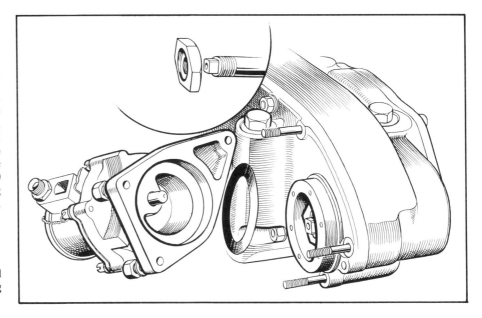

On two 1959 500cc Manx models, Doug Hele's experimental desmodromic valve gear used the existing train of cam gears. Unfortunately the project had to be shelved.

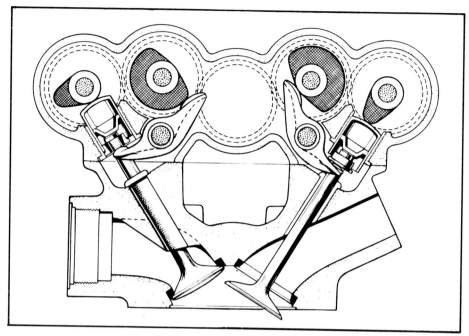

This graph shows how the gas flow through a 500cc works Norton inlet valve was substantially bettered by that through a Weslake mock-up with paired valves.

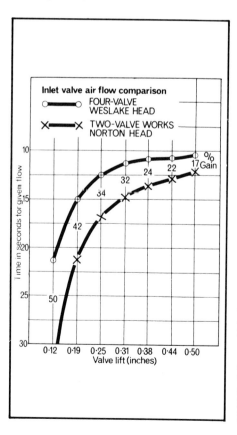

bore. In practice, the overall improvement would have been somewhere between those figures. Precisely where, it's impossible to say because, although the valves spent more time at part lift, where the percentage gain was greatest, they passed much more gas at higher lifts where the benefit, though substantial, was not so great.

However, from wide experience in relating flow tests to dynamometer results, Harry Weslake was convinced that converting the works Nortons to four valves would have boosted power by 5 to 6bhp for the five-hundred and proportionately for the three-fifty.

Hindsight lends weight to that estimate because the superiority of four-valve heads in both power and reliability was subsequently confirmed by Honda in world-championship road racing, by the Cosworth 3-litre V8 in Formula 1 car racing and by Weslake themselves in speedway. But for Joe Craig's stubbornness, Norton could have been in the vanguard of that radical development (provided the bottom half had been strengthened to withstand the higher peak revs) — and might have shared with Moto Guzzi the task of keeping the single competitive for a few years longer in the face of the Italian fours.

An altogether more enterprising approach was Doug Hele's desmodromic valve gear on a brace of experimental engines for the 499cc Manx model in 1959 — five years after the factory's withdrawal from racing. As the

drawing shows, the cambox retained its train of five spur gears — indeed the valve-opening cams remained on the front and rear shafts and operated through conventional radiused followers. The two intermediate gears, however, were no longer idlers. Instead they drove the closing cams, which raised the valves through 'underslung' rockers forked at their outer ends to embrace the stems and actuate collars secured by split collets.

Since cam modifications got no farther than the tentative stage, no significant increase in power was expected or obtained. Had the project not been shelved, however, cam developments to take full advantage of the positive operation (eg, higher lifts and fiercer accelerations) must have yielded a bonus in power as well as mechanical safety.

Pushstarting proved difficult — hardly surprising since run-and-bump engine speed on the relatively high gearing was too low for valve inertia to overcome the friction of the sliding tappets and ensure full closure in the absence of light helper springs. Again, normal development would certainly have provided a cure.

During TT practice, Bob McIntyre reeled off a couple of 95mph laps (about par in the circumstances) but in view of the engine's undeveloped state he was not overjoyed. Alas, other work at the factory took precedence and Hele had no opportunity to take the few steps that might have given the Manx models an extended lease of life.

CHAPTER 13

Honda CB450 twin

Enterprising 180-degree parallel-twin that bristled with novelties but
embodied some typical Japanese flaws

On the roadster front, the first real shot in the crazy postwar battle for ever-increasing complexity was fired by Honda with the launch of the CB750 four in 1968. Since then, they have marketed so wide a variety of extravagantly engineered high-performance engines — and in such quick succession — that it is difficult to recall the time, only a few years earlier, when the name Honda (away from the grand-prix circuits) meant step-through commuter bikes and those mild-mannered twins, the 250cc Dream and 125cc Benly, plus their sporting and odd-size derivatives.

Yet it was against that half-forgotten image of docility and relatively conventional engineering that the twin-overhead-camshaft CB450 sportster engine seemed so advanced, even heretical, when it was introduced in 1965. In retrospect, it now looks what it probably was — a convenient engine on which to unload some advanced technology from the V12 Formula 1 car-racing engines. But in 1965 it was nothing less than the 'bees' knees' — albeit over-engineered for a bike requiring a full racing crouch to nudge 100mph.

Nowadays there is scarcely a cylinder configuration that hasn't featured in a Honda brochure — four abreast, six abreast, horizontally opposed (boxer) four, transverse V-twin, in-line V-twin and four, even the once-despised upright big single. Some engines were even turbocharged. In the light of that exotic array, a medium-capacity, unblown, upright parallel twin might seem something of a yawn. But the CB450 bristled with features that flew in the face of tradition — such as double overhead camshafts, torsion-bar valve springs and 180-degree crank spacing (to neutralize the primary inertia forces and so improve the engine's dynamic balance, particularly at high revs).

Double overhead camshafts, said the traditionalists, might well be a *sine qua non* for grand-prix racing, but they were much too expensive for a catalogue roadster. Honda's answer was to cut the cost by using

neither expensive bevel gears nor a spur-gear train. Instead, the two camshafts were linked directly to the crankshaft by a single bush (*ie*, rollerless) chain — and the CB450, even after shipment halfway round the world to Britain, remained competitive in price.

For so high-revving an engine, the wisdom of using a bush chain was generally conceded, since it bypassed the risk, however slight, of a broken roller causing serious engine damage. But a bush chain was said to be noisy. Honda quietened it — not only by passing the chain over three toothed and four plain synthetic-rubber guide rollers, but also by sandwiching the 32-tooth camshaft sprockets in rubber.

The next traditionalist objection was to the use of a cam-drive sprocket on the crankshaft with as few as 16 teeth. For years 19 teeth had been regarded as the minimum if chain snatch was to be avoided. Such snatch is better understood by visualizing a sprocket with only three or four teeth. Its effective radius would fluctuate considerably three or four times each revolution so that, even for a steady sprocket speed, there would be a cyclic variation in chain speed — hence snatch. Honda damped any chain snatch with a pivoted tensioner, incorporating a thick rubber buffer, in the slack run. Adjustment was semi-automatic — slackening a bolt securing the tensioner stem allowed a spring to take up any play that might have developed.

Perhaps the most novel technicality in the CB450's valve gear, however, was the use of torsion-bar valve springs — *ie*, short, stiff lengths of spring wire subjected only to twisting (torsion). In terms of stress, no-one doubted the superiority of torsion bars over coil springs — indeed, they had long given excellent results in both car and motorcycle suspension systems. The problem was installing them in a cylinder head. Yet the CB450 layout was neatness itself.

There is no mystery in twisting a length of wire to get a spring effect. Indeed, that is the

principle of the ordinary helical valve spring — which is simply a long, thin torsion bar wound into a compact coil for ease of installation.

When it is compressed, the entire length of the wire gets twisted and it is the subsequent untwisting that extends the spring again. You'll find this twisting easier to grasp if you visualize a coarse-pitch spring. (Hairpin valve springs work on a different principle. Like clock springs, they are bent, not twisted, by the applied load.)

The reason why a straight torsion bar is superior to a coil spring in terms of stress is that its operating stresses are purely torsional, whereas in a coil spring those stresses are superimposed on the bending stresses already produced when it was wound. But the chief virtue of a torsion bar for valve closure is the elimination of the destructive surge to which coil springs are liable at very high engine speeds.

During both compression and extension, the inertia of the fast-moving coils tends to make them resist reversal, in opposition to the twisting of the wire. The resultant surging of the coils can fracture the spring.

The CB450 torsion bars were much shorter and thicker than comparable coil springs would have been if unwound. The shank of each bar (the part between the splined ends) was only 4in long and about $\frac{7}{32}$in in diameter, whereas the wire in a coil spring would have been three or four times as long and much thinner. Clearly the compact proportions of the torsion bars were necessary for easy accommodation. But there was another benefit — and that was that their natural resonant frequency was much too high for them to be troubled by engine vibration.

Finally, 180-degree crank spacing had long been commonplace for two-stroke parallel twins, where it also separated the power impulses for smoother torque and where the cylinder axes were usually closer together anyway, so reducing the rocking couple. But

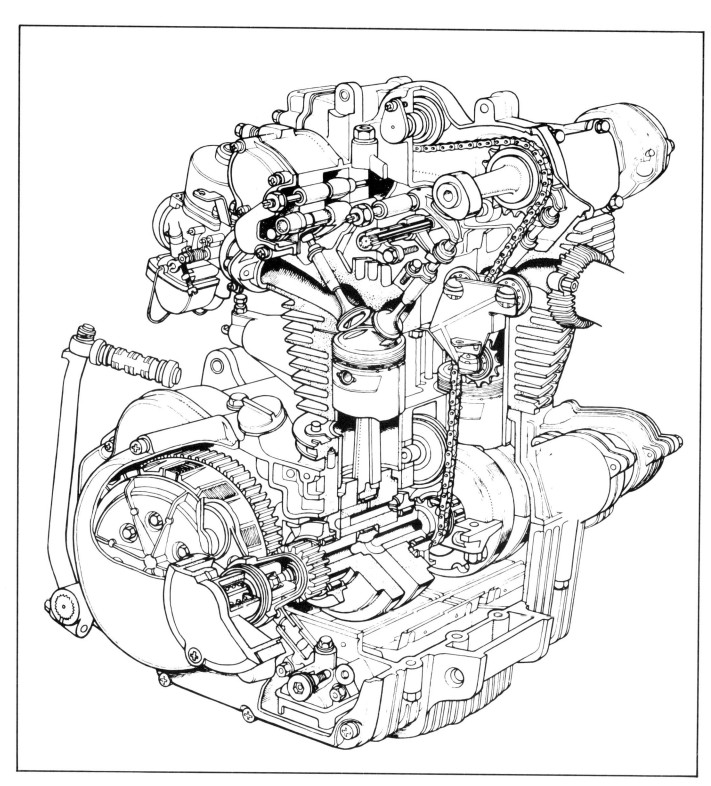

Although bristling with technical novelties, the CB450 engine suffered — especially in the lower rpm range — from inadequate flywheel effect and overwide spacing of the cylinder axes. This cutaway drawing shows how the pivoted cam levers almost doubled the lift of the lobes to about $\frac{7}{16}$ in at the valves. Also shown is the retaining clip for the right-hand exhaust-valve guide. Driving sprocket for the cam chain lies between the inner main bearings. Behind the clutch can be seen the eccentric driving the oil-pump plunger in the right-hand front of the crankcase; the centrifugal filter is outboard of the small primary drive pinion.

Technically advanced for its day (1966) this four-speed CB450 romped to 100mph on road test and achieved a mean 14.6sec/87mph for the standing quarter-mile. It was one of the Japanese industry's first high-performance mediumweights.

in a four-stroke the size of the CB450 it was predicted that the grossly uneven firing intervals (180 and 540 degrees alternately) and the larger crankshaft couple would be intolerable.

Some years earlier, on the 250cc Dream Super Sport, Honda had shown that the uneven exhaust beat could be camouflaged almost beyond notice by really effective muffling; so much so that its be-doom, be-doom character was detectable only just off idling. The aural situation on the CB450 was almost as good. But on the larger engine the 540-degree interval showed up the inadequacy of the small-diameter flywheels, sandwiched as they were between the piston skirts above and the anti-splash oil baffle beneath.

The job of flywheels is to smooth out successive firing impulses and it may be that the CB450 flywheels would have been adequate if the pistons had moved in step (360-degree intervals). But the 540-degree interval called for considerably more fly-

wheel inertia and the deficit was manifest in abnormally high non-snatch and idling speeds.

In a flat-twin engine such as the BMW the offset of the cylinder axes is so small as to render the rocking couple virtually negligible. In the CB450, however, the side-by-side layout of the cylinders and the siting of the camshaft drive, flanked by two roller main bearings, in the middle of the crankshaft dictated a wide spacing for the cylinders — and at low engine speeds the lateral rocking of the engine could be distinctly felt.

Here again the situation was aggravated by the flywheel layout. For a given weight of metal, the effect of a flywheel (ie, its inertia) is proportional to the *fourth power* of its diameter. Hence the maximum effect is obtained by concentrating the mass as much as possible in the rim and leaving the web relatively thin, as in the famous Moto Guzzi racing singles. Long before Honda, Scott had placed such a flywheel in the middle of the crankshaft of their two-speed parallel-twin

two-strokes and used its considerable inertia to damp down the inherent rocking couple most effectively. Unfortunately that ruse was incompatible with the CB450 layout, regardless of the Japanese horror of effective flywheels.

So much for generalities; now for some details. The outer end of each torsion bar was splined into a retainer bolted to the side of the cylinder head; and, to minimize overall width of the assembly, the other end of the bar was splined into the inner end of the guide tube surrounding it. Part way along this tube, external splines carried the pivot end of the forked arm that closed the valve. Although in theory the length of tubing between its inner end and the external splines was also subject to torsion, this could be ignored because of its stiffness.

To preload the bar during assembly, it was given a slight twist by a tool engaged with the retainer before it was clamped to the head.

Naturally, the geometry of the parts was

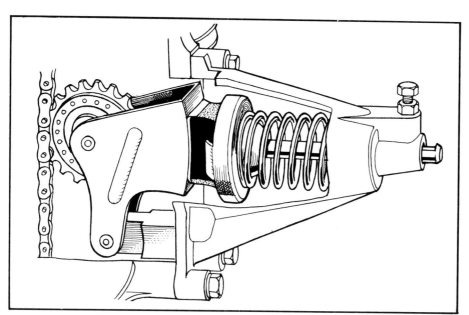

The pivoted cam-chain tensioner was normally locked by a bolt nipping the stem. Slackening the bolt enabled the spring to take up chain play automatically.

Layout of the cam chain and its seven synthetic-rubber guide rollers. The three rollers with teeth ran on needle bearings; the four carried in brackets bolted to the cylinder head had their spindles oiled from troughs formed in the brackets.

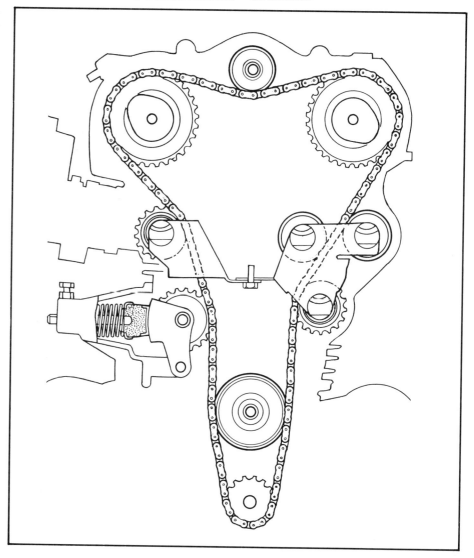

such that the operating twist in the torsion bar was not enough to give it a permanent set (a consideration that applies equally when determining the pitch of a helical valve spring). Indeed, to ensure that each torsion bar was stressed (twisted) in only one direction, every joint had a master spline so that it could be assembled in only one way. Each assembly was kept as a set — and though diagonally opposite sets could be interchanged without reversing the twist, it was impossible to switch sets directly left to right or front to rear.

Incidentally, since a conventional valve spring also helps to retain the valve guide in the cylinder head, the Honda guides had small forked clips pressing down on their flanges.

The cam boxes were integral with the cylinder head and each camshaft (exhaust and inlet) was supported, immediately outboard of the cams, by two ¾in-wide plain light-alloy bearings spigoted into opposite sides of the head. Since the curved pads on the cam followers were formed midway between pivot and tip, the lift of the cam lobe was almost doubled at the valve stem. For valve clearance adjustment, the followers were pivoted on eccentric spindles with slotted ends and locknuts.

In the camshaft drive, the three synthetic rollers with teeth (including the tensioner) were supported on needle bearings, the four others on plain spindles.

Largest of the seven was a plain one spanning the vertical chain runs in the crankcase mouth. Farther up the front (driving) run, two plain rollers and one toothed were carried in a steel bracket bolted to the underface of the head.

Components of a torsion-bar assembly, including the retainer that bolted to the cylinder head and the tubular guide that carried the forked arm for closing the valve.

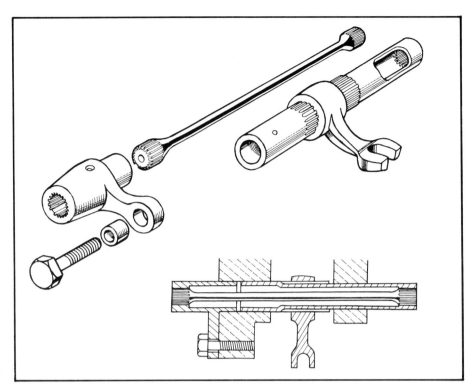

Midway between the two camshaft sprockets, the chain dipped under a plain roller in the top of the cylinder head (so increasing the arc of contact round the sprockets). Then, on its way down the slack run, it first negotiated a small toothed roller in another bracket bolted to the head and, finally, the larger toothed roller of the tensioner.

The 16-tooth driving sprocket was formed integrally with the middle portion of the crankshaft, which was pressed into the inner discs of the two pairs of flywheels. Those discs had integral crankpins, diametrically opposed to one another and supporting the steel connecting rods on caged needle rollers that bore directly not only on the crankpins but also in the big-end eyes (*ie*, no separate bearing races). Pressed on to the crankpins, the outer flywheel discs were formed integrally with the crankshaft ends.

Hard against the sides of each pair of flywheels were the caged roller main bearings — four in all — the inner two assembled on the middle part of the shaft before pressing. Here too the rollers ran directly on the shafts, while the special outer races incorporated their own attachment lugs. To relieve the crankcase joint of stress, the whole crank assembly was clamped to eight studs in the upper half of the case.

Pressure die-cast in aluminium alloy — hence superbly finished, precise in section and carrying not a gram of surplus weight — the upper and lower crankcase halves incorporated the gearcase, too. The horizontal joint passed through the axes of the crankshaft, the gearbox input shaft and the output shaft behind it. Crankshaft endfloat was limited by bronze thrust washers on both sides of the extreme-right main bearing — *ie*, one behind the 23-tooth primary-drive spur gear splined to the shaft and the other between the bearing and the end flywheel disc.

The top ends of the con-rods were also unbushed, so that the gudgeon pins ran directly in the rods. Giving a compression ratio of 8.5:1, the pistons had shallow-dome crowns recessed for valve clearance, full skirts and the usual complement of two compression rings and a slotted scraper. The top ring was chromium-faced while the

second had its lower edge ground away to give an inverted-L section. Bore and stroke were 70 × 57.8mm (445cc).

Another die-casting, the cylinder block had flanged, austenitic-iron liners with spigots just over an inch deep registering in the crankcase mouth. Besides a paper gasket at the base joint there was a rubber O-ring at

the root of each spigot.

Because of its complexity, the light-alloy cylinder head was sand-cast, with cast-iron skulls forming the deep, part-spherical combustion chambers. Valve diameters were $1\frac{7}{16}$in inlet and $1\frac{1}{4}$in exhaust; all had $\frac{9}{32}$in stems. Sparking plugs were 14mm, long reach.

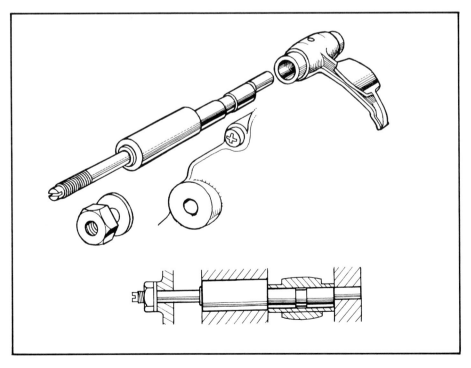

A cam lever and its eccentric spindle. Turning the spindle in its housing raised or lowered the lever pivot, so varying the valve clearance.

Incorporated in the inlet-valve cover plate was a well-baffled crankcase breather. Rubber-bonded adaptors supported the two constant-vacuum carburettors, while each finned exhaust-pipe retainer was secured on two studs.

Ignition was by 12-volt battery and two coils, with the double contact breaker on the left-hand end of the exhaust camshaft. Tapered and keyed on the same end of the crankshaft was the rotor for the 70-watt alternator, its stator housed in the crankcase side cover.

Bolted across the front of the crankcase mouth was the starter motor, its 13-tooth sprocket linked to a bronze-bushed 37-tooth sprocket floating on the crankshaft inboard of the alternator rotor. A boss on the outer face of the large sprocket drove the rotor through the customary roller-and-ramp clutch.

Giving a primary drive reduction of 3.3:1, the 76-tooth clutch gear was riveted to an eight-rubber shock absorber in the light-alloy drum, which spun on a double bronze bush on the gearbox input shaft. Also in light alloy were the seven driving plates, to which friction rings were bonded. Steel was used for the driven plates and the clutch centre was splined to the input shaft.

Behind the clutch, the shaft was supported in a double ball bearing. A similar bearing, albeit larger, supported the opposite end of the output shaft, behind the final-drive sprocket. The other ends of both shafts ran in coppered bushes.

Naturally, with the drive going in and out on separate shafts, all four gears were indirect; engagement was by conventional face dogs A long cross-shaft transmitted the motion of the left-side gear pedal to the selector mechanism on the right. As was usual those days, a kickstarter was provided in addition to the electric motor.

Since all six crankshaft bearings were of roller (ie, low-friction) type, the lubrication system operated at a low pressure; moreover, it was extremely thorough, with oil force-fed to the gearbox as well as the engine.

The 5-pint oil compartment in the bottom of the crankcase was partitioned off from the flywheel chamber by two steel pressings located by a long transverse pin. An eccentric on the back of the clutch gear drove the single 16mm-diameter aluminium pump plunger. This sucked oil through a gauze strainer and forced it into a centrifugal filter (splined to the crankshaft outboard of the primary drive gear), which kept all metallic particles out of the system, not just the ferrous ones, as does a magnet.

From the filter, the oil divided into two

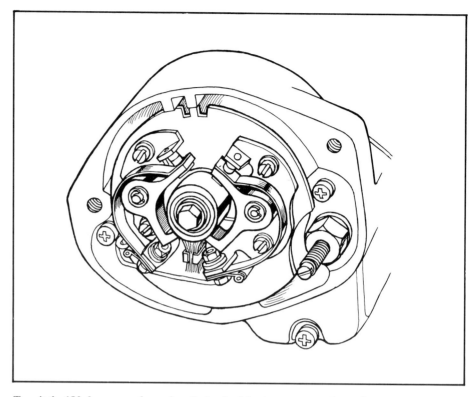

To suit the 180-degree crank spacing, the heels of the two contact-point rockers were disposed at 90 degrees around the cam.

circuits. In the upper one it passed up the right-hand pair of cylinder-retaining studs to lubricate the camshaft bearings, cam lobes and followers before spilling on to the valve stems and into troughs serving the torsion-bar sleeves. Other troughs collected oil for the spindles of the four chain rollers carried in the brackets attached to the head.

The lower circuit fed the main and big-end bearings (with splash to the cylinder bores and pistons), also the gearbox input shaft via its coppered bush. From the bore of this shaft oil got to the free gears and the clutch-drum bushes. The bores of the free gears on the output shaft got their oil from the other coppered bush, which had a trough to collect splash.

Oil return to the sump was entirely by gravity with no need for a scavenge pump. At peak-power revs (8,500rpm) circulation rate was about a gallon a minute.

Honda claimed that peak power of the CB450 engine was 43bhp, measured at the crankshaft. At 6.96:1 in top gear, overall gearing was well chosen for normal riding, with 8,500rpm attainable at 92mph. With chin and elbows glued to the tank (hardly normal riding) the revs could be pushed beyond 9,200, giving a speed of some 100mph.

Despite the engine's exciting technical specification, however, the CB450 failed to secure an enthusiastic following. It is true that factors unconnected with the engine — vague low-speed cornering, inadequate suspension damping and low-grip tyres — contributed to this situation. Nevertheless — although the engine's delightful smoothness in the higher rev ranges vindicated the manufacturer's choice of 180-degree crank spacing to neutralize the primary inertia forces — its concomitant lateral rocking and transmission snatch lower down the rpm range were less than acceptable.

Nor was servicing experience happy. The valves could be a pig to adjust, since it was well-nigh impossible to tighten the eccentric-spindle locknuts without disturbing the setting. The relative complexity of the valve gear was unwelcome, while cylinder-head removal required the cam chain to be broken and reriveted.

Although a five-speed model was introduced (with improved steering and carburation), the CB450 was soon dropped from the UK range. In the early 1970s it was reintroduced as a five-hundred (with the longer stroke necessitating deep piston-skirt cutaways to clear the flywheels) but that, too, quickly disappeared. Bold as it was, the CB450 engine was quickly consigned to the history books.

CHAPTER 14

250cc Royal Enfield GP5

Promising two-stroke racing single, designed and developed in a hurry,
but frustrated by management policy change

Royal Enfield was hardly a name you associated with road racing — not at the dawn of the 1960s anyway. Small two-strokes, sporting singles and robust parallel twins, yes. But tarmac racers — no. Then, following the company's absorption into the E. H. & P. Smith group in 1962, it soon acquired a new managing director — Leo Davenport.

Ah, wasn't he a works racer way back before the Second World War? Sure, said the oldtimers. But although more than 30 years had elapsed since Leo's racing career peaked with his victory for New Imperial in the 1932 Lightweight TT, his enthusiasm and ambition were undimmed. Royal Enfield, he decided, were going to market a racer.

By that time there was a precedent for small companies offering relatively inexpensive racing machines. For Villiers had adapted their 250cc Starmaker motocross engine for road racing by fitting a single induction tract, with $1\frac{3}{8}$in Amal GP carburettor, in place of the original splayed tract and two $1\frac{1}{8}$in Monoblocs. As a result, budding speedmen already had a choice of the Starmaker-powered Cotton Telstar and DMW Hornet, as well as the Greeves Silverstone, all for £285-295.

Davenport, however, was not content to wrap yet another frame around the Villiers engine. He wanted an engine of his own — something that, once fully developed, would make the Royal Enfield GP5 first choice for riders in that corner of the market.

Wisely he consulted Geoff Duke, six times a world champion and not long retired from international racing. When it came to suggesting an engine designer, Duke had no hesitation in choosing two-stroke specialist Herman Meier, whom he had known since 1949 when Herman arrived in the UK from his native Bremen to work for three-times Senior TT winner Harold Daniell. In May 1964 Meier started work at Redditch.

Less than a year elapsed before I called at the factory with *Motor Cycle* artist Lawrie Watts to analyse the engine, yet the produc-

Herman Meier (Royal Enfield).

tion units were already giving 34bhp at 8,000rpm — which accounts for the title of our feature article dated May 13, 1965: 'Quick-fire Results'. (Later that year the prototype development engine used by Percy Tait was not only putting out 10 per cent more power but doing so, significantly, at 10 per cent lower revs Meier claimed — and without a catastrophic drop in bhp up to 9,000rpm.)

To save time and money, Royal Enfield had stipulated a single cylinder on an Alpha bottom half, which had established a fine reputation for reliability in motocross. That understandable decision committed Meier to the Alpha's stroke of 72mm, hence a cylinder bore of 66mm, giving a capacity of 246.3cc; it also precluded the use of disc-valve induction into the crankcase. (Given more time, Meir would have preferred the oversquare cylinder dimensions of 72 × 61mm (248.4cc), for which he claimed to have calculated a power potential of 42bhp at 10,500rpm.)

Be that as it may, he started our discussion by handing me a cylinder liner — presumably for me to study the unusual transfer porting. But no sooner did he let it go than I understood the reason for his quizzical smile — the liner was featherlight, made of aluminium alloy with the bore hard-chrome plated.

'I don't get it,' I said. 'Since you plate the bore, why use a separate sleeve?' 'We don't plate the bore on production engines,' grinned Meier, 'we cast an iron liner in the aluminium jacket. What you are holding is the detachable sleeve of the prototype engine used last year (1964) by Dennis Craine in the Lightweight Manx Grand Prix and by Percy Tait on short circuits.'

It was a technique Meier had tried before joining Royal Enfield. With the engine cold, he explained, the liner could be slipped in and out by hand, which made it much easier to alter the shape and size of the transfer ports for experiment. The sleeve could then be used as a template for the cylinder.

Also, removal of the sleeve gave easy access to the transfer passages in the jacket, so that their shape could be altered experimentally by plastic metal. Of course, since the sleeve ran hotter than the jacket, there was a firm gastight fit as soon as the engine started.

'Very ingenious,' I agreed 'and what did you learn from those experiments?' 'Only that we couldn't improve on the original shapes and sizes,' was the frank answer.

The iron liner fitted to production engines at first had bulges on the sides, incorporating the transfer passages; the idea was to obviate all possibility of leakage between those passages and the exhaust port, for that would have been fatal to efficiency. But the precaution proved unnecessary and a straightforward heat-treated sleeve, with a wall thickness of $\frac{1}{4}$in, proved easily rigid enough to resist distortion and maintain complete contact with the jacket.

'Do you corrugate the outer surface of the sleeve as an extra means of location?' I asked. 'Yes,' said Meier, 'there are two ribs running right the way round. Incidentally, to ensure consistent performance all ports in the sleeve are machined in a jig before the jacket is cast on, after which the ports in the jacket are matched to those in the sleeve by hand grinding. That way, all our Grand Prix engines are within ½bhp of one another.'

'Tell me about the transfer system,' I suggested. 'In each side of the sleeve you have two extra windows, one above the other, just behind the main transfer ports. Presumably these windows are the inlets and outlets of auxiliary transfer passages, which are fed through holes in the piston skirt, as in MZ and similar rotary valve engines?'

Meier reached for a piston and showed me left and right windows milled high in the skirt, just behind the internal stiffening webs that linked the gudgeon-pin bosses to the crown. 'Right,' he agreed. 'During the transfer phase these skirt ports pass gas from under the piston crown into the lower ends of the auxiliary transfer passages; the upper ends, of course, discharge into the cylinder.

'This is the first racing two-stroke to use

Dennis Craine rounds Governor's Bridge in the 1964 Lightweight Manx Grand Prix on the prototype Royal Enfield GP5 with quick-fit light-alloy cylinder sleeve.

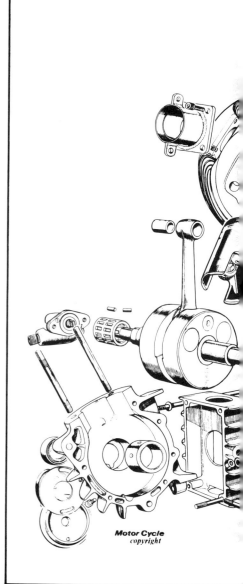

Motor Cycle
copyright

four transfer ports, to establish a predetermined gas-flow pattern, and the layout allows us to combine an auxiliary transfer system with piston-controlled induction. As you know, in a rotary-valve engine such as the MZ or any of its many copies, the auxiliary port can be placed diametrically opposite the exhaust port, where there is plenty of room in the cylinder wall. In our engine, though, the large piston-controlled inlet port occupies that position; so I've split the auxiliary transfer system into a passage on each side of the inlet port.'

'Congratulations,' I said. 'Isn't the object of the system to prevent the small-end bearing from overheating by passing some of the comparatively cool transfer gas over it?'

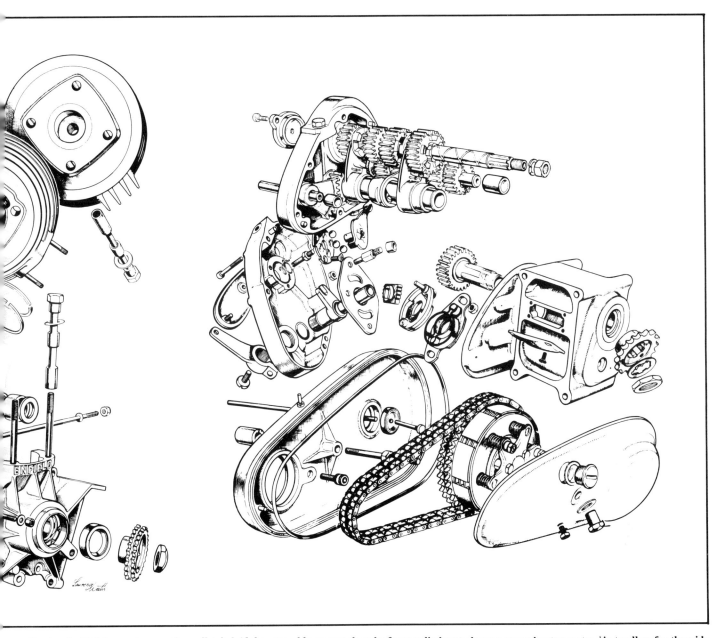

Bottom half of the engine was the well-tried Alpha assembly except that the front cylinder studs were spaced out an extra $\frac{1}{4}$in to allow for the wide exhaust port and transverse cooling fins were added to the crankcase. A finned rectangular spacer separated the case from the five-speed Albion gearbox, driven by duplex chain. The small-end bearing was bushed and the combustion chamber had a top-hat form with an annular (not half-moon) squish band.

'Primarily, yes', agreed Meier, 'but there's a power bonus too, since some of the gas under the piston crown wouldn't otherwise get up into the cylinder during the brief transfer period.'

To prove the effectiveness of the cooling of the bronze-bushed small-end bearing, Meier pointed to a highly polished connecting rod. 'This rod,' he said, 'has just done an arduous short-circuit meeting in Gordon Keith's engine, yet there's not the faintest trace of discolouration.'

As I peered up the transfer passages from the base of a production cylinder, I noticed that the main and auxiliary transfer ports were fed from wide common passages which the gas entered in the usual way via matching cutaways in the sides of the piston skirt. Above the cylinder base, however, vertical webs separated the main passages from the auxiliaries.

'To increase gas speed,' Meier pointed out, 'the cross-section area of the main passages is slightly reduced towards the top; but, to

obviate a bottleneck in the auxiliary passages, their area is increased where the lower windows feed in.'

'What about the relative port timings,' I asked, 'and the flow pattern into the cylinder?'

'All four transfer ports open and close together,' Meier assured me. 'As to gas flow, you'll see there is only $\frac{3}{8}$in between the sides of the exhaust port and the main transfer ports. So, to prevent direct charge loss to the exhaust, the main transfer passages are

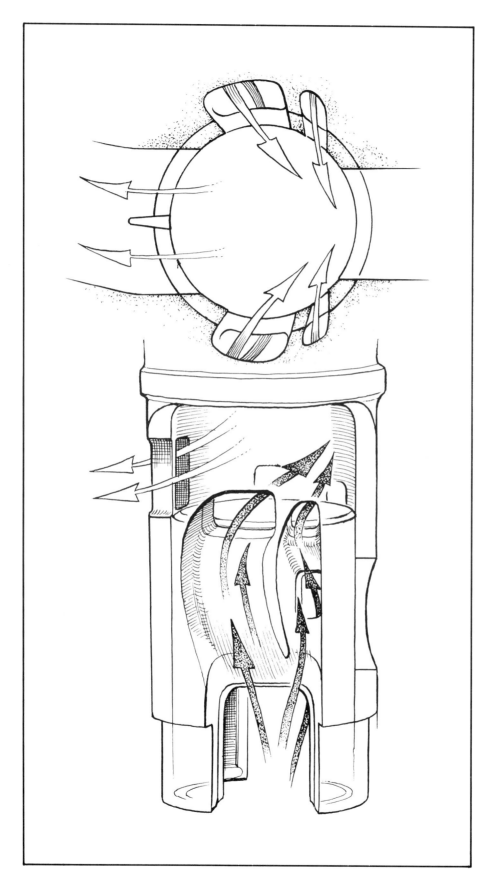

shaped to deflect the fresh gas backward more sharply than usual; they also tilt the gas streams upward about 15 degrees.

'The auxiliary ports, however, discharge in a transverse plane across the back of the cylinder. But the upward inclination in this case is much steeper (45 degrees), which lifts the whole converging column up the rear cylinder wall.'

'What about the other ports?' was my next question. 'I notice there is a vertical bridge down the middle of the exhaust port.'

'Right,' said Meier, 'that enables us to widen the port without risk of trapping a piston ring. Without a bridge, maximum safe width of any rectangular exhaust port (measured as a chord) is 62 per cent of the cylinder bore. Our port width is just over 77 per cent of the bore.

'Hence we get the fully open area we want from a port height of just over 40 per cent of the stroke, whereas it would otherwise have to be 44 per cent. In practice, the difference gives us that much extra on the length of the power stroke and a broader power band.'

If that exhaust-port height seems low by comparison with those of today's Japanese works racers (which measure 50 per cent or more of the stroke), remember that port timings are essentially time-based and the Japanese engines peak up to half as fast again as the Royal Enfield's 8,000rpm. Incidentally, the Enfield's exhaust-port height meant that its 12.5 to 12.8:1 geometric compression ratio (measured from bottom dead centre) translated to 7.9 to 8.1:1 in Japanese terms (from exhaust-port closure).

'And the inlet port?' I queried. 'Well,' said Meier, 'before we leave the exhaust port let me point out the two small holes in the top front of the piston skirt. They help to cool and oil the port bridge which, as you can imagine, has a pretty hot life.

'The inlet tract has a downward slope of 20 degrees and is machined parallel and circular, to the same bore as the $1\frac{1}{2}$in GP carburettor, throughout its full length. My reason for keeping the section constant was to simplify calculation of the tract's natural resonant frequency, which determines the best dimensions for power.

'Actually, the circular section and downdraught angle combine to give a rather deep port opening, hence a long induction period — 175 degrees of crankshaft rotation to be precise, spread symmetrically before and after top dead centre. With a rectangular port shape, that duration could restrict the breadth of the power band; but the round

These drawings show the gas-flow pattern through the divided exhaust port and main and auxiliary transfer ports with the piston at bottom dead centre.

The top face of the cylinder was corrugated to make a gastight head joint without a gasket.

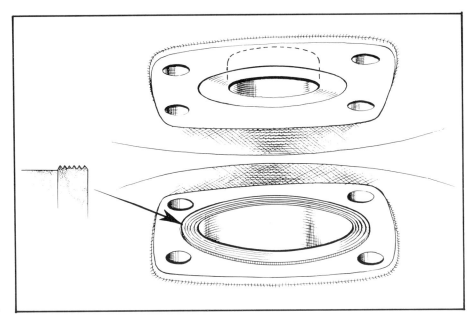

section obviates that problem by giving a slowish initial port opening.'

I asked whether the symmetrical inlet timing enforced by piston control of the port (as a result of using the Alpha bottom half) didn't involve an inordinate sacrifice in crankcase filling, by comparison with the much longer, asymmetrical induction period possible with a disc valve.

'In a production racer,' said Meier, 'two important priorities are mechanical reliability and a wide enough power band to cope with the five ratios the Albion gearbox restricts us to. Now, for long-term reliability, a 250cc single with a 72mm stroke can't be revved consistently much above 8,500rpm (which gives a mean piston speed of 4,000ft/min). And at that sort of speed, the undoubted breathing advantage of asymmetrical inlet timing is less marked than it is at higher revs. At our rpm level, too, the shorter induction period enforced by symmetrical inlet timing gives us a wider spread of power than we would get with a longer period.'

We turned to the bottom half and Meier pointed out some differences from standard Alpha practice. For example, the spacing of the front two cylinder studs was $\frac{1}{4}$in wider than usual to suit the extra-wide exhaust port. Consequently, no other make of cylinder and head would fit the crankcase.

Then the transverse cooling fins across the periphery of the case were incorporated specially for Royal Enfield. Since the engine was installed in a duplex frame (designed by Ken Sprayson, of Reynolds, and Geoff Duke) and the exhaust port was inclined 7 degrees to the left, the crankcase was well exposed to the airstream, so good use was made of the extra cooling area provided by those fins.

'Crankcase cooling is vital to two-stroke efficiency,' Meier reminded me. 'We get ample air circulation round the back of the case, too, through the hollow aluminium spacer sandwiched between crankcase and gearbox.'

'What about the Alpha crankshaft assembly?' I asked. 'Flywheel diameter,' I was told, 'is $4\frac{3}{8}$in and the crankpin and both mainshafts are a press fit. On the drive side there is a ball bearing outboard of a caged roller bearing; the other side is supported in a double row of caged rollers. The connecting rod is oval in section, with a caged needle-

This ubiquitous method of retaining the exhaust pipe in its double-wall adaptor allowed enough flexibility to absorb resonance vibration.

roller bearing at the big end and a bronze bush at the top.'

I noticed that both piston rings were of Dykes L-section, noted for the efficiency of their pressure sealing, and asked if it wasn't pointless to fit one of those in the bottom groove as well as the top.

'I don't think so,' Meier reasoned. 'On an aircooled racing two-stroke, piston-land clearance below the top ring is generous and that makes a second Dykes ring worthwhile. You'll see that the top ring is flush with the piston crown; that gives very precise control of the exhaust and transfer ports.'

Next I asked about the combustion chamber, which was shaped like a top hat. 'I first tried that in 1948,' Meier recalled, 'and it has

given me better results than other shapes. Since the diameter of the clearance space is $1\frac{9}{16}$in, that leaves a very effective squish band just over half an inch wide. Also, it is easy to machine the cylindrical recess to close limits for consistent production, and a simple matter to try various compression ratios.'

Nominally, the standard ratio was 12.5:1 (for which the ignition advance was 0.114in) and the head joint was machined to give a squish clearance of 0.030in between the shallow-domed piston crown and the matching band in the head. In practice the ratio varied a shade and the ignition timing would be set between 0.110 and 0.120in to suit.

Ignition on the production engines was by Lucas 6-volt battery and coil. Formed

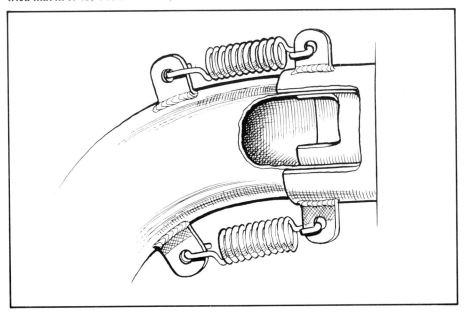

integrally with the right-hand mainshaft, the contact-braker cam gave the rather long dwell (points closed) of 240 degrees, hence ample time for the primary voltage to build up in the coil at top revs. Spark advance was fixed.

Meier was at pains to point out that the engine ran remarkably cool, which came as no surprise for several reasons. First, the 9in-diameter barrel finning got the fin tips well out in the airstream. Second, since the lower head fins measured 8in across, the outermost ½in of the top barrel fin (the one that runs hottest) was exposed to a useful flow of air as a result of the engine's forward lean. Third, the lower three head fins were rooted on the combustion chamber itself, so providing a direct heat path.

Unfortunately, there was no exhaust system handy for examination. 'As you well know,' said Meier, 'it has a crucial influence on engine performance characteristics. The precise dimensions and layout are determined first by involved calculations, then by experiment. Our exhaust comprises a plain (not tapered) primary pipe leading to a double-taper expansion box with a plain tail pipe. The offset of the exhaust port permits a fairly straight layout, crossing over from left to right beneath the engine.'

Later on, I was to learn of the ingenious method by which Meier finalized the length of the tail pipe — using a mouth organ! This instrument was, in fact, a pitch pipe, supplied and calibrated for tuning musical instruments. Now middle C, for example, is produced by a vibration frequency of 256 cycles/second (ie, 15,360 cycles/minute) and this frequency is doubled for each successive higher octave and halved for each successive lower one. Meier calibrated his pitch pipe additionally in these terms, so relating all the notes to engine rpm rates. Then, after mounting an exhaust system in a vice, he blew across the end of the tail pipe and adjusted its length until the note corresponded to an engine speed of 7,500 to 8,000rpm. The result was worth 2bhp at the crankshaft.

The almost inevitable teething troubles were concerned more with the transmission than with the engine, for the Albion gearbox was no real match for the engine's power. A snag arose, however, on the engine side, when it was found that the production exhausts had been made with the primary pipe too small in diameter. Indeed, Percy Tait's prototype development model was alone in having the designed pipe dimensions.

For the Royal Enfield's Isle of Man debut, in the 1964 Manx Grand Prix only four months after the project began, power was 32.5bhp at 8,000rpm (on a compression of 12:1). Part-throttle weakness, which impaired acceleration, was traced to the carburettors having been supplied with non-standard throttle needles and soon rectified; but in the race Dennis Craine's gearbox failed on the first lap, while Neil Kelly went out with a split tank.

Shortly after my visit to the factory (April 1965) engine power was up to 35.5bhp at 8,500rpm and the gearbox had been strengthened. 'As proof of the engine's torque,' Meier told me many years later, 'Tait and Keith pulled higher overall gearing than standard 350cc Manx Nortons in that year's TT. From the rev readings they were getting, I think they could have pulled taller gearing still if suitable sprockets had been available; but in any case riders usually find a bike easier to manage if the gearing is not quite the highest the engine will handle.'

After two laps, Tait was averaging 88.19mph in 10th position before a piston circlip came adrift; Keith retired when a battery cable broke. At the time, both men were well up on Keith's winning average of 86.19mph on a Greeves Silverstone in the previous year's MGP.

Two months later, at the Hutchinson 100 meeting at Silverstone on August 14, 1965, engine development really began to pay off when Tait, starting from the back row of the grid, finished third to the works Yamaha disc-valve twins of Phil Read and Mike Duff — averaging 82.12mph to Read's 83.07.

Besides having the only correct exhaust system, Tait's engine had the carburettor bored 0.020in oversize and an experimental head fitted. This raised the compression to 14.2:1 and housed two 10mm sparking plugs, fired simultaneously by a double-ended coil, triggered electronically for consistent timing (which becomes increasingly critical in a racing two-stroke as output rises). Spark advance was cut back to 0.078in.

'That was the trim in which the engine gave 37.5bhp at 7,200rpm,' Meier told me, 'and the porting was also modified slightly to lessen the fall-off in power beyond the peak of the curve.' (Whereas production engines, with 34bhp at 8,000 to 8,250rpm, ran out of breath rather abruptly at 8,500rpm, Tait's engine would, if need be, run on beyond 9,000rpm without flagging unduly.)

Back in the Manx Grand Prix the following month, Neil Kelly lapped at 89.36mph (only 2 seconds short of the lap record) and was just about to take over second place when the clutch failed on the Snaefell climb.

At the end of the season, to Meier's dismay, the management decided to curtail development, though some standard models were still built. Many years later, reflecting on what might have been with team-manager Geoff Duke and me in a Majorcan coffee bar, Meier produced some figures to justify his faith in the Royal Enfield's potential.

In terms of bhp/litre/1,000rpm, he pointed out, the standard engine's 34bhp at 8,000rpm translated to 17, while Tait's twin-plug engine (37.5bhp at 7,200) raised that figure to 20.8. For comparison, the remarkable Ossa 250cc disc-valve single on which Santiago Herrero gained third place in the 1969 world championship produced 42bhp at 10,000rpm, which is 16.8bhp/litre/1,000rpm.

Where power is the name of the game, of course, Meier is the first to agree that an advantage of 24 per cent in bhp/litre/1,000rpm doesn't pay off so long as the opposition has 39 per cent higher peak revs. The significance of the Enfield's 20.8 was its indication of inherent efficiency, hence the scope for development.

It is easier to add productive rpm to a two-stroke engine of high efficiency than it is to breathe efficiency into a gutless screamer (a description that does *not* apply to the Ossa!). In the first case the problem is largely to keep the big-end and small-end bearings adequately cooled and lubricated. The much more difficult task in the other case is the fundamental and highly specialized one of harnessing the resonances, to use Meier's own descriptive phrase.

The Enfield was not given the chance to fulfil its promise. Considering the progress made in little more than a year, however, it is interesting to speculate what it might have achieved by the time the Ossa was raising our eyebrows four years later.

CHAPTER 15

Twin-camshaft Bandit/Fury

Prototype twin that revealed British design strengths and management
weaknesses in contrast to the Japanese approach

Statistically, the 349cc double-knocker Triumph Bandit (and BSA Fury) engine was the first British parallel-twin four-stroke for nearly 60 years to have the pistons moving in opposite directions (one up, one down). More significantly, it was superior in design to Japanese units of the same type, which had been spearheaded by the 247cc Honda Dream Super Sport a decade before the off-beat British twin was announced for the 1971 ranges. The reason for this technical superiority was simple. The Meriden team — chief development engineer Doug Hele in particular — brought more thought to bear on the layout. Clearly recognizing both the pros and cons, Hele took care fully to exploit the former (chiefly smooth running at high rpm) while minimizing the latter (a rocking couple, uneven firing intervals and crankshaft stress problems). He even took advantage of a peculiarity in the relative camshaft motions to achieve a remarkably simple dismantling drill, of which more later.

The Bandit owed its conception to the gap left in the Triumph range by the demise of the Tiger 90 in 1969. The reason the newcomer flew in the face of established British practice and had out-of-step pistons was that the Tiger 90, with its pistons moving in step, had been unacceptably rough. And not only had the Japanese already popularized out-of-step pistons since 1961, but Hele himself had built an engine of that type soon afterwards, while he was with Norton, and was convinced that was a good way to tame vibration.

That engine was the original prototype for the 349cc Norton Navigator and I well recall my delight on learning of Doug's experiment. For, on borrowing *The Motor Cycle*'s road-test Honda Dream Super Sport late in 1961, I was so impressed by its high-speed smoothness that I decided to write an article advocating a rethink on crank layout. And when I rang round the industry I found Doug Hele was the only engineer amenable to the idea and not mesmerised by Edward Turner's choice of in-step pistons for the

trend-setting (and vibratory) Triumph Speed Twin back in 1938.

The experimental Norton engine, Doug confided on the 'phone, ran so smoothly it hardly needed to be bolted down for bench testing — in complete contrast to the conventional 249cc Jubilee parallel-twin from which it was derived. Alas, the production Navigator was denied the dynamic advantages of 180-degree crank spacing. During road testing, the mixture bias inevitable with widely overlapping inlet phases drawing on a single carburettor caused the weaker-running cylinder to seize. Clearly each cylinder needed its own carburettor (its own exhaust pipe, too) — whereas the existing cylinder-head dies were of single-carb pattern and the high cost of new twin-carb dies was out of the question.

As a fresh design, the Bandit engine escaped that particular restriction — two carbs and separate exhausts were specified from the start. An unfortunate restriction that eventually irked Hele, however, was on overall engine height. Some years earlier at Meriden, shortly before retiring as managing director, Turner himself had carried out a feasibility exercise for a 180-degree parallel-twin. And although that engine proved conclusively that his engineering skills were no match for his undoubted commercial flair (only the 63 × 56mm bore/stroke dimensions survived!) it was not thought politic to alter the overall height. That was a pity because, in the course of development, Doug would have liked to lengthen the valves if he had not already had to lengthen the connecting rods to suit a new crankshaft necessitated by failure of the original during prototype testing.

Before that stage was reached, design work by deputy managing director Bert Hopwood (also as a swansong) and project designer Brian Jones had cut production costs by reducing the number of parts and machining operations. For example, they did away with Turner's split bearings for the camshafts. They also discarded the four

gears linking the shafts, so that mechanical noise was reduced too.

Following contemporary practice in British 360-degree parallel twins, the Bandit's original crankshaft had its flywheel in the middle. But while the diametrically opposed crankpins ensured perfect static balance, their offset either side of the centre plane caused a destructive dynamic imbalance. In other words, when the shaft was spinning, centrifugal force acting on the crankpins tried to bring them into a common plane of rotation. Since the shaft was restrained by the two main bearings (one at each end) this put a tensile stress in the outer crank webs. At high rpm this was sufficient to cause fatigue fractures, hastened by the slightest imperfection in the fillets blending the crankpins into the webs, since such flaws concentrated the stresses there.

(You can demonstrate the difference between static and dynamic balance after turning a pushbike upside-down and removing the chain. The static balance of the crank assembly ensures that the pedals will remain in any set position. But if you spin them briskly the whole machine will squirm as both pedals seek a common rotational plane.)

In place of the plain flywheel, Hele's revised crankshaft had a $2\frac{5}{16}$in-thick inner web incorporating two massive offset bob-weights, diametrically opposed to the crankpins. Centrifugal force acting on the bob-weights tried to bring them, too, into a common plane and that twisting force opposed the one which had caused the trouble. Thus there was a high degree of counterbalancing within the shaft itself, so that the tensile stresses in the outer webs, along with the radial loads on the main bearings, were reduced to acceptable proportions. As an additional precaution, the fillets were rolled after machining, to give a perfectly smooth finish and so increase fatigue resistance.

The new shaft was a one-piece steel forg-

Doug Hele (BSA/Triumph).

ing in which mainshaft diameter was 30mm both sides and crankpin diameter $1\frac{5}{8}$in (as in the 650cc twins and 750cc threes), giving a journal overlap of nearly 8mm. Crankpin width was $1\frac{3}{16}$in, as in the threes; inboard of each pin was a centrifugal sludge trap.

(In view of the much reduced stresses, Hele planned to try a cast-iron version of the new shaft with the object of lowering production costs. But that experiment fell victim to the financial troubles that halted the Bandit/Fury project while 12 prototypes were still undergoing development.)

In theory, a 180-degree parallel-twin four-stroke needs 50 per cent more flywheel effect than does a comparable twin with the pistons moving in step; this is because the longest firing interval to be bridged is 540 degrees in the first case, 360 in the second. In practice, Hele contended this was significant only in engines producing high torque at low revs. With its peak torque of 21lb-ft at 6,800rpm, the Bandit engine was not in that category — and the flywheel effect provided by the robust crankshaft itself was ample.

Supporting the shaft were a 72mm-diameter ball bearing on the drive (right-hand) side and a 62mm-diameter roller bearing on the timing side. The reason for preferring a ball bearing on the side where the loads were heavier was to ensure precise axial location of the shaft for primary chain alignment. On the timing side the smaller overall bearing diameter possible with the roller type permitted closer shaft centres in the 2:1 helical reduction gearing in the first stage of the camshaft drive. (Helical gears were preferred for their relative quietness.)

Forged in Hiduminium RR56, the connecting rods had steel big-end caps, whose chief

advantage was that they halved the unwanted increase in diametral clearance as the bearings heated up. (Any consequent lack of circularity was entirely insignificant.) Other benefits were that steel caps could be made smaller, had greater beam strength and were less likely to fidget on the nuts. The split bearing shells were steel-backed lead-bronze. At the top, the rods bore directly on the $\frac{5}{8}$in-diameter, taper-bored gudgeon pins.

The lengthening of the rods (to $4\frac{3}{4}$in between centres) was necessary to prevent the piston skirts from fouling the bobweights on the middle web of the new crankshaft, since these were of much larger radius than those on the outer webs. As a result, the Bandit's rods were 4.3 times the length of the crank throw (L = 4.3R in engineering terms) whereas 4R is commonly regarded as average (ie, twice stroke length).

An advantage of long rods is that they reduce mid-stroke angularity, thereby lessening both the intensity of high-frequency secondary vibration and the cyclic fluctuation in big-end rotational speed as the rod swings backward on the crankpin at top dead centre and forward at bottom dead centre. (The latter problem is not significant with plain big ends, only with rollers.) But when I discussed rod length with Doug Hele I was interested to learn of his preference for *short* rods in engines where high torque at low rpm is a prime requirement — which it was not in the Bandit. By bringing the piston down more rapidly from tdc, Doug reasoned, the short rod achieved a mechanically advantageous angle with the crank in time to make more effective use of the rapid and brief build-up in combustion pressure.

Back to the Bandit, the pistons were sand-cast in aluminium alloy, with full skirts and flat crowns giving a compression ratio of 9.8:1 for four-star petrol. Below the two compression rings was a three-part oil scraper comprising two thin rails separated and expanded by a special spring. Drain holes were drilled both in the bottom of the groove and in the reduced land below it.

Held down by eight long $\frac{3}{8}$in-diameter studs (and three short $\frac{1}{4}$in screws at the base of the integral cam-chain tunnel), the cylinder block was cast in high-duty light alloy. It had rectangular finning and ample air space both between the cylinders and behind the chain tunnel.

In the first engines the cast-iron liners were corrugated externally and cast in the block; but this method was soon changed for the slightly more expensive one of machining the liners on the outside and shrinking them in machined bores in the block. There were three reasons for the change. First, in production it was difficult to control the

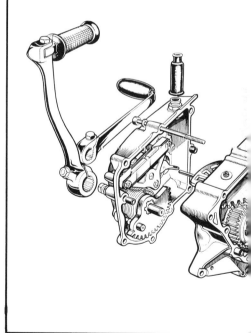

The casing for the five-speed gear cluster was integral with the left-side crankcase half, the primary chaincase with the right-side half. The cylinder axes were only $3\frac{1}{8}$in apart. The grooves across the crankshaft bobweights were for locating the shaft for ignition timing

after removing a left-side crankcase plug. The contact breaker was driven by the right-hand end of the exhaust camshaft. Note the catchment in the top of the primary chain cover for lubrication of the bottom chain run at the most effective point.

Motor Cycle
copyright

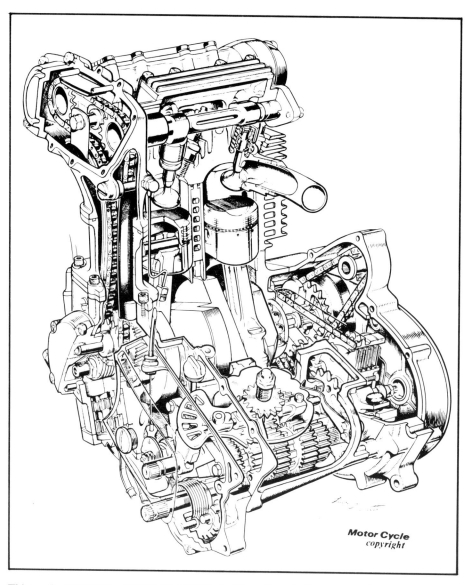

This sectioned drawing shows both pistons at mid-stroke – the left one moving downward, the other upward – also the air spaces beneath the cam boxes, behind the cam-chain tunnel and between the cylinders. Mean piston speed was a modest 3,300ft/min at the 9,000rpm peak. Maximum safe engine speed was 10,500rpm. The chain outboard of the primary drive was for the starter motor. This (earlier) drawing does not show the crankcase-breather adaptor at the top of the primary drive cover.

supported them close up to the cams; diameter of the left-side bearing was no less than $1\frac{5}{8}$in. Axial location of the shafts was by a double-forked plate engaging in grooves, whose clearance was critical in reducing mechanical noise.

Seating on sintered, iron-alloy rings shrunk in the part-spherical combustion chambers, the valves had a symmetrical included angle of 60 degrees, giving a compact clearance volume in the interests of a good torque spread and minimum heat loss.

The quick-lift cams actuated the valves through inverted cups, crowned to reduce clatter. Valve closure was by duplex coil springs inside the cups. For adjustment of the valve clearances (0.006in inlet, 0.010in exhaust) stem-tip shims, located in upward extensions of the split collets, were available in 0.002in steps. Unscrewing plugs from the inner walls of the cam boxes provided access for feeler gauges.

(Many years later, with hindsight, I asked Doug Hele if the valve gear couldn't have been made still quieter and maintenance-free by substituting finger-type cam followers, on hydraulic fulcrums, for the inverted buckets. He agreed, but pointed out that, at the time of the Bandit's design, such features were in the distant future of motorcycle engineering and would have required a long development programme.)

Made in appropriate grades of nickel-chrome steel (EN52 inlet, 21 4N exhaust), all valves had 0.3in-diameter stems supported in cast-iron guides. Throat diameters were $1\frac{5}{32}$in inlet and 1in exhaust. Lift in both cases was 0.332in; and although overall cam size was governed by the need to thread the shafts through the left-side bearings, no problem was foreseen in accommodating higher-lift camshafts for racing — either by machining grooves in the bearings to clear the cam peaks or by reducing the cam base circles or both.

The curved induction stubs were screwed into the ports and locked at the correct angle by large ring nuts. Rubber hoses and worm-drive clips attached the 26mm-choke Amal Concentric carburettors. The exhaust pipes were pulled up against copper sealing rings.

Keyed to the crankshaft, hard against the roller main bearing, were (first) the small helical timing gear, then the worm wheel to drive the duplex gear-type oil pump. Combined with the larger helical gear was the cam-drive sprocket from which the endless, $\frac{3}{8}$in-pitch, flat-sided roller chain ran up to the inlet shaft, then forward to the exhaust before returning, over the curved adjustable tensioner, to the driving sprocket.

Thrashing in the first and second runs was damped by steel strips with hard synthetic-

position of the liners in the block with sufficient accuracy while the metal was poured. Second, it was much easier to machine the lower face of the block without the liners protruding. Finally, good heat transfer from liners to muff was more predictable with shrinking than with casting.

Since the Bandit's cam drive was on one side, the cylinders were much closer spaced (at $3\frac{1}{8}$in between centres) than in Japanese versions of comparable size with the cam drive and two more main bearings in the middle. Thus the magnitude of the rocking couple was greatly reduced. A further bonus

for the Bandit in this respect was the stabilizing gyroscopic effect of the massive middle portion of the crankshaft, as compared with that from four tiny Oriental flywheels.

The cylinder-head joints were sealed by S-section copper rings seating in annular grooves surrounding the liners while a rubber ring, also in a groove, sealed the top of the chain tunnel.

Cast in the same material as the block, the cylinder head incorporated the cam boxes. Indeed, the hollow camshafts (which had integral 16-tooth sprockets) bore directly in plain holes in both sides of the casting, which

Secret of the quick-dismantling drill. At one mid-stroke position every two crankshaft revolutions all valves in the Bandit/Fury engine were closed for 60 degrees, hence the camshafts were unloaded and could be withdrawn easily (top diagram). There is no such period in a parallel twin with 360-degree crank spacing (bottom).

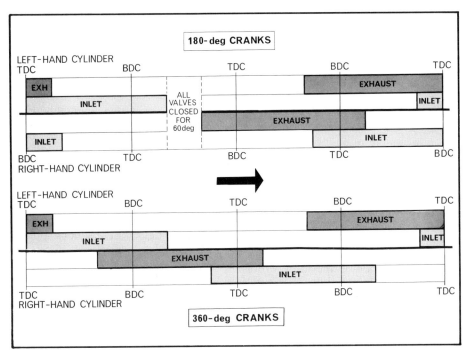

With the cranks spaced at 180 degrees, the primary (but not the much smaller secondary) inertia forces cancel out. The magnitude of the resulting rocking couple depends on the spacing of the cylinders.

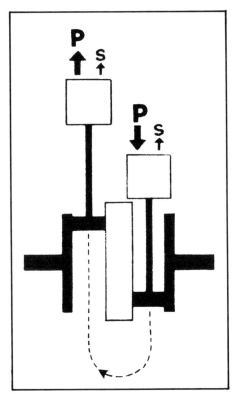

rubber facings bonded on. The rear strip dangled from a bolt in the cylinder head and had a rubber buffer at the bottom; the top strip located in grooves in the sprocket cover. Pivoted at the bottom, the tensioner blade had its hard-rubber facing riveted on; the slotted top mounting was locked by the bolt that secured the camshaft-retaining plate.

The secret of Hele's quick-dismantling drill was a 60-degree period when all valves were closed, so that both camshafts were free from valve-spring pressure. As the valve-phase diagram shows, this occurred around mid-stroke with the left-hand piston rising on compression and the other descending on the firing stroke. (There is no such period where the pistons move in step.)

With all valves closed it needed only the withdrawal of the bolt from the tensioner slots for the blade to swing down, giving enough slack for the chain to be lifted off the camshaft sprockets; the retaining plate then came away, leaving the camshafts free to be withdrawn. Thus head and block removal was simpler than with a pushrod twin.

Furthermore it was possible to set the valve clearances with the head off the engine, although they could not be corrected without withdrawing the camshafts. That was of little consequence, however — the need for adjustment was rare with so few points of contact to wear and the rubbing areas large and swamped in oil.

At 9,000rpm, the oil (SAE20-50) was circulated at a rate of 25 gallons an hour — ample for cooling and lubrication without wasting power through excessive drag. Normal running temperature was 80 to 90 degrees C.

From the tank, the delivery gears drew oil past an anti-siphon ball valve and pumped it through a full-flow paper filter into the timing cover, where a relief valve limited the pressure to 70 to 80psi. The main feed from there was into the end of the crankshaft

(sealed by a synthetic-rubber garter) for the big ends, cylinders and pistons. A small jet squirted oil on to the worm gears while the remaining two feeds were to the spindle supporting the larger helical gear and, through an external pipe, to a banjo connection on the cylinder head.

Drillways took the oil from there to both left-side camshaft bearings, from which it was metered into the shafts to emerge from the cam base circles before draining from the cup guides and cam boxes into the chain tunnel.

To prevent an accumulation of oil in the sump, the scavenge gears were 60 per cent wider than the delivery gears. A long, tongued coupling at the top of the oil-pump shaft drove the revmeter.

On the crankshaft, just outboard of the ball main bearing, were the $\frac{3}{8}$in-duplex primary drive sprocket (splined), the driven sprocket in the electric-starter drive (on needle rollers) and the Lucas 12-volt, 120-watt RM21 alternator (keyed). The reduction-gear housing for the starter spigoted into the back of the primary chaincase, while the left-hand end of the motor itself was clamped to the crankcase. Total reduction in the epicyclic gearing and the single-strand chain drive to the sprag clutch on the outer face of the engine sprocket was 14:1.

A special contact breaker was called for, with the points spaced 90 (and 270) degrees apart. This was situated at the right-hand end of the exhaust camshaft where, for greater accuracy, the auto-advance unit was clamped to a parallel extension of the shaft

The ill-fated 350cc double-knocker engine installed in the BSA Fury chassis.

In the original crankshaft (below) fatigue fractures in the outer webs resulted from tensile stress at high rpm as the offset crankpins sought a common plane of rotation under centrifugal force. In the revised crankshaft (bottom) this centrifugal effect was largely neutralized by the opposing effect of the bobweights on the middle web. This crankshaft was virtually a 360-degree one, with large central counterweight, split down the middle and twisted through 180 degrees.

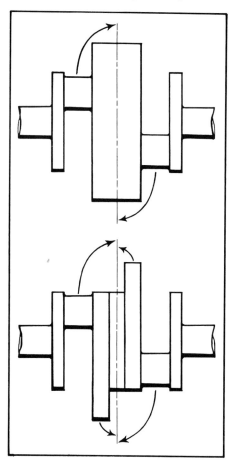

and driven by a peg rather than taper-driven in the usual way.

With its volume practically constant, crankcase breathing was naturally easier than if the pistons had moved in unison. In Meriden fashion, the case breathed through the drive-side main bearing into the primary chaincase where, from an adaptor in the cover, the fumes were led to the air filter.

There was nothing haphazard about primary chain lubrication, oil flung around the case being collected in a catchment at the top and drained through a pipe to drip on the bottom run, just behind the engine sprocket.

The five-plate clutch incorporated a vane-type rubber shock absorber in the hub and was withdrawn by the customary three-ball ramp mechanism. Five speeds were chosen with an eye to racing as well as fashion; since the engine had a good spread of torque, there was no point in considering more. A 3-degree undercut on the flanks of the dogs prevented the gears from slipping out of engagement. Support for the mainshaft comprised two ball bearings, and for the layshaft two needle rollers. Lubricant was EP80 oil.

The internal ratios were 1, 1.156, 1.413, 1.872 and 2.7:1. Overall gearing had not been finalized, but would probably have been around 6.7:1 in top. At the time of my original analysis (*Motor Cycle*, February 3, 1971) top speed was 104mph, while the engine gave 34bhp at 9,000rpm on test.

Alas for the most exciting British engine since the 750cc BSA/Triumph three, the Bandit/Fury twin was killed in the middle of prototype development. While the accountants blithely imagined they could solve their financial problems by rushing straight into production, their timescale was unrealistic to say the least. Several problems had still to be licked, tooling was incomplete and there was no short cut to stocking the dealers' showrooms. Money and time ran out.

For the most part, the Japanese reverted to in-step pistons for their parallel-twins once they rediscovered crankshaft-driven balance shafts patented by Dr Fred Lanchester at the turn of the century. They could have saved themselves the switch by giving their 180-degree versions the calibre of thought that went into the Bandit power plant.

CHAPTER 16

Six-cylinder Honda CBX

Classic example of a supremely successful lightweight grand-prix configuration that failed to survive the transition to heavyweight roadster

Of the three manufacturers who sought prestige through big six-abreast roadsters (Benelli, Honda and Kawasaki in that order) Honda could at least claim to have achieved racing successes at the highest level (more than a decade earlier) with engines of the same basic configuration. Any such claim, however, was more of an advertising ploy than a technical justification for the 1,047cc CBX roadster. For the CBX, however handsome and smooth-running, was high and wide with it and so sacrificed some measure of chuckability, especially as it scaled nearly 600lb on the road.

The racing six, on the contrary, was not only light but also a masterpiece of miniaturization, no wider across the fairing flanks than contemporary singles of the same capacity. Consequently the engine could be slung much lower to the benefit of nimble handling.

Unlike the massive CBX, Honda's 250cc racer virtually had six cylinders thrust upon it by the rapidly advancing two-stroke technology of the mid-1960s. With the two-stroke's established superiority in bhp/litre/1,000rpm, Yamaha's air-cooled, disc-valve parallel twin (virtually an Oriental MZ) had extended Honda's once-invincible 14,000rpm double-knocker four to the limit of its speed potential and found it wanting. The only way within the FIM rules for the four-stroke to offset the two-stroke's built-in advantage was to raise peak rpm by using smaller cylinders, hence more of them.

Starting late in 1964 with 54bhp at 16,000rpm, the resulting 24-valve engine needed only Mike Hailwood's masterly touch on the twistgrip and a pretty rapid power hike to 60bhp to restore Honda's superiority in emphatic fashion — though Yamaha soon narrowed the gap with their more-powerful but mettlesome water-cooled V-four.

In 1966, Hailwood's dominance of both the Lightweight 250cc TT and the class world championship was little short of contemptuous. In the 350cc class, too, the engine's inherent merit was underlined. Bored and stroked from 39 × 34.5mm (249cc) to 41 × 37.5mm (only 297cc) it shrugged off its 53cc deficit for Mike to beat Giacomo Agostini's 12-valve MV Agusta three for that world title as well, though the 65bhp Honda's early retirement from the Junior TT (with faulty ignition and a sticking valve) handed Ago that prestigious race on a plate.

The following year (1967) brought even greater glory to Honda's sweet-revving six when Hailwood retained both the 250 and 350cc world championships after scoring walkovers in the relevant two TT races.

Four world individual titles and three TT victories in two years had amply proved Honda's prowess in six-cylinder technology — and the incomparable melody of those half-dozen megaphones in high-pitch unison lingered in the memories of grand-prix racegoers for years after Honda quit the classic scene at the end of 1967. Notwithstanding the family likeness in the CBX engine, however, the technology didn't translate too readily because of the vast difference in emphasis between the two designs.

Whereas the problem of width had been surmountable in the 250cc racer, each 64.5mm cylinder bore in the CBX engine was an inch wider; the plain crankshaft bearings were wider too, as was the primary drive from the middle of the crankshaft to the jackshaft behind the crankcase — by inverted-tooth chain for quietness.

In the racer, power was all-important and there was room enough to arrange the six carburettors parallel to one another, each dead in the centre plane of its cylinder for equal flow through the two inlet valves. Not so in the CBX, where the 28mm constant-vacuum carburettors were at knee height and the two clusters of three had to be canted inward to clear the rider's legs.

In a four-valve cylinder head, an inlet tract angled in this way tends to favour the remote valve (the outer one in this case) at the expense of the nearer one — though the four-valver's bonus of relative freedom from valve float is unaffected (the CBX valve gear was safe to 10,300rpm). Fortunately, the compromise on cylinder filling was unimportant in a 1-litre touring engine producing 105bhp at 9,000rpm. Indeed, if the CBX engine had matched the 250cc racer for specific power (bhp/litre) it would have delivered well over 200bhp!

Crankcase width was trimmed not only by mounting the generator and electronic ignition unit, respectively, on the left and right ends of the short jackshaft, rather than on the crankshaft ends, but also by chamfering both end crank webs. The CBX was the first catalogued Honda with transistorized ignition; and to prevent backlash in the primary drive from affecting the spark timing, the chain was automatically tensioned by a blade under the bottom run actuated by a spring-loaded plunger with hydraulic damping.

Because of the high inertia of the heavy generator and the absence of a flywheel on the (fully counterweighted) crankshaft, the generator drive incorporated a slipping clutch (a spring-loaded pair of friction plates) to protect the jackshaft and primary drive from the effects of violent acceleration or deceleration. Incidentally, a more powerful generator and larger-capacity battery were standardized on the later B model to cure the undercharging inevitable when a high-performance machine is habitually run at low rpm with plenty of use of the lights.

The cam drive, by two inverted-tooth chains, started from a narrow sprocket just to the right of the primary drive sprocket. Each camshaft was in stiff left and right halves, united by Oldham (tongued) couplings. The first chain drove the exhaust camshafts while the other (shorter) chain took the drive back from there to the inlet shafts; the revmeter was driven by the right-hand exhaust shaft.

Both chains were tensioned by spring-loaded blades of semi-automatic type, in

A picture to recall a 16,000rpm symphony of sound as Jim Redman (left) and Mike Hailwood play a total of 12 trumpets to an appreciative Hockenheim audience during the 1966 West German 250cc GP.

The remarkably slim 249/297cc grand-prix engine that established Honda's prowess in six-cylinder technology with four world championships for Mike Hailwood.

One of the most exciting sights and sounds in the long history of the Isle of Man TT – Mike Hailwood swinging his Honda six to an emphatic victory in the 1967 Lightweight 250cc event. The subsequent dominance of the two-stroke has robbed the races of incomparably sweet music.

Schematic drawing of an early Honda four-valve racing layout showing (inset) the bifurcated inlet port. For optimum cylinder filling the inlet tract needs to be square to the two valves, not angled to one side.

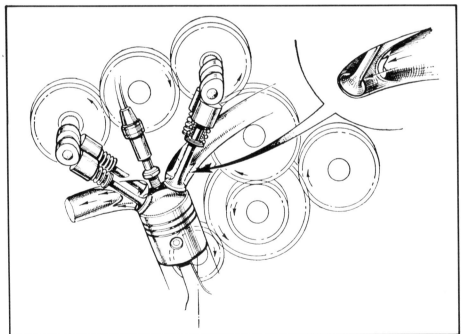

butterflies and a diaphragm-type accelerator pump on the third float bowl from the left fed all tracts.

Mounted above the five-speed, all-indirect gearbox, the starter motor drove through the usual double reduction to a large-diameter thin gear in the middle of the jackshaft. To the right of that gear, the pinion that drove the drum of the wet multiplate clutch incorporated an anti-rattle device; this comprised a thin toothed ring spring-loaded against the left-hand face of the pinion itself, but having one tooth fewer. Since the toothed ring also meshed with the clutch-drum gear, the effect was to resist rapid changes in the direction of backlash and so damp out chatter.

From a sump holding 5½ litres (9.6 pints) of oil, two trochoid-type pumps lubricated the engine, clutch and five-speed gear cluster, with return by gravity. At 4,000rpm the total oil supply was said to circulate 16 times a minute, hence the provision of an oil radiator. The major circuit forced oil through a disposable filter on the front of the crankcase, into the crankshaft and up to the camshafts, where plates collected the oil in troughs for the cams and their followers. The second circuit, having three-quarters the flow rate of the first, fed the damper for the primary chain tensioner, the bar that sprayed the underside of the top run, the gearbox and the oil cooler (whence it drained to the sump).

which release of a locknut enabled the spring to take up any backlash that may have developed. The shorter chain had a rubbing strip on the top run to prevent flutter. Customary inverted buckets transmitted cam motion directly to the valve stems; the return springs were wound in two different pitches to give a twin-rate effect.

With small squish segments front and rear, the piston crowns were flat for most of their area and gave a compression ratio of 9.3:1. The connecting rods were short enough to require the sides of the piston skirts to be shortened appreciably to clear the crankshaft balance weights.

A central cable controlled all six throttle

Status symbol – the 1,047cc straight-six CBX roadster. The ungainly width of the engine necessitated canting the two clusters of carburettors inward – a lesser evil than amputating the customers' knees!

Contributing to the engine's width were cylinder bores of more than $2\frac{1}{2}$ in each, six plain big-end bearings, seven plain mains and inverted-tooth transmission and cam chains. To save some width the generator and ignition unit were on the ends of the shorter jackshaft, not the crankshaft, while the end crank webs were chamfered. Note the anti-rattle ring on the inner face of the clutch-drive gear and the friction drive to the alternator. The starter motor (above the five-speed gearbox) drove the jackshaft through double reduction gearing. The valve springs were twin-rate and the piston skirts shortened to clear the crank webs. The camshafts were in right and left halves; note the revmeter drive in the middle of the right-hand exhaust shaft.

What with its mechanical complexity and the need to balance the six carburettors with pressure gauges, the CBX earned no laurels for servicing. Produced on only a small scale, it was imported into the UK from the beginning of 1978 until April 1982, during which period only a few modifications were made, chiefly to surpress mechanical noise. Despite its illustrious track ancestry, it was not every rider's cup of tea.

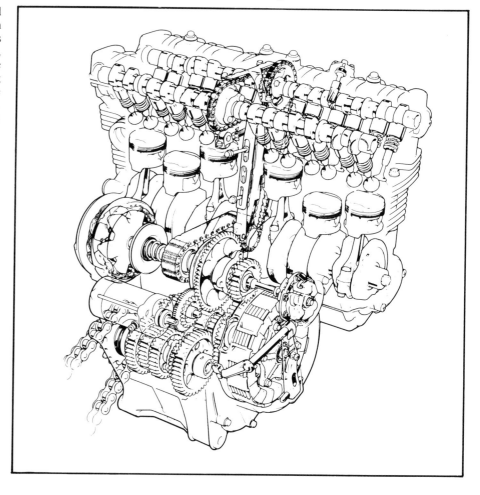

118

CHAPTER 17

Prototype NSU Wankel

Bold and revolutionary rotary-piston engine of immense charm, born
too late and scuppered by rocketing oil prices

With Wankel interest now in a relatively low key, it is difficult to recapture the devastating effect of NSU's disclosure of their revolutionary rotary-piston engine as 1959 took its leave and ushered in a promising new decade. Throughout the industrialized world, wherever internal-combustion engines were made, the tantalizing new prospect was hailed on the one hand with an enthusiasm befitting the invention of perpetual motion, yet bluntly denounced on the other by hard-headed sceptics.

The hopefuls claimed that the reciprocating engine was at best a triumph of development over design — vibratory and clattery, too. Eagerly they predicted its demise and quoted the 29bhp at 17,000-18,000rpm of NSU's first 125cc Wankel prototype. Pragmatic engineers retorted that the engine's capacity was really 375cc, since its three working compartments — regardless of sharing the same sparking plug and porting — were simultaneously carrying out different phases of the four-stroke cycle. (As we shall see, the capacity argument is futile from both standpoints.)

The sceptics' main stand, however, was simply that so many rotary engines had been designed and come to nought that the Wankel, notwithstanding its promise of unprecedented smoothness and mechanical quietness, could safely be dismissed as yet another forlorn hope. As Harry Mundy (then *Autocar's* technical editor, later Jaguar's chief engineer) told me: 'Con-rods were good enough for my father and grandfather before me and they're good enough for me.'

Some measure of the Wankel's initial impact was the alacrity with which the world's automotive giants —such as General Motors, Daimler-Benz, Curtiss-Wright, Toyo-Kogyo (Mazda), Citroen, Fichtel and Sachs, Suzuki, Yanmar Diesel, Outboard Marine Corporation, Rolls-Royce and others — hedged their bets by shelling out vast sums of money for licences to manufacture and develop the new engine for every

conceivable application. If the end of the road was in sight for the reciprocating engine, they all wanted a part of the new action.

Within a relatively few years the Wankel was into cars, motorcycles, aircraft (including models), snowmobiles, outboards, chainsaws, military auxiliaries, heavy compressors, gas engines, generators, indeed industrial engines of all sorts. In size it ranged from the 4.9cc of the single-rotor Graupner model-plane engine, producing 0.6bhp at 16,000rpm, to the 41 litres (yes, 41,000cc!) of the twin-rotor Ingersoll-Rand natural-gas engine, giving 1,000bhp at 1,000rpm.

But it was the deeply entrenched vested interests in the reciprocating engine and its production technology — as much as the Wankel's inherent problems of gas sealing, ignition and thirst (highlighted by repeated explosions in crude-oil prices) — that eventually brought the Wankel down to earth.

Early in 1960, however — notwithstanding the 600cc parallel-twin Prinz car they were also producing — NSU owed their sky-high reputation almost entirely to their motorcycling achievements: spectacular world road-racing championships, speed records galore, advanced streamlining and cam gear, and production of a high-quality range of mopeds, scooters, roadsters and racers. Naturally, therefore, when artist Vic Berris and I flew to Stuttgart to be met by Dr Walter Froede, imaginative chief of NSU's research department, I automatically envisaged a new range of two-wheelers as flag bearers for the Wankel engine.

As it turned out, NSU never produced a rotary-engine motorcycle; that was left mostly to Suzuki (single-rotor RE5), Hercules (single-rotor W2000, marketed as a DKW in Britain) and Norton (twin-rotor Interpol 2), while Van Veen put a Comotor (Citroen-NSU) twin-rotor car engine in their limited-production OCR1000. (The Yamaha twin-rotor RZ201 seemingly got no farther than the Tokyo Show.) All Wankel-powered NSUs had four wheels — first (in

1960) a Prinz 3 chassis fitted with an experimental engine of 250cc giving 30bhp; then, four years later, the first production model, the Spider sports two-seater with 500cc and 50bhp; and finally, another four years on, the 115bhp twin-rotor Ro80 saloon voted Car of the Year by both *Car* and *Autovisie* magazines.

But all those developments were far in the future when Dr Froede shepherded me into his research department. Indeed, even if my crystal ball had told me of NSU's impending switch to cars, my enthusiasm would have been undimmed; so radical was the Wankel concept that it was the engine alone that fascinated me, almost regardless of the use to which it would be put.

At the time of my visit there was widespread misunderstanding of the way the engine worked. Angry that their secret, painstaking developments of several years past had just become public knowledge — through a premature disclosure by Curtiss-Wright, the first American licensees — NSU had issued a hurriedly prepared press release, which itself was far from accurate, thus compounding the general guesswork. Indeed, confusion as to the Wankel's workings was nothing new to NSU, for some countries' patent offices had rejected their applications as impracticable and had to be convinced by working models (one of which I still possess).

Mechanically, no internal-combustion engine could have been simpler for there were only two moving parts — the output shaft and a three-flank rotor that delivered power impulses to an eccentric boss formed on the middle of the shaft (this boss corresponding to the crank in a reciprocating engine). But the internal *shape* of the rotor housing containing the ports and sparking plug, though resembling a very dumpy figure eight, was far from simple except to a geometrician; likewise the precise shape of the rotor; and the way in which it advanced by one flank on its own axis for each revolution of the output shaft while orbiting

119

the housing in such a manner as to keep all three apexes in constant contact with the housing wall, thus isolating each chamber from its neighbours.

Eager that my analysis in *The Motor Cycle* should dispel all misconceptions, Dr Froede first baffled me by asserting that the engine's housing shape was a two-lobe epitrochoid, then introduced me to the esoteric world of cycloids and trochoids in all their varieties.

If, like me, you are cursed with an over-dose of intellectual masochism, you too can put your sanity at risk by tracing this family of geometric curves with the aid of scissors, cardboard, drawing pins, pencil and a pair of compasses until a man in a white coat comes to take you away in a plain van.

Suffice it to say that a cycloid can be traced by rolling a circle along a straight line. If you choose the centre of the circle as your tracing point you will, of course, merely draw another straight line (parallel to the base line). But if the tracing point is eccentric (*ie,* between the centre and circumference of the circle) you will draw a wavy line called a prolate cycloid.

Move the tracing point to the circumference and you will get a series of humps similar to the path of any point in the middle of a rolling tyre tread (this is called a common cycloid). Now extend any radius of the circle beyond the circumference and choose a tracing point on that extension and your humps will be linked by overlapping loops (curtate cycloid).

Suppose we now substitute a base circle for the base line. Clearly we can roll a free circle round the outside or the inside of the base circle; either way, if we again choose the centre of the rolling circle as our tracing point we shall merely describe another (concentric) circle. If we use an eccentric tracing point, however, the figure we produce is a trochoid — an *epitrochoid* if the rolling is external, a *hypotrochoid* if it is internal.

The ratio of circle diameters determines the number of lobes in the epitrochoid (or the number of sides on the hypotrochoid). And for a given type of figure the precise shape depends on the ratio of radius to eccentricity in the rolling circle. For a two-lobe epitrochoid (as in the Wankel engine) the diameter of the rolling circle must be half that of the base circle; and the smaller the eccentricity relative to the radius the less pronounced is the epitrochoid's waist. (In practice, the shape is a compromise between overall engine size, combustion-chamber shape, compression ratio, output-shaft diameter, centrifugal loading on the apex seals and their angularity on the housing wall).

So much for the shape of the rotor housing; what of the rotor itself? Technically its shape is known as the epitrochoid's inner envelope, which is the figure inside the area swept by the epitrochoid when the functions of the fixed and rolling circles are interchanged.

As to the rotor's orbiting-cum-spinning motion, the first of these (orbiting) is clearly imparted by the eccentric on the revolving output shaft. The rotor's forward rotation on its own axis, however, comes from male-and-female gearing. In one side of the rotor bore (alongside the bearing track) is an internally toothed gear that meshes with a stationary gear having two-thirds the number of teeth and fixed to the inner face of the adjacent housing wall. It is this 3:2 ratio that advances the rotor by one flank for each orbit, thus bringing it back to its original attitude every three turns of the output shaft.

Of the countless combinations investigated by Felix Wankel and Dr Froede, the two-lobe epitrochoid and three-flank rotor was the one that best suited the four-stroke cycle, with the inlet port feeding one lobe, the exhaust port scavenging the other, the plug in the opposite side of the housing and all three compartments constantly varying in volume to take care of induction, compression, expansion and exhaust.

At a superficial glance a three-flank hypotrochoid (traced by rolling a one-third-diameter circle round the inside of the base circle) and its outer envelope (the figure it sweeps when the circle functions are interchanged) looks substantially similar to the Wankel layout. A closer look shows why this combination is unsuitable, however: the rotor apexes are rounded, not pointed, hence the contact points move back and forth and cannot be sealed.

Building that first 125cc experimental engine was a protracted affair. Not only had all the geometric variables to be explored and tooling, jigs, test rigs and techniques to be developed; but also the layout of the engine itself was a ghastly complication compared with all its successors.

Meanwhile, to maintain interest and check rotor sealing, a two-lobe Wankel compressor was improvised. On test this proved superior to all known types, producing pressures up to 120psi and giving NSU a commercial safety net should the engine not make the grade. Operating at well under half capacity (*ie,* 40-45psi) that compressor boosted the power of a modified Quickly moped engine from 1.6 to 13bhp, thereby enabling Hermann Müller to push the world 50cc record beyond 122mph in a fully streamlined NSU 'flying hammock' at Utah in 1956.

The reason for the extraordinary complexity of the original engine was Felix Wankel's insistence on a purely rotary motion for the rotor (no orbiting) so that sealing efficiency should not be compromised by the reversal of centrifugal loading on the apex seals as they negotiated the housing waist. This meant arranging for both rotor and housing to spin on separate axes in the same direction and at different speeds, connected by 2:3 external gearing.

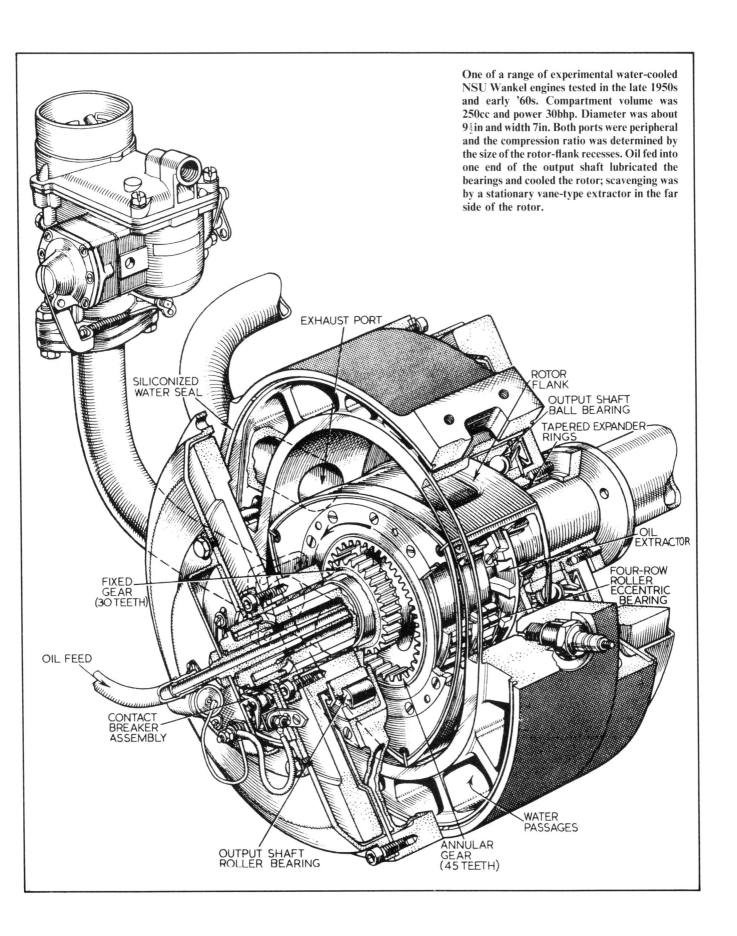

One of a range of experimental water-cooled NSU Wankel engines tested in the late 1950s and early '60s. Compartment volume was 250cc and power 30bhp. Diameter was about $9\frac{1}{2}$ in and width 7in. Both ports were peripheral and the compression ratio was determined by the size of the rotor-flank recesses. Oil fed into one end of the output shaft lubricated the bearings and cooled the rotor; scavenging was by a stationary vane-type extractor in the far side of the rotor.

EXHAUST PORT

SILICONIZED WATER SEAL

ROTOR FLANK

OUTPUT SHAFT BALL BEARING

TAPERED EXPANDER RINGS

OIL EXTRACTOR

FOUR-ROW ROLLER ECCENTRIC BEARING

FIXED GEAR (30 TEETH)

OIL FEED

CONTACT BREAKER ASSEMBLY

OUTPUT SHAFT ROLLER BEARING

ANNULAR GEAR (45 TEETH)

WATER PASSAGES

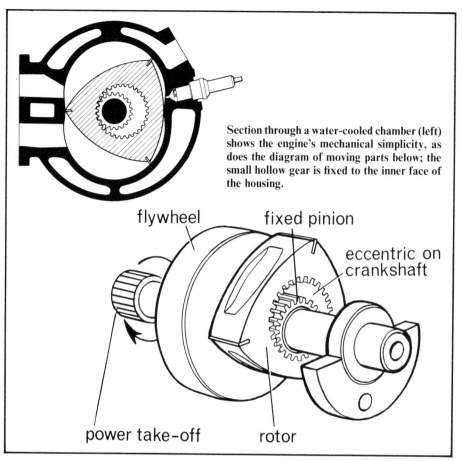

Section through a water-cooled chamber (left) shows the engine's mechanical simplicity, as does the diagram of moving parts below; the small hollow gear is fixed to the inner face of the housing.

flywheel

fixed pinion

eccentric on crankshaft

power take-off

rotor

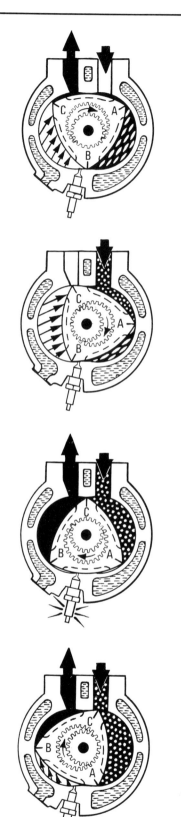

The price paid for this simplified seal loading was a nightmare of induction, exhaust and ignition systems. Mixture from the carburettor was fed into one end of the hollow rotor shaft, through ports in the rotor sides and transfer passages in the housing sides to the working compartments. Exhaust gases escaped through a peripheral port in the housing into the annular space between it and the fixed outer casing. And in the middle of each rotor flank was a sparking plug fed from a slip-ring on the other end of the shaft. Power was taken from the gearing counter-shaft running at housing speed.

Red letter day for that precious contraption was February 1, 1957. First it was motored round to check breathing efficiency and mechanical losses; then it was shut in a safety tunnel and buzzed round at an unprecedented 25,000rpm — happily without

How it works. Different phases of the four-stroke cycle take place simultaneously in the three rotating compartments. Since the bore of the rotor bears on an eccentric boss on the output shaft, successive power impulses on the rotor flanks turn the shaft, while the 3:2 gearing advances the rotor by one flank for each orbit of the chamber.

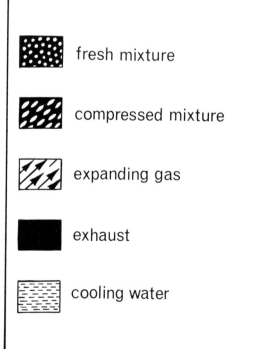

fresh mixture

compressed mixture

expanding gas

exhaust

cooling water

disintegrating. Finally, amid considerable trepidation, it was set to run under its own power. All tension evaporated as it howled up the scale to produce 29bhp at 17,000-18,000rpm, a brake mean effective pressure of 125psi at 8,000rpm and a specific fuel consumption of 0.55 pints/bhp/hour — all encouraging figures for the first test of such a revolutionary device.

Elation notwithstanding, however, there were two obvious snags. First, the engine's extreme complexity ruled it out for commercial production. Second, its operating speed was much too high for any road vehicle (whether two-wheeled or four) — posing problems not only in overall gearing but, more particularly, in accessory drives.

The enormous simplification of a stationary housing and a planetary rotor motion not only swept away the complicated induction, exhaust and ignition layouts; it also provided another incentive for lowering engine speed (through port areas and timings) since the rotor no longer had a simple motion around a fixed axis.

Felix Wankel was bitterly opposed to the change. His apex seals had proved equal to combustion pressures and he feared they might perform less well when subjected to continuously fluctuating centrifugal loading — they might even lose contact with the housing wall as the loading was momentarily reversed at the housing waist.

Firmly overruling these objections, Dr Froede supervised the design (by Dipl Ing Paschke) of the first planetary engine, of identical capacity and geometry. Completed in 1958, it brought a crop of headaches. Insofar as the seals gave no trouble, Wankel's fears proved groundless; but power was down, oil consumption heavy, the exhaust smoky and the plain eccentric bearing showed signs of tightening.

The power loss was traced to poor positioning of the plug (in the leading half of the combustion space) and the use of a small side inlet port with poor timing. In subsequent experiments, combustion was improved by moving the plug to the trailing half of the combustion chamber, so that the advancing rotor apex squirted the rapidly expanding gases violently through the shallow rotor-flank recess into the leading half, thereby creating turbulence and enhancing burning. Some Wankel engines (notably in Mazda cars) have two plugs per chamber, one in each half, with differential timing. In either case, since a conventional plug hole in the housing wall would allow the burning gases in one compartment to leak back over the passing apex seal into the compressed charge in the following compartment, it is usual to recess Wankel plugs and connect them to the combustion chamber by a very

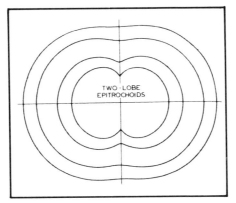

TWO-LOBE EPITROCHOIDS

narrow hole, as Gilera did in their grand-prix fours in the mid-1950s.

As to the inlet port, a peripheral location gave much better breathing and boosted bmep to 157psi at 5,500rpm (in an early 250cc engine) even on low-grade petrol. A side inlet was found to use the fuel more economically, however, because there was less direct loss to the exhaust port during the overlap period; naturally, the smaller the port area the lower in the rev scale was peak torque developed.

The cause of the heavy oil consumption was pinpointed equally quickly. In the original engine, both rotor and housing had been cooled by water — fed through the space between the two hollow shafts and thence through passages in the housing. In the planetary engine, however, while it was even simpler to circulate water round the

stationary housing, another way had to be found to cool the rotor; so oil was pumped into it through the output shaft and eccentric bearing. Unfortunately, oil built up in the rotor, escaped at the sides and leaked past the side seals into the working compartments, in much the same way as it gets past the piston rings in a reciprocating engine when there is too much oil in the crankcase.

The remedy was to put a stationary, curved-vane extractor in the side of the rotor remote from the annular gear; as the rotor turned, the steel vanes scooped out surplus oil and led it away axially. This modification slashed oil consumption below that of a conventional engine and eliminated the exhaust haze.

Another disadvantage of oil in the rotor was the cocktail-shaking effect, which was found to be responsible for much of the engine's mechanical losses. Not surprisingly, therefore, eliminating the oil cooling — a move initiated by Curtiss-Wright — reduced specific fuel consumption without any penalty in overheating, whether the rotor was made of aluminium alloy, steel or iron.

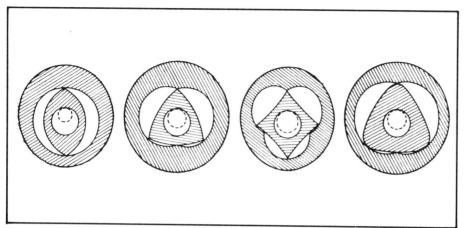

Some of the many trochoidal forms investigated. From the left, the first three are single-lobe, two-lobe and three-lobe epitrochoids with their inner envelopes. Correctly geared, all three inner envelopes can orbit their epitrochoids while maintaining continuous contact at the apexes; the two-lobe form was chosen for the NSU Wankel engine. The fourth — a three flank hypotrochoid and its outer envelope — is unsuitable for an engine as the contact points move back and forth around the apexes and cannot be sealed.

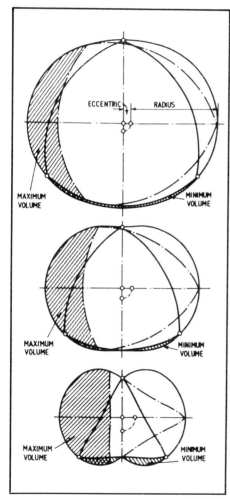

Pros and cons of epitrochoid proportions, determined by radius-to-eccentric ratio. For a given capacity, the top arrangement gives the highest compression ratio, the lowest the smallest engine bulk. Drawbacks of the bottom layout include greater angularity of the apex seals, reversal of centrifugal force on the seals at the waist and restricted diameter of the output shaft.

Subsequently, some licensees (Fichtel and Sachs in the first place) bypassed oil-associated problems by channelling the ingoing charge through the rotor to cool it (charge cooling). While this was acceptable where high specific power had a low priority, it was a mixed blessing in a high-performance engine because the consequent heating of the charge reduced its density unless (as in the twin-rotor Norton) it was then partially cooled before it reached the combustion chambers. An additional bonus of charge cooling, Norton found, was more thorough vaporization of the charge, enabling leaner mixtures to be used safely to the benefit of fuel consumption.

At first, oil was also mixed with the petrol to lubricate the apex seals; but when the proportion was cut from one part in 50 to one in 200 without increased wear, the way was open to eliminate the addition altogether by suitable combinations of material for the seals and housing surface. Indeed, research into compatibility of mating materials has been a major factor in reducing the wear rate on Wankel apex seals to an acceptable level.

The quick answer to the picking-up of the plain eccentric bearing was to substitute a roller bearing — first with crowded needles, then with four rows of caged rollers. But the problem stemmed less from bearing type than from centrifugal distortion of the light-alloy rotor as each apex in turn was subjected alternately to maximum and minimum centrifugal loading. The consequent kneading action distorted the rotor in an ever-changing direction, which also gave rise to tooth breakage in the annular gear besides interfering with the free working of the side seals. Naturally, hollowing the apexes improved matters by lessening the loads, while steel and iron gave greater inherent rigidity.

In principle, rotor seals (both side and apex) work in much the same way as conventional piston rings. That is to say, a side

clearance of about 0.001in in their grooves allows gas pressure to get behind them and force them into contact with the housing; in

This exploded drawing of a water-cooled engine shows how few parts it had. The two flywheels were locked on the output shaft by wedge-shape expander rings. The rotor-flank recesses were offset to make room for the oil extractor; their depth was a compromise between a high compression ratio and an ample passage for gas squirt during initial combustion. Round-section ports were kinder to apex seals than were rectangular sections.

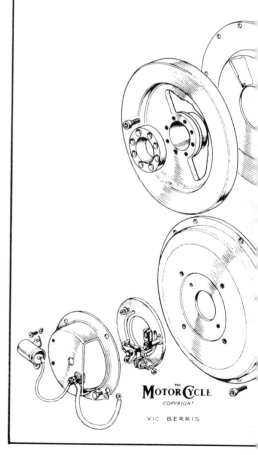

the case of the apex seals, of course, gas pressure is supplemented by centrifugal force. Sealing a Wankel rotor effectively, however, presents problems undreamed of in a conventional engine.

For a start, the springiness a piston ring derives from its shape is absent and so some other means has to be found to provide initial contact for starting. In the NSU Wankel the seals were lightly loaded by beryllium-bronze springs (chosen for their retention of elasticity when hot). Next, while any gas blowing past the top piston ring may be trapped by the second, a Wankel rotor has only one line of defence.

Third, while the side seals can have a rectangular section (as in a piston ring) since they remain square to the sides of the housing, this luxury is denied the apex seals, which are square to their mating surface only when passing through the housing's major and minor axes (ie, at the waist and the middle of each lobe). Rocking as they do some 20 to 30 degrees each side of the perpendicular (depending on housing shape) these seals have to be curved on their outer faces.

Finally, the trickiest parts to seal proved to be the six rotor corners, where the seal grooves met and gas escaped from the bottom of the grooves until spring-loaded trunnions were devised to check it.

To determine whether seal failure would set the engine alight — as burning gases from one chamber ignited the following fresh charge to send flames licking back to the carburettor — or whether the worst consequence would be a drastic loss of performance, it was decided to spoil a set of apex seals by filing. There was no fire, though starting and power were impaired. Once, indeed, when a broken seal flew out of the exhaust port the engine continued to run, albeit erratically!

Typical of the complexity of the development problems encountered was the appearance, at the end of a 100-hour test, of chatter marks on the housing wall at the

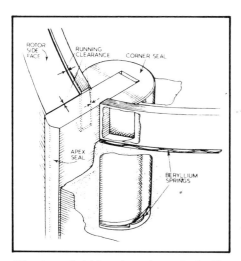

All rotor seals (side and apex) were backed by gas pressure and lightly spring-loaded. The trunnions sealed the overlap points.

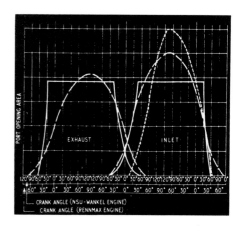

Comparison of port-opening areas, showing the advantage of a Wankel engine with peripheral ports (solid lines) over the same engine with a side inlet port (short-dash line) and the world-beating 1954 NSU Rennmax racing engine (long-dash lines).

beginning of the induction lobe. Since the housing had just been changed from cast iron to chromium-plated light alloy, material compatibility could be suspect; but so could the engine's basic geometry (affecting the extent of reverse loading on the apex seals); and so could the strength of the seal springs, since there were no chatter marks in the other lobe where the seals were backed by high gas pressure.

For cooling the rotor housing, NSU had a strong preference for water circulation with the flow pattern tailored to equalize, so far as possible, the temperatures of the two lobes. Nevertheless, air cooling was investigated (notably in conjunction with Fichtel and Sachs) with the depth of finning similarly tailored and the blast generated by a crank-shaft-mounted fan and directed by close-fitting cowls, as in the Hercules (DKW) W2000. Understandably, NSU were loath to grant licences for less precise cooling arrangements; indeed it was many years before Norton, in a bid to save weight, noise and complexity, chased the bugs out of direct air cooling. This they did by mounting two housings side by side, hot lobes forward, in a frame with no front down tube (thus making best use of the restricted airflow behind the front wheel) while finning the housings deeply to provide an ample heat sink for congested traffic conditions.

The geometric configuration of the Wankel engine endows it with both advantages and disadvantages in comparison with conventional reciprocating engines. Most fundamental drawback is the attenuated shape and high surface/volume ratio of the combustion chamber, resulting in above-average absorption of combustion heat into the surface, to the detriment of fuel consumption. Naturally this ratio becomes more favourable as chamber volume is increased. In any case there are compensations in a lower octane requirement, less risk of detonation, higher potential compression ratio and lower nitrogen-oxide emission in the exhaust. Moreover, since engine design is essentially a compromise, there is scope for improved combustion through experiments in the shape of the rotor-flank recess connecting the leading and trailing halves of the combustion chamber, not to mention fuel injection and stratified charge.

Next, since the crank throw of a Wankel is only about 40 per cent of that in a piston engine of equivalent capacity, gas-pressure loads on the eccentric bearing are higher. Against that, the more destructive centrifugal loads are correspondingly lower, while bearing speed is only two-thirds of the shaft and wear is spread more evenly round the outer track.

On the credit side, a less obvious peculiarity of the Wankel is the fact that each full stroke (from minimum to maximum volume and *vice versa*) occupies 270 degrees of the output shaft, not 180. Thus, ignoring lead and lag, the Wankel has half as long again to get the charge in and out, to the benefit of deep breathing, while the less abrupt application of power to the output shaft makes for smoother torque. So, for some purposes, Dr Froede told me, to get any sort of comparison with reciprocating engines, the Wankel was regarded as having a thermodynamic speed of two-thirds the shaft speed.

Which brings us back to the futility of the capacity argument mentioned at the beginning of the chapter. 'Show the original planetary engine to a Chinaman,' said Dr Froede (no fear of being labelled a racist those days!), 'and he sees one inlet port, one exhaust port and one sparking plug. Tell him there is a power impulse for each revolution of the crankshaft and he concludes it is a 125cc two-stroke.

'If you then reveal that it works on the four-stroke principle he will say it must be a 250cc twin — and for some purposes that seems the best way of looking at it. But considering the engine as a 375cc four-stroke implies a rotational speed of two-thirds that of the output shaft; since no part of the engine revolves at that speed, the argument falls flat.'

What really matters, he agreed, is an engine's cost, size, weight, endurance and — the Wankel's Achilles heel — the amount of work it extracts from a given value of fuel. He saw the new engine as lighter, smaller, simpler and potentially cheaper to make than a comparable piston engine. It is commendable that against all the odds — entrenched commercial opposition as well as its own inherent problems — it has survived at all, for which the faith and dedication of Mazda's Kenichi Yamamoto are largely responsible.

It seems arguable that if, at the end of the last century, the pioneers of internal combustion engineering had been able to choose between the Wankel, with all the problems mentioned, and the piston engine — with the clatter, vibration, valve breakage, piston seizure and con-rod bearing failure that plagued its early years — they might well have settled on the Wankel.

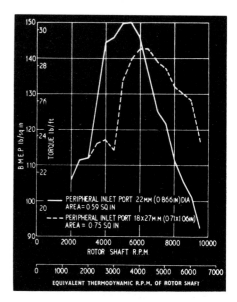

These graphs for a 250cc NSU Wankel engine show the effect of inlet-port area on power characteristics.

CHAPTER 18

Moto Morini 3½

Plain designation for a delightful and ingenious Heron-head V-twin
embodying advanced combustion technology

The survival of the Italian motorcycle industry, albeit on a very small scale, long after the collapse of its British counterpart is generally attributed to the protection of its home market by government import restrictions. True though it is, that simple explanation obscures the considerable credit due to those postwar Italian designers who, scorning new fashions from the Far East, retained their traditional individuality while continuing to gild sound engineering with artistic flair.

Typical of that fertile breed were Moto Morini's Gino Marchesini, grown old in the ways of his craft, and the younger Franco Lambertini, whose obvious professional talents were matched by an eager enthusiasm. My call at the small Bologna factory in the summer of 1975 was unannounced, since I had only just contrived a free day during a planned visit to Fabio Taglioni at Ducati. Yet Lambertini proudly answered my every question on their fascinating 344cc (62 × 57mm) V-twin engine — delighting me repeatedly with evidence of an uncommon degree of foresight in its design. Deservedly, that foresight had paid off in instant acceptance of a captivating machine and the very minimum need for detail modifications after its launch.

Whether deliberately or otherwise, the makers understated the new model in 1971 by calling it simply the 3½. Yet in both Strada and Sport guises it was not only handsome, compact and a joy to handle — as one would expect in view of its race-bred chassis and 320lb dry weight — but its engine had an unusually charming combination of qualities. It was silky smooth, thanks to good mechanical balance, and free-revving by virtue of robust construction and valve gear of low reciprocating mass — while sophisticated porting and combustion made it both punchy and economical. And notwithstanding a potential of nearly 95mph in Strada trim and comfortably over a ton with the Sport camshaft, jets and higher-compression pistons, it was as easy on the ears as on the pocket.

In motorcycle engineering the Morini twin broke new ground in having so-called Heron cylinder heads — characterized by a flat underface, two parallel valves and the combustion recess formed in the piston crown — a feature Moto Guzzi adopted in the V35, V50 and V65 twins later on. Other features that helped lift the 3½ out of the rut included a toothed belt to drive the camshaft, a forged one-piece crankshaft, transistorized ignition and the extensive use of beautiful pressure die-castings. With initial production scheduled for no more than 3,000 units a year, great pains were taken to keep down production costs, not only by adopting Heron heads but also by using identical cylinders, heads, pistons, connecting rods and other parts front and rear.

Choice of a V-twin rather than a parallel-twin stemmed from a determination to give the engine character and quality as well as smooth running; but the selection of a 72-degree cylinder angle was sheer compromise. It was, Lambertini insisted, very little less silky than the ideal 90 degrees (for perfect primary balance) and had slightly more even firing intervals. And while the angle was narrow enough for compact installation in the duplex-loop frame, it was wide enough for the camshaft to be located high in the V of the crankcase.

Even so, to make room for the camshaft it had been necessary to space the cylinders apart slightly at the base so that their axes intersected not at the crankshaft centre line but a little below it. Such offset cylinders are known as *desaxé* and in the 3½ the effect was double: positive in one cylinder, negative in the other. I queried the effect on firing intervals (nominally 432 and 288 degrees) and was told that these worked out at 433 degrees 19.14 minutes and 286 degrees 40.46 minutes, respectively. Such precision!

Although cheaper production was the chief reason for choosing Heron heads — since the underside had only to be planed, not sphered — there were technical advantages, too, in fuel economy and high torque,

which Morini claimed with some justification to have exploited more than anyone else. In the car world, such heads already had an impressive pedigree. Among the power units that had featured them were those in the Jaguar V12, the Rover 2200, the Alfasud and some Fords and Audis.

It is true that Heron heads subsequently lost favour for car engines. Ford, for example, found the NOx content in the exhaust too high for the stringent emissions laws in their international markets (a problem not applicable to the Italian motorcycle industry). There were complaints of rough combustion, too, even of pistons burning with some little-known brands of fuel. Probably all these problems stemmed from the makers' failure to control the compression ratio sufficiently accurately in production. For Ford had made further economies by leaving the piston crowns as cast, rather than machining them, and ratios were found to vary by as much as one unit above or below the nominal figure — *ie*, a designed 10:1 might, in practice, be as low as 9:1 or as high as 11:1. The extra-high ratios were, of course, the culprits. But Morini forestalled such problems by evolving an unusually sophisticated combustion chamber; by machining that part of the piston crown that controlled the squish clearance and compression ratio; and by arranging for the electronic auto-advance to retard the ignition timing by 4 degrees at top revs.

Predominantly, high-performance two-valve heads had long been of crossflow pattern, with large valves set at an angle in part-spherical combustion chambers. Parallel inlet and exhaust valves had perforce to be smaller and, before the advent of the Heron head, were therefore associated with lower performance levels. If, for example, both head face and piston crown were flat, the combustion chamber was almost pancake-shaped, with a high surface/volume ratio (hence excessive heat loss), low compression ratio and long flame path — all of which combined to add high consumption to

Franco Lambertini (Moto Morini).

engine used by Tarquinio Provini when he well-nigh robbed Jim Redman and his Honda four of the world championship in 1963, then by the up-and-coming Giacomo Agostini to skittle all Provini's Italian lap and race records at the start of his illustrious career. The caption to the engine told, in metric terms, of a brake mean effective pressure (*ie*, productive work on the piston crown throughout its four strokes and net of mechanical and pumping losses) equivalent to a phenomenal 206psi at 10,500rpm — evidence of exceptional high-speed breathing and burning efficiency.

Lambertini told me they had continued their exhaustive research into porting and low performance. Some designs avoided these snags by recessing the valves in some form of 'inverted bathtub' — so concentrating the combustion space and raising the compression ratio, though in some cases breathing was then impaired by the masking of the valves. By transferring the combustion recess from head to piston crown, the Heron arrangement retained the high compression ratio and ample squish area (for added turbulence), yet the valve heads were completely unmasked once the piston started to move down from top dead centre.

That lack of masking, and the fact that the business ends of the Morini's ports were more nearly parallel to the valve stems than in a crossflow layout, compensated considerably for the relatively small valve sizes by using much more of the valve periphery than is usually the case with crossflow, where little more than half of it may be effective.

Porting and combustion were a Morini speciality from way back, as I was reminded by the display of their famous 250cc double-knocker single-cylinder racing engine in the reception hall when I arrived. It was the

Cylinders, heads, pistons and con-rods are identical front and rear but only the front piston has an expander spring behind the oil-scraper ring. The heads have a flat underface and the piston crowns three levels. Eleven teeth and eight keyways in the small cam-drive pulley provide vernier timing adjustment. Both stiff and light, the valve rockers incorporate an 8:11 leverage ratio. The crankshaft is a one-piece forging and pressure die-castings abound. Note the simple but effective oil separators.

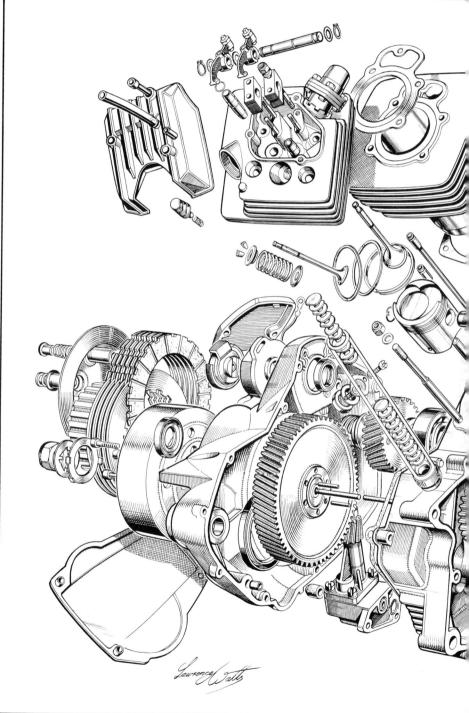

Lawrence Watts

combustion with the Heron heads — and the result showed up clearly in the small diameter of the exhaust valve; the peculiar shape and pronounced taper of its port; the uncommonly large (*ie*, gradual) radius blending stem into head on both valves; and the strange form of the piston crown.

The small exhaust valve, Lambertini explained, was 'fantastic for torque'. The curved port opened out from 18.5mm at the valve throat to 25mm at the outlet. As a result, gas speed through the throat was very high, creating a deep depression there during valve overlap. Allied to the ram effect of the inlet tract (which narrowed from 25mm in the carburettor to 23.5mm before opening out to 26mm at the valve throat) that produced extremely good cylinder filling, even at low revs, while the port layouts minimized any loss of fresh charge to the exhaust. It was, incidentally, the high gas speed that dictated the large underhead radius on the valves for the smoothest possible flow.

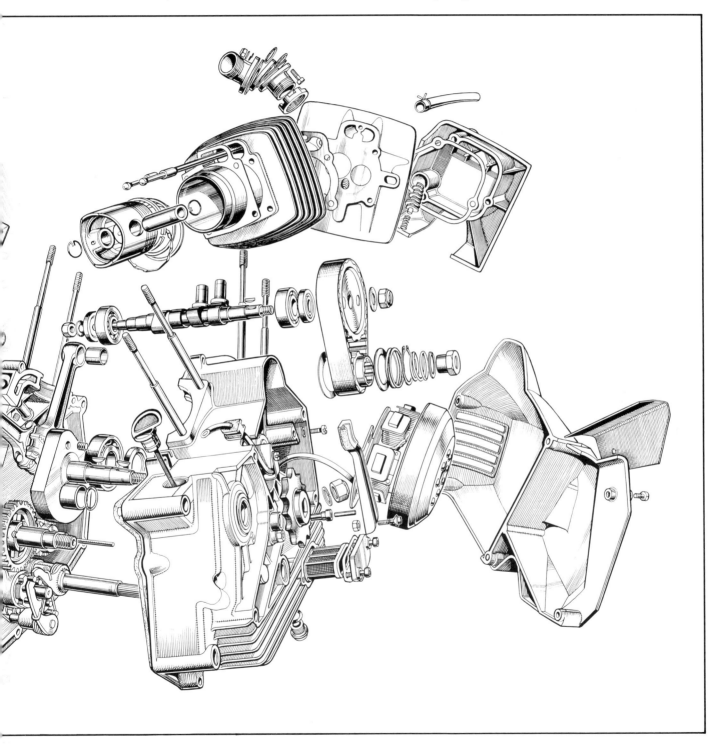

Moto Morini's charming 3½ V-twin in Strada guise.

The piston crown's contribution to high torque and low thirst stemmed from high compression, a low surface/volume ratio (at tdc) and the unusual combustion pattern it promoted. There were, in fact, three levels to the crown. The top level, surrounding the valve heads and sparking plug, had a new-moon shape adjacent to the plug and a peaked shape opposite. It was the height of this level (the sole difference between Strada and Sport pistons) that determined the squish clearance and compression ratio. In

Controlled combustion. As the flame front spreads from the plug points, the peak on the piston splits it into two vortices which turn back to meet the ends of the advancing front.

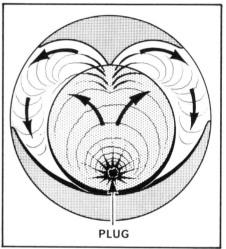

the Strada the clearance (from the cylinder head) was 3mm, giving a ratio of 10:1; in the Sport the clearance was only 2mm, the ratio 11:1.

The middle crown level (2mm lower on the Strada, 3mm on the Sport) was kidney shaped under the valve heads. A further 2mm down, the bottom level was circular, not quite in the middle of the crown but set slightly towards the plug.

The resulting combustion pattern was ingenious. As the flame front radiated out from the plug points (like ripples on a pond) maximum gas pressure occurred at the point of the peak on the opposite side. This split the flame front into two vortices, which rotated outward and back towards the ends

This section through the ports shows the curvature and pronounced taper of the exhaust tract, also the comparatively small size of the valve. The inlet port has 30 degrees down-draught and 34 degrees offset; the exhaust has 18 degrees updraught and 30 degrees offset.

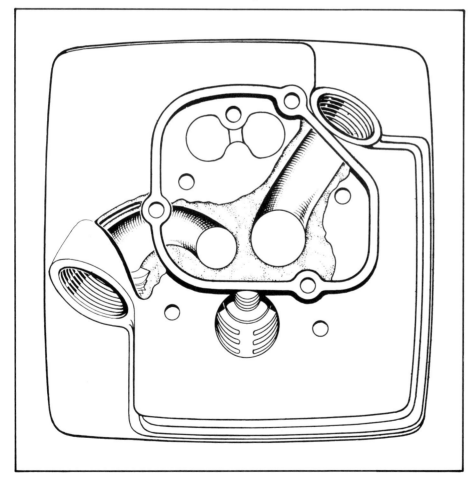

of the advancing flame front, so promoting turbulence and ensuring thorough, quick combustion.

With this sophisticated approach, Morini were well in the vanguard of contemporary research into combustion characteristics and the effects of controlled turbulence in chambers of various shapes. Indeed, their engine was keenly studied by eminent research establishments, including Ricardo Consulting Engineers, based in England with contracts worldwide.

Before the benefits of really large squish areas were exploited, the chief source of turbulence in two-valve (non-Heron) cylinders was the spiral swirl imparted to the ingoing charge by the offset and downdraught angles of the inlet port (allied, in some cases, to small peripheral squish bands). Judged by subsequent standards, this arrangement gave relatively slow burning, requiring a fairly large degree of ignition advance. As a result, squish was at first denigrated in many quarters as lagging too far behind the spark to be of much use.

Later, however, the much more vigorous turbulence generated by large squish areas, in conjunction with specially shaped clearance volumes (designed both to control the pattern of gas movement and to shorten the maximum flame travel), was found to speed up the burning to such an extent that much less ignition advance was required, thus practically eliminating the lag between spark and squish. This permits considerably higher compression ratios without detonation, to the benefit of engine efficiency.

So effective is this method, indeed, that some of the most advanced car engines are able to dispense with spiral swirl generated by inlet-port offset (thus allowing more compact installation) and yet use very high compression ratios and short ignition advance. At the time of writing, two notable flat-top-piston examples are the Michael May Fireball combustion chamber in the 5.3-litre V12 Jaguar HE (High Efficiency) engine and the Porsche TOP (Thermally Optimized Porsche) design in the 2.5-litre 944 straight-four. In the first case the combustion space (containing the plug in one side) is concentrated under the head of the exhaust valve, which is recessed above the cylinder-head face. The rest of the head face (including the inlet valve) and the closely approaching piston crown combine to squirt the charge through a carefully shaped slot which gives it a strong spiral motion as it enters the clearance volume. As a result, a compression ratio of 12:1 or more can be used with pump petrol despite a cylinder volume of 445cc. (A basically similar layout, though without a specially formed slot, is used in the Ricardo HRCC design.)

In the Porsche head the clearance volume is wedge-shaped, with the plug in the middle of the shallow side face and close to the cylinder axis. There are two broad squish segments — one outboard of the plug, with a 2.2mm clearance, and the other diametrically opposite with a clearance of only 0.9mm. Thus the movement of the converging streams of highly turbulent gas around tdc is biased towards the plug, where it is further controlled by curvature of the wall on both flanks of the plug. In this case a compression ratio of 10.6:1 is standardized despite a cylinder volume of 620cc.

Although different in detail, both these layouts produce some stratification of the charge, in which the mixture at the plug points is richer than the remainder. This propagates the flame rapidly enough for an overall lean mixture to be used at part throttle, so enhancing fuel economy without slow burning and consequent overheating.

Enough of digression. On bench test, Morini's faith in their research was justified not only by high specific power and a wide spread of torque but also by a commendably low specific fuel consumption. The relevant figures were 35bhp at 8,200rpm (Strada) and 39 at 8,500 (Sport) — giving approximately 102 and 113bhp/litre, respectively (and a punchy 12.4 and 13.3 bhp/litre/1,000rpm). Torque peaks (23.67lb-ft at 5,900rpm and 24.75 at 6,300) told only part of the tale for the Strada's torque exceeded 20lb-ft from 4,200 to 8,750rpm while the Sport's topped

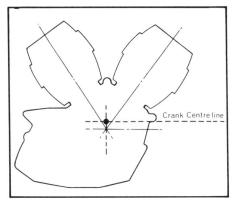

Desaxé means the cylinder axis is offset from the crankshaft centre line. The Morini 3½ has both positive and negative desaxé so that the two axes meet below the centre line to provide room for the camshaft between the cylinders.

22 from 5,000 to 8,650. No less remarkable were specific consumption figures of 0.43lb/bhp/hr (Strada) and 0.4 (Sport).

(The figures for peak power and peak torque were taken from the handbook supplied by Harglo Ltd, the British Concessionaires, where Lawrie Watts made his drawing. Graphs obtained in Bologna later — from which the torque spread and specific consumption were derived — suggest the handbook in no way overstated the performance.)

All of this indicates that Moto Morini, as distinct from so much of the automotive industry, did not need the shock of repeated explosions in world oil prices to recognize the crucial importance of what takes place in

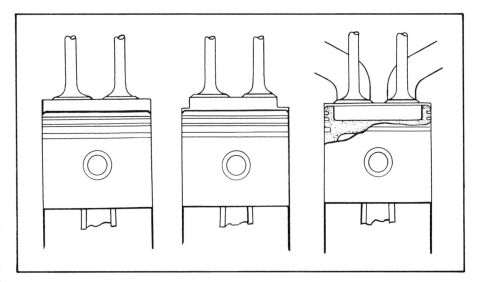

Schematic drawing of three types of combustion chamber with parallel vertical valves. The inefficient pancake shape (left) gives a high surface/volume ratio, low compression ratio and long flame travel. The inverted bathtub (middle) mitigates those defects but masks the valves. The Heron head (right) moves the combustion space into the piston, so practically eliminating masking.

the combustion chamber and its associated porting.

Compared with conventional pistons, those in a Heron layout run hotter because there is more crown area exposed to combustion heat (and correspondingly less in the cylinder head). For that reason Lambertini specified a vertical slot down one face of the skirt so that it could expand circumferentially and avoid the need for a large cold running clearance. Also there was plenty of metal in the crown to serve as a heat sink and provide an ample heat path down to the ring grooves.

Spacing the cylinders apart to provide room for the camshaft naturally altered the leverage of the connecting rods — in opposite directions of course. To restore the leverage to normal, the gudgeon-pin bosses were moved slightly inward. In the front cylinder, however, this resulted in a tendency for the piston to rattle because of the increased slap at top dead centre. This was cured by reducing the radial depth of its slotted oil-control ring sufficiently to put a thin expander spring behind it.

Since the crankshaft was forged in one piece, the steel con-rods were split across the big-end eye (with the caps located by serrations). Running two rods side by side on a common crankpin normally offsets the cylinders by the width of one big-end eye. But in order to get the exhaust ports farther out in the cooling breeze, this stagger was increased to 30mm in the $3\frac{1}{2}$ by offsetting the con-rod shanks and small ends relative to the big-end eyes.

Lateral location of the crankshaft was taken care of by a large ball bearing on the drive side (the left). Unusually, though, thermal expansion of the case was not accommodated in a roller bearing on the opposite side; instead, a smaller ball bearing there was a sliding fit on a crankshaft sleeve.

Although the crank cheeks were formed into bobweights for balance purposes, there was no separate flywheel (except that the hefty steel rim on the aluminium alternator rotor on the right provided some inertia). As Lambertini observed, a V-twin has less need of a flywheel than other twins since both pistons are never at rest at the same instant; while each is stationary the other is moving at full speed and so serving as a flywheel.

Clamped against the left-hand main bearing was the helical gear for the clutch drive (a 29:66 reduction) and, outboard of that, the worm drive for the half-speed oil pump. Outside the other main bearing (and protected by an oil seal on the crankshaft sleeve) was the steel pulley for the cam-drive belt — its combination of eight keyways and 11

teeth providing a fine vernier adjustment for the valve timing. The 22-tooth pulley on the camshaft was made of cast iron with the object of preventing belt snatch by stabilizing shaft rotation. Since the belt itself was not long enough to accommodate any provision for tensioning, renewal was recommended every 20,000km (12,500 miles) or whenever backlash exceeded 6mm.

A ball bearing at each end supported the camshaft, and the four hollow, flat-base steel followers ran directly in the aluminium crankcase, since that was a compatible bearing combination. In any case, the followers had a large bearing surface and rotated in use, being slightly offset to the cams. Moreover, side thrust was minimized by forming the cups for the steel ball-ends of the solid duralumin pushrods right down in the base of the followers.

Tunnels for the short rods were cast in the cylinders and heads and steel cups at the top of the rods engaged adjustable ball-ends in the rockers. Slim and straight, these were notable on three counts. First, a full-length shank above the spindle boss ensured ample stiffness in spite of low weight; second, they made line (not point) contact with the valve tips; third, they incorporated a leverage ratio that multiplied cam lift by 1.375 at the valve, so that the Sport camshaft's 7mm lift translated to a valve lift of more than $9\frac{1}{2}$mm. The effect of the shorter travel of the cam followers and pushrods was to ease the problem of keeping the valves under full control at high revs; in practical terms, valve float was pushed beyond 9,200rpm, even with comparatively weak springs.

In established Italian practice, lubrication was simplified by housing the gear cluster in the crankcase, where it received oil flung out of the big ends; and by carrying the oil ($2\frac{1}{2}$ litres) in an integral sump rather than a separate tank so that return was by gravity, not by scavenge pump. The $3\frac{1}{2}$ had a further simplification, however, for oil (drawn through a 14sq-in fine-gauze filter) was pumped only into the crankshaft, and crankcase pressure was relied on to force oil mist up the pushrod tunnels to the valve gear. Incidentally, each valve stem had a groove round the middle for oil retention. An oil separator with seven staggered baffles was housed in the breather in each rocker cover, while two similar separators (with 11 baffles each) were inserted in the large-bore plastic breather pipe venting the gear compartment at the rear.

Supplied by Ducati Elettrotecnica, the capicitor-discharge ignition was powered by the alternator lest anyone should want to remove the battery for racing. The rotor was

driven by the left-hand end of the camshaft and the stator mounting was slotted for timing adjustment. Range of the electronic auto-advance was from 10 degrees after tdc (static) to 34 degrees before it by 6,000rpm, then backing off to 30 degrees beyond peak revs. The revmeter was powered by one of the high-tension coils (which was slightly stronger for the purpose). Of the six coils in the ventilated alternator stator, one served the ignition, the others the lighting.

In view of the engine's remarkable tractability, the provision of six speeds must be regarded as a concession to sporting fashion rather than a necessity. Supported in ball bearings, the input and output shafts were separate — thus the drive was indirect in all gears and crossed over from left to right. Internal ratios were: 3.2, 2.0, 1.47, 1.21, 1.047 and 0.95:1. Unusually, the three selector forks were made of aluminium and given a special surface treatment. The six-plate clutch was dry.

So sound was the design of the $3\frac{1}{2}$ that the only changes, early in its production, were slight strengthening of the gear-cluster pinions and the use of bolts and nuts to secure the big-end caps instead of screwing the bolts into threads in the con-rods. It was no surprise when the original models quickly produced a string of descendants. First was a 123cc (59 × 45mm) six-speed single in roadster and enduro forms (front cylinder only). Then came a 239cc (69 × 64mm) five-speed single-cylinder roadster, which was later discontinued in favour of a roadster and sports twin of the same capacity (59 × 43.8mm), with a compression ratio of 11.7:1. Finally came a 478cc twin (69 × 64mm), first with five speeds, then six, and a compression ratio of 11.2:1; subsequently the stroke was lengthened by 4mm in a 507cc off-road version. Conclusive proof of the crankshaft's robustness was provided when an experimental version of the 478cc twin withstood the considerable extra stresses of turbocharging without modification.

I have never known a grand-prix engineer who did not find that the challenge of world-championship competition provided the highest level of intellectual fulfilment — Giulio Carcano at Moto Guzzi and Walter Kaaden at MZ were outstanding examples. But, in the Moto Morini $3\frac{1}{2}$ and its derivatives, Gino Marchesini and Franco Lambertini showed that, when the need arises, a series-production brief and a clean sheet of paper can provide ample scope for the expression of sound, imaginative engineering, enthusiasm and pride.

CHAPTER 19

Kawasaki Z1300 six

Up-to-the-minute, civilized heavyweight engine that somehow strayed
into a motorcycle chassis

In launching the massive six-abreast Z1300 in 1979, Kawasaki achieved the incongruous distinction of sacrificing a sophisticated and wholly admirable engine to an overall concept totally alien to the very essence of a motorcycle, at least as understood in Europe. Some 700lb of material for the standard model — let alone 930lb for the lavishly over-equipped Voyager version that followed — could better have made two light, lithe and much less thirsty single-trackers.

The makers seemed to be catering predominantly for riders on the sundown side of the Atlantic with sufficient masochism to relish the worst of both worlds: *ie,* the vulnerability and exposure to the weather of a solo motorcycle and the obesity, unwieldiness and thirst of the traditional American limousine.

In a sleek sports car, the refined 120bhp engine would have made a lot of sense; in a road-going solo, however, its primary appeal was to the deplorable worship of surplus power and weight as virility symbols.

Be that as it may, the power plant itself commended respect for its refinement, advanced design and the clever way it anticipated increasingly restrictive legislation on noise and exhaust gases, especially in California.

The smooth torque and perfect mechanical balance inherent in a straight-six were complemented by four transmission shock absorbers. Water cooling made for mechanical quietness, as did inverted-tooth chains, helical bevel gears and several combinations of steel and plastic gears.

Boldest of all, however, Kawasaki broke new ground in the way they tackled the severe Californian clean-exhaust legislation projected to 1984.

Among the American car giants, the hysterical rush to produce exhaust gases fit to bottle as baby food had spawned various engine accessories, including a pump to feed air into the exhaust manifold to prolong combustion and so reduce the level of unbur-ned hydrocarbons and carbon-monoxide discharged into the atmosphere.

The Z1300's afterburning system (fitted to the US version only) was not only the first ever on a motorcycle; it was also the first on any vehicle to work automatically rather than use a pump. And — to meet the long-mileage requirements of the clean-air laws — it was backed up by refined carburation (later superseded by fuel injection) and fully transistorized battery ignition.

When *Motor Cycle Weekly* artist Lawrie Watts and I visited Kawasaki's Slough headquarters to analyse the new engine we were spared the usual dismantling. Instead, a beautifully sectioned display unit was mounted on a bench for our inspection.

Widest part of the engine, the crankcase measured 25in across the covers. It seemed immaterial whether that was more or less than the width of Honda's Gold Wing flat-four or 1,047cc CBX straight-six, for all three were too broad in the beam and any difference could have been only marginal.

Supported in seven plain bearings, the 120-degree crankshaft was not only fully balanced (every web counterweighted rather than full disc); there was also a bonded-rubber torsion damper at the left-hand extremity to smooth out the effects of the slightly uneven linear spacing of the firing impulses applied to the shaft (firing order was 1, 5, 3, 6, 2, 4).

Just inboard of the torsion damper was the double-reduction drive from the starter motor housed behind the end two cylinders. Mounted on the opposite extremity of the crankshaft was the 220-watt AC generator.

From the middle of the crankshaft a wide inverted-tooth chain took the drive back to a jackshaft. This, in turn, distributed it four ways — first back to the clutch (via another wide inverted-tooth chain on the right); second, down to the eccentric-rotor oil pump (through plastic and steel gears on the left); third, up to the two overhead camshafts (via a narrow inverted-tooth chain just to the left of the primary chain); and fourth, not so far up to a short traverse shaft, via a single-strand bush (*ie,* rollerless) chain just to the left of the cam chain.

This short shaft drove the water impeller (on the front of the cylinder block) through plastic and steel bevel gears; and the ignition trigger unit (under the carburettor serving the right-hand pair of cylinders) via steel and plastic spur gears outboard of the bevels.

Considering the distribution drives individually, that to the clutch incorporated the first transmission shock absorber in the form of a spring-loaded two-lobe face cam on the right flank of the large jackshaft sprocket.

The cam chain was automatically tensioned by a roller mounted in a spring-loaded non-return bracket behind the rear (slack) run, while the front and top runs were damped by rubber-faced metal strips. The bevel-shaft chain, too, had a spring-loaded tensioner in the rear run; the use of a bush chain there was typical Japanese practice to obviate the possibility of a broken roller falling in the works. No tensioning was considered necessary for either of the wide chains.

Wet liners were used in the cylinder block, both to minimize its weight and width and to enhance cylinder cooling. A further aid to keeping block width in check was the choice of considerably undersquare cylinder dimensions — 62mm bore × 71mm stroke. Farther back, between the rider's knees, width was even more critical so only three carburettors were fitted, each having a parallel pair of 32mm chokes to serve adjacent cylinders.

In the part-spherical heads, all the sparking plugs were inclined outward (three to the right, three to the left) while the shallow-dome pistons gave a compression ratio of 9.9:1. Each camshaft, formed integrally with its central sprocket, was supported in four plain bearings, the two on each side spaced between the three cams.

An external clue to the ingenious after-

Anomalous American dream bike — the original Z1300 with 120 (later 130) bhp, chiefly used for 55mph cruising with so many electrical accessories that the makers had to fit a second generator.

burning system was provided by the two exhaust-cam covers (left and right), both of which were fed, through plastic piping, with filtered air from the top of the filter box behind the carburettors. Trapped under each cover was a plate containing three downward-opening reed valves — one above each exhaust valve.

Behind each exhaust valve, a cored passage in the cylinder head connected the small reed-valve chamber with the top of the port, close to the valve-seat insert. Consequently the fluctuating pressure in the port was communicated to the reed valve.

So long as that pressure was above atmospheric the reed valve was forced up on to its seat; but as soon as the low-pressure wave was reflected back to the port from the end of the exhaust pipe, the reed was pulled open and fresh air was drawn into the port from the air filter. To prevent any port from sucking gas from its neighbour (instead of air from the filter box) the reed-valve chambers were isolated from one another by vertical walls on top of the cambox. Thus a continuous stream of air was distributed to the six exhaust ports to prolong the burning of the gases in the pipes and so reduce to the legal level the surplus carbon monoxide and hydrocarbons finally discharged.

Unsightly blueing of the chromium plating on the pipes (as a result of the extra heat fed into them) was prevented by a double-wall construction.

It was necessary to cut out the afterburning system whenever the throttles were closed — otherwise there would have been popping in the silencers, similar to overrun popping when a leaky exhaust system admits air. This cut-out was effected by a valve in the pipeline from airbox to cam covers.

Normally the valve was held open by a coil spring, so permitting a free flow of air; but the spring chamber was connected by small-bore piping to the middle two inlet tracts (numbers 3 and 4). Hence, when the throttles were closed, the consequent depression in those tracts sucked the valve on to its seat (against the spring pressure), so closing off the air supply to the cam covers. Since the middle two pistons moved in step, so working 360 degrees out of phase, the suction on the valve was constant enough to prevent it from fluttering.

Flexibly mounted, the double-barrel Mikuni carburettors were of the constant-vacuum type and breathed through three separate compartments in the air-filter box. A short, cable-operated cross-shaft controlled the butterfly throttles via adjustable vertical link rods, while the idling stop was set by an accessible handwheel at the bottom.

A common diaphragm in each carburettor actuated both throttle slides, with air (not oil) damping to give the necessary enrichment for acceleration. There was a separate quality screw for each tract but only three cold-start jets, operated by a lever (marked 'choke') on the left. In the half-choke position, the lever automatically propped the butterflies open slightly for a fast tickover.

When the ignition was switched off, a solenoid automatically cut off the petrol

The wet cylinder liners help save some width. Each constant-vacuum carburettor feeds adjacent ports through twin chokes (with the two throttles controlled by a common diaphram). The plumbing over the engine is for the afterburning, which necessitates double-wall exhausts (at bottom) to prevent blueing. The original generator is on the right-hand end of the crankshaft. Note the width of the transmission chains, also the pivoted tensioner behind the cam chain.

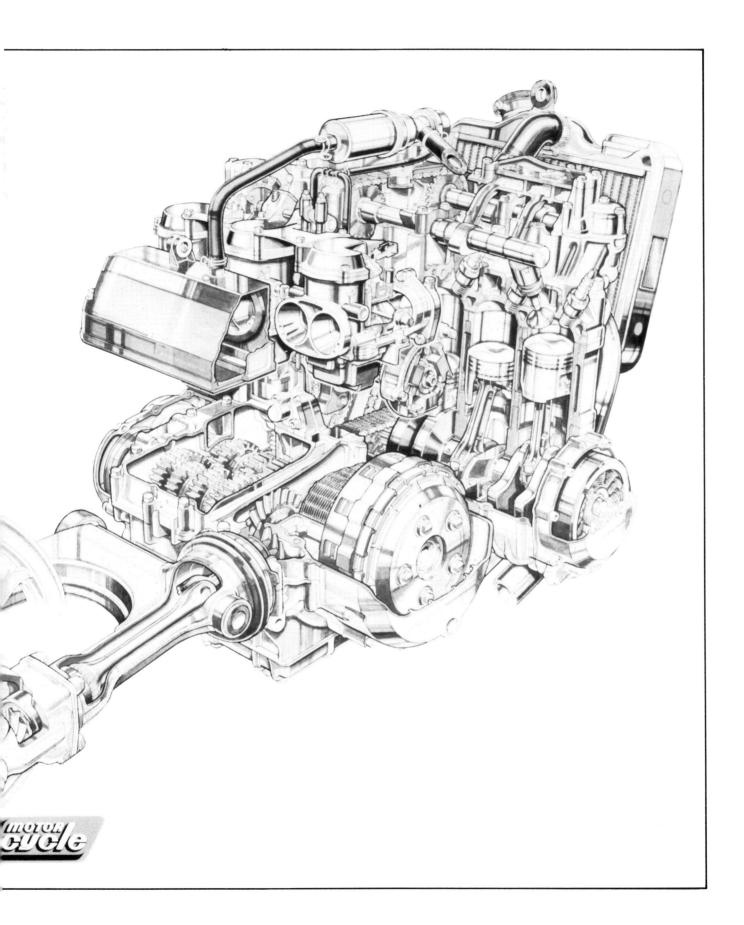

Sectioned display model of an admirable engine better suited to a small sports car. Below the inlet manifold is the automatic solenoid fuel switch. On the end of the gearbox output shaft is one of the large-diameter spring washers of the third transmission shock absorber.

On the end of the crankshaft (outboard of the starter-motor reduction gearing) is the bonded-rubber torsion damper — later discarded in favour of the second generator (American specification) or the relocated ignition unit (British spec).

supply to the gallery feeding the three float bowls.

With its pick-ups spaced at 120 degrees, the triple ignition trigger unit beneath the right-hand carburettor ran at engine speed so that each cylinder had an idle spark at tdc overlap besides the required one at tdc compression; auto-advance was controlled centrifugally, not by vacuum.

Since the radiator was close in front of the cylinder head, the coolant hoses were commendably short. The thermostat was in the outlet from the head and bypassed the water straight down to the impeller inlet for quick warm-up when the engine was cold. Behind the radiator was a temperature-sensitive white plastic fan that automatically boosted airflow through the rad during low-speed, high-temperature conditions.

The second transmission damper comprised a set of rubber blocks in the hub of the seven-plate, five-spring die-cast aluminium clutch. Withdrawal thrust came from a three-ball ramp on the left via a rod in the hollow gearbox input shaft.

A window in the clutch cover provided a check on oil level; both engine and gearbox were lubricated by the same supply and the unit breathed from the top of the gearbox shell, via an oil separator, to the induction system.

In the light of experience in Germany, where a combination of long, fast autobahn trips and infrequent checks led to the oil level falling low enough to cause big-end failure, sump capacity was later increased from 4.5 to 6.2 litres and a warning light provided.

Unusually for an all-indirect gearbox, both input and output were on the same side (the right); by taking advantage of the overall width of the engine to overlap the output bevel gear with the clutch and its drive chain, the designers thereby brought the final-drive shaft closer to the rear wheel than it could have been on the left.

To handle the engine's high torque (85lb-ft at 6,500rpm) the five pairs of gear pinions were massive — and there was ample backlash in the face dogs to ensure a dependable change. The most ingenious feature of the box, however, was the use of a double output shaft (a solid shaft inside a hollow one) as a means of providing the third transmission shock absorber.

Naturally, the five driven pinions were on the hollow shaft, which was attached at the extreme left to the driving element of the three-lobe face-cam shock absorber. The driven element was splined to the inner shaft which, at the extreme right, carried the output bevel. The necessary spring loading of the two elements was by two pairs of large-diameter back-to-back spring washers.

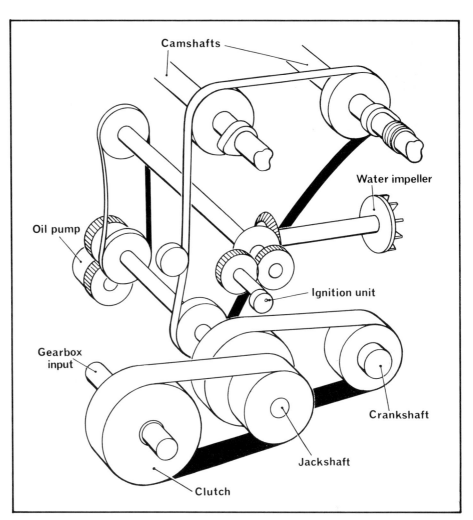

The primary chain drives the jackshaft. From there power is distributed directly to the clutch, camshafts and oil pump, and indirectly to the water impeller and ignition unit (before its relocation on the crankshaft).

At both ends of the final-drive shaft (which was enclosed in the arm of the fabricated steel fork and sealed at the front by a plastic gaiter) the bevel teeth were helical — a form that spreads the load and reduces noise. The universal joint was co-axial with the fork pivot.

At the rear the crownwheel drove the seven-spoke cast-aluminium wheel through a set of large cush rubbers — the final transmission shock absorber. On the opposite side of the hub was the perforated brake disc — 300mm (11¾in) in diameter and 6mm thick — with the perforations unevenly spaced to eliminate squeal with the sintered-metal pads chosen for wet-weather efficiency. The caliper was clamped directly to the left fork arm, however, an arrangement that tends to cause wheel hop under hard braking.

Besides the increase in sump capacity men-

tioned earlier, a few other modifications were dictated by experience. Statesiders who adorned their Z1300s with every conceivable electrical gadget, then dutifully observed the 55mph speed limit, found the generator unable to match the demand on the battery at such low revs. So, for the American market, Kawasaki fitted a second alternator — on the left-hand end of the crankshaft, where it replaced the seemingly dispensable torsion damper, thus avoiding any increase in engine width.

The UK model, too, lost its torsion damper when the ignition unit was moved across from its original location behind the cylinder block.

On both sides of the Atlantic, fuel metering was refined by the adoption of electronic fuel injection, with its proven benefits in exhaust cleanliness, economy, warm-up and drivability from cold. The American model was the first to lose its carburettors — and its

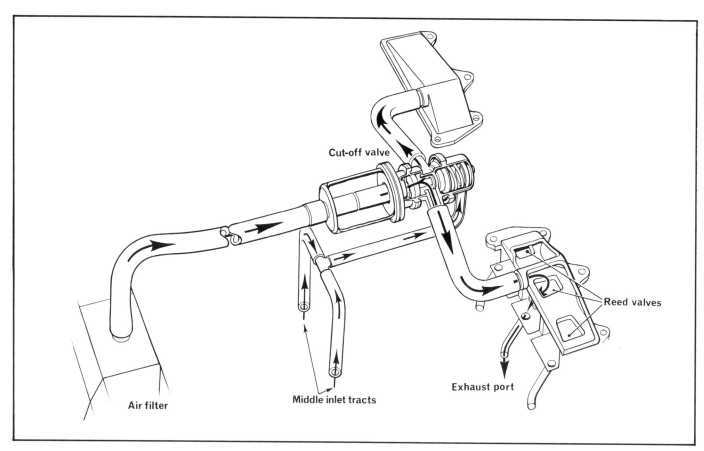

Cut-off valve

Reed valves

Exhaust port

Air filter

Middle inlet tracts

The successive depressions in the six exhaust ports combine to draw filtered air from the air-filter box, through the large-bore T-pipe and the individual reed valves under the cam covers. This air burns surplus carbon monoxide and hydrocarbons in the exhaust pipes. When the throttles are closed the cut-off valve in the T-pipe blocks the flow of air to the cam covers to prevent popping in the silencers. This valve (normally held open by a spring) is closed by suction from the middle two inlet tracts, via the small-bore pipes.

Factory performance curves on the original cam form. Peak torque translates to 85lb-ft and minimum specific fuel consumption to a creditable 0·46lb/bhp/hour — both at 6,500rpm.

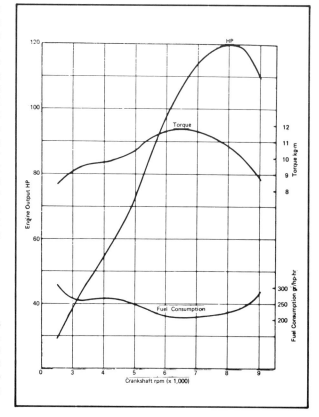

injection system was, predictably, more elaborate than the UK version. While both systems injected into six separate chokes, the UK version worked in a single mode, whereas a dual-mode provision enabled Statesiders to select for either power or economy through a two-way switch which changed the overall mixture strength accordingly. A revised cam form was also said to have raised peak power to 130bhp, still at 8,000rpm.

If properly serviced, especially in respect of oil level, the Z1300 engine was eminently dependable — as was to be expected in view of its surplus potential for most purposes. In engineering terms, the complete engine-transmission unit was a credit to the automotive industry, let alone the motorcycle division.

Its complexity and size, however, made the bike as a whole much too heavy and cumbersome for mature European tastes, long nurtured on effortless handling and man-handling.

The only European highways on which the engine could be given its head were the West German autobahns — and in that country power was already limited to 100bhp by law anyway. The main market for the prestigious straight-six was the USA, where its 140mph potential was incongruous, to say the least, in the context of an overall 55mph limit.

CHAPTER 20

Suzuki RG500 square-four

Unblushing copy of MZ disc-valve layout that brilliantly confirmed the
potential of the East German formula

In the development of the grand-prix two-stroke engine no circuit played a more decisive role than the $37\frac{3}{4}$-mile Isle of Man Mountain course with its wide altitude range, its short steep climb up Snaefell and its punishing assortment of bends, bumps, humps and drops. For example, in the early 1960s Yamaha's 250cc air-cooled disc-valve twin — ridden so spectacularly by Fumio Ito and so cagily by Phil Read — had the measure of the previously invincible Honda fours on just about every other circuit in the world-championship calendar; but the TT repeatedly exposed its lack of stamina through serious mechanical failures.

It is in the light of the TT's reputation as a two-stroke killer that the record of Suzuki's water-cooled RG500 disc-valve square-four in the Senior (500cc) event seems so phenomenal: seven victories on the trot and all with different riders. They were Read in 1977, Tom Herron in '78, Mike Hailwood in '79, Graeme Crosby in '80, Mick Grant in '81, Norman Brown in '82 and Rob McElnea in '84. In 1983 there was no separate Senior TT and the combined Senior-Classic 1,000cc race was won by McElnea on a full-size twin-camshaft Suzuki four-stroke; but the previous year's Classic race (as well as the Senior) fell to an RG500, ridden by Dennis Ireland.

From 1976 to 1982, moreover, the RG500 won four world individual championships — through Barry Sheene in 1976 and '77, Marco Lucchinelli in '81 and Franco Uncini in '82. It must be conceded, however, as a partial explanation of the engine's fine IoM record, that a decade or more before the birth of the RG500 all two-stroke race-engine designers had learned the two fundamental lessons of the TT — first, that water cooling, preferably with an impeller, is indispensable to minimize cylinder distortion and permit smaller piston clearances; second, that the piston's heat problems diminish with cylinder size, hence the smallest individual size permitted by the FIM formula for a given total capacity pays dividends in stamina as well as specific power.

Since designer Makoto Hase could never disguise the fact that the RG500 engine was virtually a quartet of East German MZ 125cc singles (or a pair of MZ 250cc parallel-twins) driving a common underslung power take-off shaft, the Suzuki's record reflects enormous credit on Walter Kaaden's pioneering work in the MZ race shop where, on a veritable shoestring, he had evolved all the engine's salient features — long, asymmetric inlet timing, highly resonant induction and exhaust systems, auxiliary transfer porting opposite the exhaust and a large squish area in the cylinder head matching the shallow-dome piston crown — more than a dozen years earlier.

In a subtle sense Suzuki's achievements with the RG500 may be regarded as some sort of atonement. For their grand-prix competitiveness (initially in the 50 and 125cc classes) — indeed Japanese two-stroke competitiveness as a whole — stemmed from their ruthless poaching of MZ star Ernst Degner, whose sensational defection to Japan they organized in 1961, thus acquiring the cylinder, piston, crankshaft, connecting rod and valve disc of a 125cc race engine that was streets ahead of the floundering opposition.

Even so, it is only fair to acknowledge Hase's courage in choosing the square-four layout at all, logical though it was since disc-valve cylinders could be coupled only two abreast. For Suzuki's first square-four, a water-cooled 250cc disc-valver based on Hugh Anderson's 1963 Honda-beating 125cc air-cooled parallel-twin, had proved to be the most embarrassing flop in grand-prix history (the fiasco of Honda's 32-valve NR500 four-stroke four came some 15 years later). It almost seemed that the plethora of advance ballyhoo from Hamamatsu during the 1963-64 close season had offered providence too great a temptation. In fact the engine was plagued on the track by intractable carburation and ignition problems, while the absence of a water impeller was a mistake, as was the inheritance of an unnecessary oil pump from roadster practice.

The RG500 was essentially a catalogue racer (available to anyone with 4,500 greenbacks to spare) with the works machines a step or two ahead in development. Despite the hairy handling of the original chassis and the suddenness with which the power rushed in at the critical engine speed, it quickly became the overwhelming choice of top and middle-ranking privateers; indeed many of its successes were achieved by standard over-the-counter machines.

Compared with the ill-fated two-fifty, it benefited from interim improvements in carburation and ignition, also from the use of a water impeller. Strangely, though, it retained a pump feeding oil through the crankshafts to the big ends, as a supplement to the 3-percent mixture of oil in the fuel. The object of pump oiling in a two-stroke (besides obviating the need for roadside ready-mix) is to reduce the supply to the engine under light-load conditions by linking pump stroke to throttle opening, thus minimizing carbon deposits in street riding. Since these conditions don't apply in racing, a pump is superfluous. Given proper design, the petroil mixture should take care of the big-end bearings as well as the pistons and cylinders. Indeed, the RG500's big ends enjoyed better conditions than most; for in addition to the usual slotting and scalloping of the con-rod eyes, they had a large side clearance, which reduced frictional heat — since the rods were located laterally at the small ends, where the angular rubbing was much smaller. Predictably the pump was soon discarded (and the petroil ratio changed from 30:1 to 20:1).

So far as power characteristics were concerned, the most significant of the few detail differences from MZ specification was probably the use of the typical Japanese cylinder dimensions of 56mm bore and

139

Makoto Hase (Suzuki).

Early 1976 drawing of Barry Sheene's spare engine, showing two-abreast crank assemblies with side-by-side thin gears driving the common jackshaft gear. The thrust washers flanking the small-end eyes locate the con-rods at the top instead of the bottom. The inlet discs spin in fibre sandwiches. Early modifications included wider squish bands for higher compression; two extra side transfer ports; a smaller magneto; elimination of the oil pump; and a change from oversquare to square cylinder dimensions (reversed much later with the adoption of Power Chamber exhaust-port valves). Cylinder liners were discarded later in favour of Nikasil plating of the aluminium bores, and single-ring pistons.

50.5mm stroke rather than Kaaden's 54 × 54mm. Ostensibly this was intended to boost peak power by permitting 7 per cent higher revs for the same mean piston speed. Even so, the initial peak of 90bhp at 10,000rpm (180bhp/litre) was 10 per cent short of the 200bhp/litre produced by Degner's one-two-five in the year of his defection! It was 1976 before MZ's 1961 specific output was matched by the standard RG500 (with 100bhp at 11,000rpm).

Ironically that was the year when Sheene's works engine led the change to square cylinder dimensions (54 × 54mm) for greater low-speed torque. That change — in conjunction with an extra transfer port each side (making seven in all, with identical timing) and an increase in the width of the annular squish band, raising the trapped compression ratio from 7.7 to 8.4:1 (in geometric terms, from 14 to 15:1) — gave Sheene a power boost from 6,000rpm upward and an increase in the peak to 103bhp at 11,250rpm.

Another works modification at the same time (for reliability, not power) was to use a one-piece construction for the power take-off shaft — which drove the impeller (through a worm) and magneto (through a taper) on the left; the clutch (through an idler) and initially the oil pump (another worm) both on the right. Standard engines for a time retained the less expensive two-part flanged shaft, united by four bolts and nuts, but with bolt diameter increased from 6mm to 8mm to cure breakages.

The accompanying exploded drawing was made by Lawrie Watts early in 1976 from a spare engine in Sheene's old Wisbech workshop, under the watchful eye of father Frank since Barry was away racing in America. Subsequent developments have embraced both obvious changes in construction and progressive refinements in porting, bearing quality, piston alloy (up to 19 per cent silicon content), weight saving and suchlike. Before discussing those developments and their concomitant power increases, then, let us examine that 1976 engine.

Beneath the separate cylinders and heads (secured by 16 long studs) were three main light-alloy castings (first changed from aluminium to magnesium in Sheene's works engine): these were the upper crankcase half, containing the bottom part of the side transfer passages; the lower crankcase half, in which the four separate flywheel assemblies sat; and a tray housing the power take-off shaft (alternatively called the primary drive shaft or jackshaft), the short idler shaft and the input and output shafts of the six-speed, all-indirect gear cluster. (Incidentally, the tiny worm shown on the right-hand extremity of the jackshaft drove the tachometer.) The two joints between the castings passed through the planes of all the shaft axes; and while any crank assembly could be lifted out independently after removal of the cylinders and upper crankcase half, the much more frequent task of changing internal gear ratios involved a complete strip and reassembly taking a disproportionate three hours.

The squish bands shown (if any) seem to be the original minimal ones used with the 56mm bore. Cylinder porting here is pure

MZ, with two transfer ports each side (virtually wide single ports divided by a vertical wall to prevent ring trapping) and the auxiliary port fed through a window in the piston skirt. The exhaust port adaptors comprise short double-wall tubes into which the pipe ends are slotted and retained by a pair of tension springs; this construction permits quick pipe changes for test-house experiments besides providing enough flexibility to prevent cracking.

Since all the crankshafts rotated in the same direction (forward in the engine illustrated) it is clear that the rear exhaust ports were in the cylinder thrust face (on the power stroke) whereas the front exhausts were in the non-thrust face. As a consequence, the rear two cylinders were marginally the more efficient — a difference of $2\frac{1}{2}$bhp was measured. While some of this difference has been attributed to the straighter run of the rear pipes, tests with rear pipes on the front cylinders failed to reverse the discrepancy. In fact, as Walter Kaaden established many years earlier, the piston provides a better seal between crankcase and exhaust when it is hard against the port, giving crisper port control and more torque.

Besides the normal cutaways at the sides of the piston skirt to clear the main transfer passages, there were two tiny holes in the skirt, diametrically opposite the window, to lubricate and cool the hot-running exhaust-port bridge. Surprisingly for a grand-prix engine, each piston had two rings — the top one of keystone type (bevelled upper face) to prevent sticking and improve sealing, the other of plain section and only half as thick.

Equally surprising, the standard con-rods

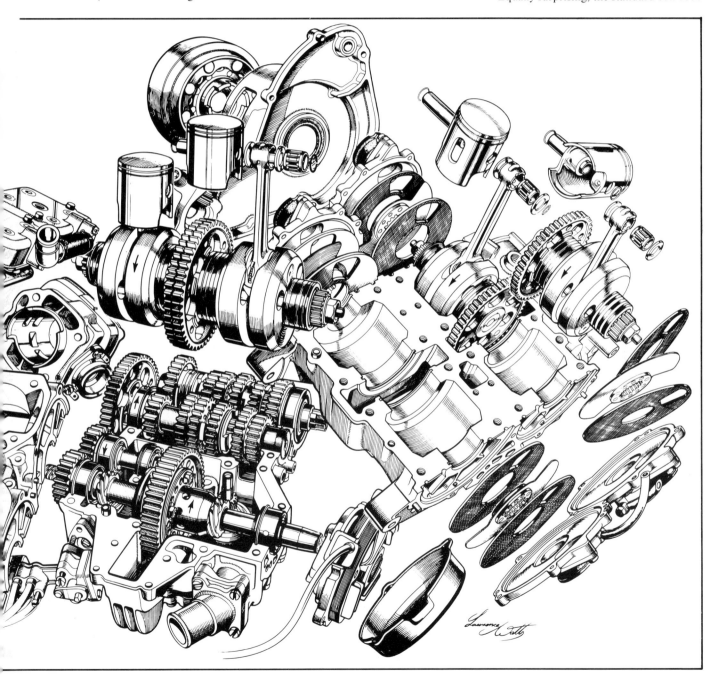

141

Lower engine casting with jackshaft and transmission gears. The jackshaft was changed to one-piece construction for the 1976 works engines (but stronger clamping bolts for production models). Two years later the idler gear between jackshaft and clutch was discarded in a crankcase redesign, so reversing engine rotation. Left and right crank assemblies were also united in full-width driving gears.

In this 1978 engine the lower front cylinders indicate the crankcase redesign for rapid access to the gear cluster. Carburettor choke size is 34mm.

had a rough finish, only the works rods being polished. Both top and bottom rod bearings were of caged needle-roller type — those at the top cooled by fresh gas passing from under the piston crown, through the window into the auxiliary transfer passage. The fly-wheel discs were bevelled round the outer edge, supposedly to prevent obstruction of the inlet passage; but in fact the bevelling was insufficient to prevent the flywheel face from intruding into the tract. Indeed, the outer segment of the unplugged balance holes could be seen above the floor of the tract. A minor point, perhaps, but surprising con-sidering the competitiveness of grand-prix engineering. However, when Roberto Gallina subsequently removed the obstruc-tion by steepening the bevel in the Italian team's engines, it was found they would no longer sustain full revs in top gear because of the reduction in flywheel inertia!

Each pressed-up flywheel assembly had a thin gear pressed on its inner end, so that adjacent gears ran closely side by side to mesh with the primary drive gear. Naturally, the inner main bearings were of considerably larger diameter than the outers; and all eight were located laterally by rings in matching grooves, as were the shaft bearings in the tray.

On the outer end of each crankshaft was a splined boss carrying the thin steel inlet valve. Unlike the MZ discs, though, they spun between ported fibre plates pegged in position rather than directly between the crankcase and the side cover. Rubber sleeves on the outside of the covers insulated the 34mm carburettors from vibration.

For good mechanical balance diagonal pairs of pistons moved in step, hence fired simultaneously (through a pair of double coils). However, the electronic ignition sys-tem triggered both coils together every 180 degrees, so that all cylinders also got an idle spark at bottom dead centre. As part of the lightening process, magneto size was reduced from the 1976 works engines onward.

External plumbing was kept to a mini-mum in the cooling system. From the bottom of the radiator a hose led water to the impeller, which sent it through cored pas-sages in the tray and lower crankcase half, then up into transverse passages in the upper half, between the front and rear crank cham-bers. From there the water rose through jackets in the cylinder and head castings — finally emerging from the sides of the heads, which were coupled front to rear for the two returns to the top of the rad.

By 1977 the makers were claiming 118bhp, presumably through internal developments, but the following year there was an obvious major change in construction, apparent

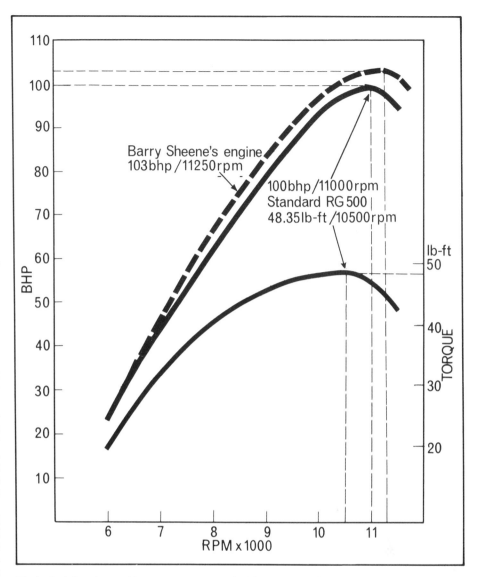

Typical of the edge available to works riders is this graph showing standard power and torque curves (solid lines) with the power curve of Barry Sheene's 1976 world-championship engine, boosted by higher compression, modified porting and square (54 × 54mm) cylinder dimensions.

through the much lower level of the front two cylinders. In effect, the tray had been combined with the lower crankcase half in a single casting making a stepped joint with the upper crankcase half. Thus, although crankshaft access was unaffected, the gear cluster could be withdrawn from the right after removal of a side cover — slashing the time required to change internal ratios from three hours to 10 minutes! At the same time the idler gear was discarded, so shortening the engine and reversing the direction of rotation of the crankshafts — which trans-ferred the benefit of thrust-face exhausts from the rear cylinders to the front. A bonus was that the revised engine layout enabled the axes of the chain sprocket and fork pivot

to be brought closer together to minimize chain snatch due to suspension movement.

Originally there were three choices of gear cluster, giving different ratios for the lower three gears. Next came five choices, with the differences covering the bottom four ratios. Finally all gears could be varied indepen-dently, with a choice of three ratios for each.

Another modification about the same time was to dispense with the separate thin crankshaft gears and press the left and right shafts halfway into a common (though less than double-width) gear. This layout retained the revised tooth form introduced with the one-piece jackshaft, the net result being not only greater accuracy of ignition timing but also greater consistency between

Barry Sheene in action on the works RG500 Suzuki during his second world-championship year — 1977.

None of the RG500's Senior TT victories was more popular than Mike Hailwood's in 1979, the second year of his sensational IoM comeback after more than a decade's absence.

left and right cylinders. Vibration was lessened too.

Interestingly, all these 1978 modifications were tried experimentally the previous year in a 652cc engine (62 × 54mm) to ensure that nothing would be overstressed in the grand-prix engine. Peak power climbed a further 4bhp to 122, still around 11,000rpm.

The main change in 1979 concerned the cylinders, which lost their flanged, dry, cast-iron liners in favour of Nikasil plating of the aluminium bores. This not only saved weight but stabilized piston clearances at different temperatures, too, as a result of improved heat flow. Hand-in-hand with the new cylinders went single-ring pistons with smaller running clearances. Meanwhile the engine was narrowed slightly by various means, such as substitution of the flanged disc-valve covers by plain covers recessed in the crankcase sides and sealed by large O-rings.

By 1980 top power was quoted as 125bhp at 10,800rpm. Meanwhile experiments had been proceeding with exhaust valves aimed at spreading useful torque farther down the rev range, so that cylinder dimensions could revert to 56 × 50.5mm for more top-end power without sacrifice of mid-range acceleration. The bore/stroke change was introduced in 1982, but teething troubles delayed the adoption of the valves for some time.

Unlike Yamaha's Power Valve, which lowered the height of the exhaust port mechanically below a predetermined engine speed (so preventing excessive loss of fresh charge with the burnt gases, to the benefit of torque), the Suzuki Power Chamber valve had no effect on port height, though it too had only two positions — open and closed. Linked left to right for simplicity of operation, the valves were situated in cylindrical

housings in the port roof and slotted through diametrically. With the valve closed the slot lay parallel to the port roof, leaving the port unaffected for full power. But when, below a selected engine speed, the valve was rotated through 90 degrees (by a battery-powered electric motor and push/pull cables) the slot lined up with similar slots in the port roof and an auxiliary chamber, so connecting them for improved low-speed tractability (and starting).

Contrary to a widespread belief, the effect was due not to a reduction in the resonant frequency of the exhaust box as a result of the increase in its total volume, but to the auxiliary chamber itself reflecting a positive pressure pulse back to the port to resist charge loss at a time when the normal pulse from the reverse-cone section of the box was out of phase.

Control of the valve was electronic and the engine speed at which it closed could be varied between 6,500 and 9,000rpm by changing a resistor. Usually it was set to close in the lower-7,000rpm range. In the event of control failure the valve remained closed so that the rider retained full power at the cost of some tractability.

The first problem was predictable because the auxiliary chambers were incorporated in the cylinder-head castings, so feeding heat from the exhaust gases back into the engine. It is probably no coincidence that the consequent overheating was first experienced at Assen (in 1983) where the many corners must have resulted in the valves spending a disproportionate amount of running time in the open position.

Separating the chambers from the heads was a promising move and the Italian team got the valves working satisfactorily during the latter part of the 1984 season. But the British Heron Suzuki team's hopes for that season were frustrated, for Barry Sheene had all the available valve equipment, yet raced 1983 engines without it (considering it not worth using) while the team used 1982 engines.

At the time of writing, Suzuki were claiming about 130bhp for the works engines. From cylinders of the same size (important for a valid comparison) it is pertinent to note that Walter Kaaden was approaching that level of specific power some 15 years earlier, before MZ decided to quit the grands prix and devote their pathetically slender resources to the much less demanding but commercially more relevant task of monopolizing the European 250, 350 and 500cc cross-country championships.